Battle Honours
of the
Royal Navy

Being the officially authorised and complete listing of Battle
Honours awarded to Her/His Majesty's Ships
and Squadrons of the Fleet Air Arm
including Honours awarded to
Royal Fleet Auxiliary Ships
and merchant vessels

Compiled by
Lt. Cdr. Ben Warlow Royal Navy

First published in the United Kingdom in 2004 by Maritime Books, Lodge Hill, Liskeard, Cornwall, PL14 4EL

Contents

Introduction..7

Foreword...9

Author's Note..11

Preface..13

Part 1: Battle Honours and their Ships/Squadrons..21

Part 2: Single Ship Actions...59

Part 3: Ships and their Honours...63

Part 4: Fleet Air Arm Squadrons and their Honours...217

Part 5: Royal Marines Battle Honour...223

List of Sources/Bibliography..224

List of Illustrations

Badges

WARSPITE
SWIFTSURE
UNICORN
800 Squadron, Fleet Air Arm

Battle Honours Board

INVINCIBLE

Photographs

ANTELOPE
ARROW
S.S. ATLANTIC CONVEYOR
BAMBOROUGH CASTLE
BETONY
CALDER
CENTURION
EAGLE
EURYALUS
FAULKNOR
GREY GOOSE
JERVIS
NUBIAN
ORION
PRINCE OF WALES
REPULSE
H.M.C.S. SACKVILLE
SHROPSHIRE
R.F.A. SIR TRISTRAM
H.M.A.S. SYDNEY
TRITON
URSULA
VICTORIOUS

Introduction

By Admiral Sir Alan West, GCB, DSC, ADC
First Sea Lord and Chief of Naval Staff

For many years the complete records of Battle Honours of ships and Fleet Air Arm Squadrons of the Royal Navy have lain unpublished in the archives of the Naval Historical Branch of the Naval Staff. Some minor and partial lists have been released covering Honours awarded to particular ships and for particular campaigns, but there has never been a published comprehensive record.

I commissioned the Naval Historical Branch to undertake a complete review of Royal Navy Battle Honours with a view to this publication of this complete list, including, in addition to warships, Fleet Air Arm squadrons, and ships flying the Red and Blue ensigns. A quick glance will show how many ships have served gallantly in the defence of our islands during the past hundreds of years. And yet, more serious students of naval history will be aware that this record is only the tip of the iceberg; many ships and squadrons have been involved in other important actions which have not been deemed to have met the arduous criteria required to merit the award of a Battle Honour. Many more have been employed on more routine, but still vital, tasks where their very presence has deterred aggression and permitted trade to be conducted in safety and without hindrance.

This record shows also how some names seem to have acquired a surprising tendency to carry their ship's companies into the thick of naval actions throughout the centuries, appearing in the record repeatedly. This is part of the heritage that is vital to the maintenance of the tradition whereby the Royal Navy has fought without hesitation against odds, and, more often than not, despite the logic and reason of the situation, triumphed.

It is time that this record is placed fully in the public domain, and I congratulate Lieutenant Commander Ben Warlow, who I first met in the cold waters off the Falkland Islands in 1982, on his efforts to ensure that this has been achieved.

Foreword

By Captain C.L.W. Page, MA, FIMechE, Royal Navy Rtd
Head of the Naval Historical Branch

This book is the officially authorised record of the Battle Honours awarded to H.M. Ships and Fleet Air Arm Squadrons. The only previous official publication was an Admiralty Fleet Order issued in 1954, which was concerned only with ships and squadrons whose names/numbers were extant at that time. This, of course, was not readily available to the public. All the official records were, and still are, held in the Naval Historical Branch of the Ministry of Defence, who issue the information as required. This is usually when a new ship or squadron is commissioned. This work encompasses all Battle Honours awarded since the Battle of Armada in 1588 up to the present time, and which includes all ships and squadrons who have received a Battle Honour. It is to be hoped that this will be a valuable source of information to historians and researchers.

Whitehall
2004

Author's Note

Battle Honours were not defined until they were first published in Admiralty Fleet Order 2565/54, which listed the Honours to which ships in the Fleet at the time were entitled. This Order was the result of years of diligent work, during which the Honours to which other ships, whose names were not then extant, were established. There have been some subsequent minor revisions. During this review a new Area Battle Honour, 'East Indies 1940-45' has been introduced to give the same recognition to the many operations carried out in that theatre as is given to those in other areas, (Atlantic, North Sea, Mediterranean, etc). It has also been found appropriate to extend the limits of the area defined for the Area Battle Honour 'Malaya 1942-45' in order to encompass those actions which took place further south and east in the region of Java. A codicil has also been added to that Battle Honour to cover the cable cutting operations carried out by midget submarines off Saigon and Hong Kong in 1945. Nevertheless, the original main work still stands as the 'master list'.

The time has come for this 'master list' to be published in full, so that officers and men of the Navy, and others interested in such matters, can have access to the complete listings.

The original listings contained details of 'numbered' vessels – MTBs, MLs etc. Details of these have been retained in Parts 1 and 2, but only submarines and steam gunboats (some of which were later given names) have been included in the alphabetical lists in Part 3

The original listings contained ships and squadrons of the Members of the Commonwealth and Dominions who are now independent. These names have been retained in this publication, but any decisions on amendments to their Battle Honours now rests with their own authorities. The Naval Historical Branch remains, as always, ready and willing to provide any assistance to these authorities in any researches they may conduct into this topic.

Doubtless, as has always been the case, the Navy will be called to stand in peril in the future, and further Battle Honours will be added, but this is the complete list to date, compiled from unpublished sources in the Naval Historical Branch. In conducting this work I have felt proud to have been able to honour in a minor way those, including my father, who gave their all for the Country in the Service.

In all this work I have been ably guided, supported and assisted by Captain Chris Page and his staff in the Naval Historical Branch, to whom I owe a debt of thanks.

Ben Warlow
Burnham-on-Crouch
2004

Preface

The award of Battle Honours to Her/His Majesty's ships is intended to foster esprit de corps among their officers and ships' companies, who are thereby encouraged to take a personal interest in the war-time exploits not only of their present ship, but also of ships of the same name which have distinguished themselves in the past.

The Battle Honours Committee is comprised of The Head of the Naval Historical Branch together with a Senior Officer of the Second Sea Lord's Department. The Committee makes recommendations for awards to the Navy Board, which will authorise any official Honours considered appropriate.

It was decided that the earliest action of which sufficient is known, and which is in all respects worthy of inclusion, was 'ARMADA 1588'. The actions and campaigns listed as Battle Honours are displayed on a scroll, mounted in a suitable position in the ships which are eligible for these Honours.

There is a tendency to regard Battle Honours in terms of general naval history and to include many actions and incidents which, meritorious in themselves, are not of sufficient importance to be ranked as Battle Honours. If awards are made too freely, they lose much of their value. Moreover, limitations of space prevent everything from being included on the scroll. A selection has therefore to be made – several incidents being often summarised into a single short-titled Battle Honour – in a manner similar to that adopted when determining the Battle Honours which appear on a Regimental Colour.

Battle Honours have been granted to those ships (including former ships of the same name) which took part in certain actions or campaigns. These engagements with the enemy fall under the following headings:

(i)	Fleet or Squadron Actions
(ii)	Single-ship or Boat Service Actions
(iii)	Major Bombardments
(iv)	Combined Operations (i.e. with the Army)
(v)	Campaign Awards
(vi)	Area Awards

Definition

Battle Honours have been awarded generally for successful war service rather than as a record of service. Successful war service implies, not only the actual sinking or capture of an enemy warship, but also the following:

(i)	Sinking of enemy merchant ships in escorted convoy.
(ii)	Engagements with enemy light forces, when both sides often incurred losses.
(iii)	Operations which resulted in the more or less complete frustration of the enemy's intention at the time, even though no warship may have been sunk.

In deciding which actions are to rank as Battle Honours, the following general rules have been adopted, though exceptional cases require a departure from a rigid observance of them.

(i)   A Battle Honour will be awarded for those actions resulting in the defeat of the enemy, or when the action was inconclusive but well fought, and in the exceptional cases where outstanding efforts were made against overwhelming odds.

(ii)   A Battle Honour will not be awarded for a British defeat, or when the action was inconclusive and badly fought.

In the past, some ships have displayed 'Battle Honours' which had not been formally ratified. Only those approved by the Ministry of Defence are permitted.

The qualification entitling a ship to a particular Battle Honour is that she was present during the action – the extent of her participation is immaterial. In the days of sail, physical or visual contact with the enemy, except as mentioned below, was normally a sine qua non. However in the wars of the 20th Century, when wireless communication enabled patrols and scouting groups to operate effectively at much greater distances than was possible with visual signalling only, this qualification required modifying. For example, the operational range of aircraft often led to the carrier being more than 100 miles from the scene of close action. For these reasons the word 'present' has been taken to mean presence at sea under the direct orders of the Senior Officer controlling the operation, although some ships may not have actually opened fire on the enemy. The award is therefore based on the mention of the ship in the dispatch of the Commander-in-Chief; Flag Officer's War Diary; a Battle Summary of the Naval Staff History (BR 1736 series); the Report of Proceedings of the Commanding Officer; or the ship's log. Examples of the exception referred to above will be found in the Campaign awards, where a ship was employed over the whole range of a Foreign Station (e.g. China), many of the actions in which she took part being, in themselves, of minor importance only, though they contributed to the main strategic effort. However, the presence of a ship or squadron for just a short transitory period in an area of conflict will not necessarily entitle the ship or squadron to the Area Battle Honour. The Battle Honours Committee will consider each case on its merits based on the general criteria above.

Some ships have many Battle Honours to their credit, others only a few. The Royal Marines have, traditionally, just the one Battle Honour – 'Gibraltar' – with no date. The more fortunate ships are not, however, limited to any arbitrary maximum number of Honours which may be displayed. If a ship is renamed at any time she will assume the Honours which go with her new name, and will no longer be entitled to those previously awarded under the old name. The exception to this principle is when ships launched with 'numbers' instead of names are subsequently named. They then can wear the Battle Honours of their name, and also any they earned prior to their naming. Ships with numbers only are included in Parts 1 and 2, but only numbered submarines and steam gun boats are included in the alphabetical lists in Part 3, with cross references where they received names later in their careers.

The Battle Honours applicable to one of His/Her Majesty's Ships are not eligible for use by a Royal Fleet Auxiliary (RFA) of the same name, and vice versa. On rare occasions mercantile vessels were awarded Battle Honours. The RFAs and mercantile vessels concerned are identified in Sections 1 and 3.

Single-ship and Boat Service Actions

A number of single ship actions during the Napoleonic Wars were recognised later by the award of a clasp to the General Service Medal (Navy) 1793-1840. The criterion for these awards was that a promotion was made at the time, irrespective of the importance or magnitude of the event. The more outstanding of these actions, when the enemy was of equal or superior force, are considered to be worthy of a Battle Honour and have been shown by quoting the name of the enemy captured (or sunk) with the year date. No special recognition by means of a medal and clasp was made for any successes before 1793, though promotions were made in compliment of the victory. These earlier actions have also been considered on their merits.

Bombardments etc

Battle Honours for major bombardments have been granted only when there was appreciable opposition on the part of the enemy. Other bombardments, when the enemy reply was negligible, have been included among the various minor affairs for which a separate, named Battle Honour will not be awarded, and which are merged, when appropriate, with an Area Award.

Fireship attacks have been recognised either by a separate, named Battle Honour (e.g. 'BASQUE ROADS') or by being merged with the Battle Honour awarded for a series of engagements, of which the fireship attack is only one. Thus, the fireship attack on the Spanish fleet in Calais Roads in 1588 is included in the general Battle Honour 'ARMADA': similarly, the destruction of the French ships at La Hougue in 1692 is merely a non-stop continuation of the battle of Barfleur.

Combined Operations

The capture of a fortress (Havana) or of a large island (Martinique), in conjunction with military forces, has been recognised by the award of a named Battle Honour. In some of these operations a large number of seamen and Marines was landed to assist the Army. However, where the Navy had little to do beyond the safe conveyance of the troops to the point of attack, the support fire of the ships (including Fleet Air Arm Squadrons) being no more than a minor contribution to the success of the operation, a Naval Battle Honour has not been awarded, notwithstanding that a participating regiment quite properly wears the Honour on its Colour.

Campaign Awards

Starting with the First Burma War (1824-6), Battle Honours have been awarded for certain campaigns as a whole, and not for individual actions during those campaigns. For example, the successful operation of the Light Squadron in the Sea of Azov in 1855 is one of the series of actions embraced by the campaign award 'CRIMEA'.

1914-18 War

The selection of Battle Honours for the 1914-18 War is based on the award of clasps with the British War Medal, though not all of the campaigns or area events which were distinguished by a clasp are suitable for the grant of separate Battle Honours. Here, also, several clasp awards have been combined into a single Campaign or Area Battle Honour.

1939-45 War

The Battle Honours for the 1939-45 War are set out in Part 3. The following are explanatory notes on the award of Area Battle Honours:- (a) defining the area limits, and (b) the ships eligible:

ATLANTIC
1939-45

a) The North Atlantic, from the Equator to the Arctic Circle
b) All ships and submarines which were employed as escorts to ocean convoys in the North Atlantic and also those ships of Support Groups which took part in a successful action.

BISCAY
1940-45

a) Between the latitudes of Ushant and Cape Ortegal from 12°W to the coast of France
b) Ships and submarines which were employed on patrol duty in the area and took part in a successful action. The interception and sinking of enemy blockade runners is not a qualification for the award.

NORTH SEA
1939-45

a) The North Sea and all waters to the eastward, between Southend and the Shetland Islands, except coastal waters of Norway.
b) All ships which were employed as escorts to coastal convoys on the East Coast of the United Kingdom. Also ships and submarines, which were employed on patrol duty in the area and took part in a successful action.

ENGLISH
CHANNEL
1939-45

a) The English Channel and all waters on the South Coast between Southend and Bristol, the western limit being a line drawn from Ushant to the Scilly Islands, and thence to the North Coast of Cornwall.
b) All ships which were employed as escorts to Channel coastal convoys, and also other ships and submarines which took part in a successful action in the area. Successes achieved in connection with Operation Neptune are recognised by 'NORMANDY 1944'.

NORWAY
1940-45

a) The coastal waters of Norway, as far north as the latitude of Tromso.
b) All ships and submarines which were engaged in the Norway operations from 8 April to 8 June, 1940, and also those which took part in a successful action in these waters at later dates.
Recognition of Fleet Air Arm attacks, such as those on the *Tirpitz*, is normally restricted to the carriers and squadrons

concerned; the covering escorts on those occasions are not eligible for the award.

ARCTIC
1941-45

a) Within the Arctic Circle, except for the coastal waters of Norway to the southward of Tromso.
b) All ships, including the covering forces which were employed as escorts to or in support of the convoys running to and from North Russia; also those ships and submarines which operated in the area and took part in a successful action.

MEDITERRANEAN
1940-45

a) The whole of the Mediterranean, the western limit being a line joining Cape Spartel and Cape Trafalgar.
b) All ships and submarines which took part in successful actions that are not covered by any of the named Battle Honours for the area. That is to say, the destruction of an enemy ship or submarine which was effected during and in connection with a recognised campaign, e.g. SICILY 1943, is regarded as an incidental item of the campaign, and not as qualifying for a separate Battle Honour award. If, however, the success was unconnected with any named operation for which a Battle Honour is granted, then it will qualify for the general award of MEDITERRANEAN with the year date(s). Minor bombardments will also qualify for this award.

EAST INDIES
1940-45

a) The Indian Ocean, including the Red Sea, Bay of Bengal and the Arabian Sea
b) Those ships which conducted successful attacks against enemy shipping or significant enemy shore installations.

MALTA
CONVOYS
1941-42

a) The Mediterranean, as above.
b) All ships and submarines which are mentioned in the pub lished dispatches as having taken part in Operations Excess, Substance, Halberd, Harpoon and Pedestal; also those which took part in Operations M.F.3, M.F.4, M.G.1 and the supply of aircraft and stores to Malta.

LIBYA
1940-42

a) Inshore, between Port Said and Benghazi.
b) All ships and vessels of the Inshore Squadron (formerly Force W) - but excluding the heavier covering forces - which were employed in maintaining Tobruk and other places on the coast, and generally in supporting the Army in the Western Desert. Fleet Air Arm Squadrons, both carrier-borne and shore-based, are also eligible.

AEGEAN
1943-44

a) All waters of the Aegean Archipelago between 35° and 42°N and between 22° and 39°E.
b) Ships and vessels which were engaged with the enemy in

the area between 7 September 1943 and 28 November 1943, and also during 1944.

ADRIATIC
1944

a) All waters in the Adriatic to the northward of 40°N.
b) Ships and vessels which were engaged with the enemy in the area during 1944.

MALAYA
1942-45

a) Malacca Strait and waters adjacent to the Malay Peninsula and Sumatra, between 7°N. and 9°S. and between 95°-118°E. The cable cutting operations off Saigon and Hong Kong in 1945 are also exceptionally included in this Battle Honour.
b) Ships and submarines which took part in a successful action in the area.

OKINAWA
1945

a) The Far East
b) All ships and submarines which are mentioned in the published dispatch as having taken part in Operation Iceberg.

JAPAN
1945

a) The mainland of Japan.
b) Fleet carriers and their aircraft which took part in the final attacks on Japanese warships and shore positions, together with those ships which carried out bombardments of the Japanese mainland.

Post 1945

In the following (a) defines Area limits and (b) the ships eligible:

KOREA
1950-53

a) The coast of Korea
b) Ships entitled to the Korea Medal

FALKLAND
ISLANDS
1982

a) Below 35°S and North of 60°S in the South Atlantic between 2 April and 14 June 1982
b) All Ships, submarines, Royal Fleet Auxiliaries and Ships Taken Up From Trade.

KUWAIT
1991

a) In the Central and Northern Gulf to the west of the meridian 51°E at any time between 17 January and 28 February 1991.
b) All HM Ships, and Royal Fleet Auxiliaries

Note: In all the above, the expression 'all ships' includes Fleet Air Arm Squadrons when they are carrier borne. On these occasions it is usual for the aircraft carrier also to receive the award, but if the actual action takes place at a distance from the carriers, the escorting ships will not be eligible for the Award (e.g. Norway and the attacks on the Tirpitz). When the Squadrons are shore based they will normally receive the Battle Honour where it is concerned with naval operations (e.g. Libya), but other non-naval operations (e.g. The Battle of Britain) are not recognised in this context. It will be for the Battle Honours Committee to consider each case on its merits and make the appropriate recommendations to the Navy Board.

The Scroll

The Scroll and the lettering and numbering thereon are to be made of teak. Its dimensions and lay-out will depend upon the position chosen for its display in the ship, and the number of Battle Honours to which the ship is entitled and wishes to display. The outside dimensions should not, however, exceed the following:

Capital Ships, Aircraft Carriers and Fleet Shore Establishments:	10ft x 6ft (3.07 m x 1.84 m)
Cruisers, large Depot, Repair & Maintenance Ships:	6ft. x 5ft (1.84 m x 1.53m)
Other classes of ships, including Destroyers, Frigates and Ocean Minesweepers. Fleet Air Arm Squadrons:	4ft. x 3ft. (1.22 m x .98 m)

The Badge of the ship or squadron is to be carved into the Scroll as an integral part thereof. The smaller ships which are eligible only for a Type Badge will have their Type Badge carved on the Scroll.

Battle Honours are normally to be displayed in BLOCK LETTERS: the single- ship and boat service actions listed in Part 2, however, are to be displayed in lower case letters between inverted commas. This enables the necessary distinction to be made between a fleet action, named after a place, and the name of a single enemy ship, when the two names are the same (e.g. 'CHESAPEAKE 1781' and "*Chesapeake* 1813'). The name of the enemy ship or submarine sunk/damaged during the 1939-45 War is not shown, the action being denoted by a place name in BLOCK LETTERS. Exceptions to this rule are '*Admiral Hipper* 1940', '*Scharnhorst* 1940', '*Admiral Scheer* 1940', '*Bismarck* 1941', '*Kormoran* 1941', '*Hokoku Maru* 1942', '*Tirpitz* 1943' and '*Takao* 1945'.

When the dates of a campaign or area Battle Honour extends over a period of more that two years only the terminal years are shown on the Scroll, notwithstanding that the ship may have a break in her service in respect of that particular Battle Honour. For example, a ship which is entitled to the Battle Honour 'ARCTIC' for the years 1941, 1943 and 1945 will display 'ARCTIC 1941-45', and so forth.

Scrolls denoting the Battle Honours of Fleet Air Arm Squadrons should be displayed flanking those of the Carrier in which they are embarked. For Squadrons based at Naval Air Stations such Scrolls should be displayed in a suitable position near the ship's quarterdeck where they can be under the supervision of the regulating and/or gangway staff. To facilitate movement between ships and air stations the Battle Honours scrolls of Fleet Air Arm Squadrons are held on the charge of the Squadron and transferred as necessary.

Scrolls denoting the Battle Honours for submarines are normally displayed in harbour on a board on the conning tower/fin casing below the ship's bell.

Battle Honour Scrolls taken from ships that are being prepared for sale are returned to store for use in other ships of the same name.

PART 1
BATTLE HONOURS AND THEIR SHIPS/SQUADRONS

The following are the Fleet Actions, Campaigns, etc., for which a Battle Honour is awarded, together with their qualifying dates and a list of the entitled ships/squadrons:

ARMADA 1588   21-29 July 1588

This battle comprised a running series of actions, which stretched from the Cornish Coast to the North Sea, and included actions with fire-ships. Almost half of the Spanish fleet failed to return home as a result of the action and stress of weather.

Queen's Ships:- Achates, Advice, Aid, Antelope, Ark (Royal), Brigandine, Bull, Charles, Cygnet, Disdain, Dreadnought, Elizabeth Bonaventure, Elizabeth Jonas, Fancy, Foresight, Galley Bonavolia, George, (Golden) Lion, Hope, Mary Rose, Merlin, Moon, Nonpareil, Rainbow, Revenge, Scout, Spy, Sun, Swallow, Swiftsure, Tiger, Tramontana, Triumph, Vanguard, Victory, (White) Bear, White Lion.

Merchant Ships under Drake:- Bark Bond, Bark Bonner, Bark Buggins, Bark Burr, Bark Hawkyns, Bark Manington, Bark St. Leger, Bark Talbot, Bear Young, Chance, Delight, Diamond of Dartmouth, Edward Bonaventure, Elizabeth Drake, Elizabeth Founes, Flyboat Yonge, Galleon Dudley, Galleon Leicester, Golden Hind, Golden Noble, Griffin, Heartsease, Hope Hawkyns, Hopewell, Makeshift, Merchant Royal, Minion, Nightingale, Roebuck, Spark, Speedwell, Thomas Drake, Unity, Virgin God save her, 1 small caravel.

Merchant ships from the City of London:- Antelope, Anthony, Ascension, Bark Burr, Brave, Centurion, Diana, Dolphin, George Noble, Hercules, Jewel, Gift of God, Golden Lion, Margaret and John, Mayflower, Minion, Moonshine, Pansy, Passport, Primrose, Prudence, Red Lion, Release, Rose Lion, Royal Defence, Salamander, Thomas Bonaventure, Tiger, Toby.

Merchant ships under the Lord High Admiral:- Anne Frances, George Bonaventure, Jane Bonaventure, Samuel, Solomon, Susan Parnell, Vineyard, Violet.

Merchant ships in Queen's pay:- Black Dog, Edward of Maldon, Katharine, Lark, Marigold, Nightingale, Pippin.

Victuallers to the Westward:- Bearsabe, Elizabeth Bonaventure, Elizabeth of Leigh, Gift of God, Hope, John of London, Jonas, Marigold, Mary Rose, Pearl, Pelican, Richard Duffield, Solomon, Unity, White Hind.

Coasters under The Lord High Admiral:- Aid of Bristol, Bark of Bridgewater, Bark Potts, Bark Webb, Bartholomew of Apsam, Crescent of Dartmouth, Galleon of Weymouth, Gift of Apsam, Handmaid of Bristol, Hearty Anne, Hart of Dartmouth, Jacob of Lyme, John of Chichester, John Trelawney, Katharine of Weymouth, Little John, Minion of Bristol, Revenge of Lyme, Rose of Apsam, Unicorn of Bristol.

Coasters under Lord Henry Seymour:- Anne Bonaventure, Bark Lamb, Daniel, Elizabeth of Dover, Fancy, Galleon Hutchins, Grace of God, Grace of Yarmouth, Griffin, Handmaid, Hazard of Feversham, John Young, Katharine of Ipswich, Little Hare, Marigold, Matthew, Mayflower, Primrose of Harwich, Robin of Sandwich, Susan, William of Colchester, William of Ipswich, William of Rye.

Voluntary ships:- Bark Halse, Bark Sutton of Weymouth, Carouse, Elizabeth, Elizabeth of Lowestoft, Flyboat, Fortune of Aldborough, Frances of Fowey, Gallego of Plymouth, Golden Ryall of Weymouth, Grace of Apsam, Greyhound of Aldborough, Heathen of Weymouth, John of Barnstaple, Jonas of Aldborough, Margaret, Raphael, Rat of Wight, Samaritan of Dartmouth, Sampson, Thomas Bonaventure, Unicorn of Dartmouth, William of Plymouth.

AZORES 1591   31 Aug-1 Sept 1591

Revenge. *(See Single Ship Actions)*

CADIZ 1596   21 June 1596

Queen's ships:- Ark Royal, Charles, Crane, Dreadnought, Lion, Lion's Whelp, Mary Rose,

Mere Honour, Moon, Nonpareil, Quittance, Rainbow, Repulse, Swiftsure, Tramontana, Truelove, Vanguard, Warspite, Witness.

Merchant ships (English and Dutch):- Alcedo, Amulo, Archangel, Bark Rose, Blue Pigeon, Brave, Brown Fish, Centurion, Chameleon, Cherubim, Corbett of Ipswich, Darling, Delight, Desire, Elizabeth of Hampton, Elizabeth of London, Elizabeth Jonas of Hull, Endeavour, Exchange, Expedition, Experience, George, Gift of God, Golden Dragon, Grace of God, Great Katherine, Green Dragon, Hercules of Rye, Howard, Hoy of Sandwich, Hunter of Enkhuysen*, Hunter of Schiedam*, Jacob of Enkhuysen(bis)*, Jacob of Rotterdam*, John and Francis, Jonas, Jonathan, Joshua of Hamburg*, Lioness, Mary Ann, Mary Margaret, Marygold, Mermaid, Mermaid of Dartmouth, Minion, Peter of London, Phoenix of Amsterdam*, Pleasure of Bristol, Popinjay, Posthorse, Primrose, Prudence, Prudence of Plymouth, Roebuck, Roger and Katherine, Ruben (or Ruby), St. Jacob of Akersloot*, St. Peter of Enkhuysen*, Swan (bis), Unicorn of Bristol, Vineyard, Violet of London, Yager of Schiedam*.

These ships, although bearing post-war names, appear to be Dutch.

DOVER 1652   19 May 1652

Adventure, Andrew, Assurance, Centurion, Fairfax, Garland, Greyhound, Happy Entrance (Entrance), James, Martin, Mermaid, Portsmouth, Reuben, Ruby, Sapphire, Seven Brothers, Speaker, Star, Triumph, Victory, Worcester.

MONTECRISTO 1652   28 August 1652

Constant Warwick, Elizabeth, Paragon, Phoenix.

KENTISH KNOCK 1652   28 September 1652

Andrew, Diamond, Garland, Greyhound, Guinea, James, London, Nightingale, Nonsuch, Pelican, Resolution, Ruby, Sovereign, Speaker.

(List incomplete)

PORTLAND 1653   18-20 February 1653

Advantage, Adventure, Advice, Amity, Angel, Ann and Joyce, Ann Piercy, Arms of Holland, Assistance, Assurance, Brazil frigate, Centurion, Charles, Chase, Convert, Convertine, Cullen, Cygnet, Diamond, Discovery, Dolphin, Dragon, Duchess, Eagle, Elizabeth and Ann, Exchange, Expedition, Fairfax, Falmouth, Foresight, Fortune, Gift, Gilliflower, Guinea, Hannibal, Happy Entrance (or Entrance), Katherine, Kentish, Laurel, Lion, Lisbon Merchant, Martin, Mary ketch, Merlin, Nicodemus, Nightingale, Nonsuch, Oak, Old Warwick, Paradox, Paul, Pearl, Pelican, Plover, President (or Great President), Princess Maria, Prosperous, Providence, Rainbow, Raven, Reformation, Richard and Martha, Rosebuck, Ruby, Ruth, Sampson, Sapphire, Satisfaction, Speaker, Speaker's Prize, Success, Sussex, Tenth Whelp, Thomas and Lucy, Thomas and William, Tiger, Triumph, Tulip, Vanguard, Victory, Waterhound, Welcome, William and John, Worcester.

GABBARD 1653   2-3 June 1653

Adventure (bis), Advice, Andrew, Arms of Holland, Amity, Ann and Joyce, Anne Piercy, Assistance, Assurance, Bear, Benjamin, Blossom, Brazil, Centurion, Convert, Convertine, Crescent, Crown, Culpepper*, Diamond, Dolphin, Dragon, Dragoneare, Duchess, Eagle, Eastland Merchant, Employment, Essex*, Exchange (bis), Expedition, Fair Sisters, Falcon, Falmouth, Foresight, Fortune, Fox, George, Gift, Gilly Flower, Globe, Golden Fleece, Guinea, Hamburg Merchant, Hampshire*, Hannibal, Happy Entrance (Entrance), Heart's Ease, Hopeful Luke*, Hound, Hunter, Industry, James, John and Abigail*, Jonathan, Kentish, King Ferdinando, Laurel, Lion, Lisbon Merchant, London, Loyalty, Malaga Merchant, Marmaduke, Martin, Mary, Merlin, Mermaid, Middleboro', Nicodemus, Nonsuch, Oak, Paul, Pearl, Pelican, Peter, Phoenix*, Portsmouth, President (or Great President), Princess Maria, Prosperous*, Providence, Prudent Mary, Rainbow, Raven, Reformation, Renown, Resolution, Richard and Martha, Roebuck, Ruby, Samaritan, Samuel Talbot, Sapphire, Sarah, Society, Sophia, Speaker, Stork*, Success, Sussex, Swan*, Tenth Whelp (Whelp)*, Thomas and Lucy, Thomas and William, Tiger, Triumph, Tulip, Vanguard,

Victory, Violet, Waterhound, Welcome, William*, William and John, Worcester.

* 3 June only

SCHEVENINGEN 1653 31 July 1653

Advantage, Andrew, Assurance, Crescent, Diamond, Dragon, Duchess, Exeter Merchant, Expedition, Foresight, Gift, Golden Cock, Hannibal, Hound, Hunter, James, John and Katherine, Laurel, London, Malaga Merchant, Mary Prize, Mayflower, Merlin, Norwich, Oak, Pelican, Phoenix, Portland, Portsmouth, President (or Great President), Prosperous, Rainbow, Raven, Recovery, Renown, Resolution, Seven Brothers, Sophia, Tiger, Triumph, Tulip, Vanguard, Victory, William, Worcester.

PORTO FARINA 1655 4 April 1655

Amity, Andrew, Bridgewater, Foresight, George, Kent, Merlin, Mermaid, Newcastle, Pearl, Plymouth, Princess Maria, Success, Unicorn, Worcester.

SANTA CRUZ 1657 20 April 1657

Bridgewater, Bristol, Centurion, Colchester, Convert, Fairfax, Foresight, George, Hampshire, Jersey, Langport, Lyme, Maidstone, Nantwich, Newbury, Newcastle, Plymouth, Ruby, Speaker, Swiftsure, Unicorn, Winsby, Worcester.

LOWESTOFT 1665 3 June 1665

Adventure, Amity, Anne, Antelope, Assistance, Assurance, Bear, Bendish, Blackamore Merchant, Bonaventure, Breda, Briar, Bristol, Castle frigate, Centurion, Charity, Clove Tree, Coast frigate, Colchester, Constant Katherine, Convertine, Diamond, Dolphin, Dover, Dragon, Drake, Dreadnought, Dunkirk, Eagle, Fame, Forester, Fountain, Garland, George, Gloucester, Golden Lion, Guernsey, Guinea, Hambro' Merchant, Hampshire, Happy Return, Henrietta, Henry, Horseman, Hound, Jersey, John and Abigail, John and Katherine, John and Thomas, Katherine, Kent, King Ferdinando, Leopard, Lion, London, Loyal George, Loyal Merchant, Maderas, Marmaduke, Martin, Mary,

Maryland Merchant, Mary Rose, Milford, Monck, Mountague, Newcastle, Nightingale, Old James, Oxford, Pembroke, Plymouth, Portland, Portsmouth, Princess, Providence, Prudent Mary, Rainbow, Reserve, Resolution, Return, Revenge, Royal Charles, Royal Exchange, Royal James, Royal Katherine, Royal Oak, Royal Prince, St. Andrew, St. George, Sapphire, Satisfaction, Society, Success, Swallow, Swiftsure, Tiger, Triumph, Unicorn, Vanguard, Yarmouth, York, Young Lion.

FOUR DAYS' BATTLE 1666 1-4 June 1666

Amity, Antelope, Assurance, Black Bull, Black Spread Eagle, Bonaventure, Breda, Bristol, Clove Tree, Convertine, Diamond, Dragon, Dreadnought, Essex, Expedition, Gloucester, Greyhound, Happy Entrance, Henrietta, Henry, Hound, House of Swyte (of Sweeds), Leopard, Lilly, Little Katherine, Little Unicorn, Loyal George, Mary Rose, Plymouth, Portland, Portsmouth, Princess, Rainbow, Reserve, Revenge, Richard, Royal Charles, Royal James, Royal Katherine, Royal Prince, St. George, St. Paul, Sevenoaks, Spread Eagle, Swallow, Swiftsure, Triumph, Vanguard, Victory, Young Prince.

ORFORDNESS 1666 25/26 July 1666

This action fought during the Second Dutch War was a major victory. It is the more remarkable having been fought so soon after the demanding Four Days' Battle.

Abigail, Adventure, Advice, Aleppine, Amity, Anne, Antelope, Assistance, Assurance, Baltimore*, Blessing, Bonaventure, Breda, Briar, Bristol, Cambridge, Castle*, Centurion, Charles, Charles Merchant*, Coronation*, Crown, Defiance, Delph, Diamond, Dover, Dragon, Dreadnought, Dunkirk, Eagle, East India London*, East India Merchant*, Elizabeth, Expedition, Fairfax, Fanfan, Foresight, Fortune, Fox, George*, Gloucester, Golden Phoenix, Great Gift, Greenwich, Guilder de Ruyter, Guinea, Hampshire, Happy Return, Helverson, Henrietta, Henry, House of Sweeds, Jersey, John and Thomas*, Katherine*, Kent, Land of Promise, Leopard, Lion, Lizard, London Merchant*, Loyal London, Loyal Merchant*, Marmaduke, Mary (bis), Mary Rose, Mathias, Monck, Mountague, Newcastle, Old James, Paul,

Plymouth, Portland, Portsmouth, Princess, Providence(bis), Rainbow(bis), Resolution, Revenge, Richard, Richard and Martha*, Royal Charles, Royal James, Royal Katherine, Royal Oak, (Royal) Sovereign, Ruby, Rupert, St. Andrew, St. George, St. Jacob, Samuel, Sancta Maria, Slothany, Swallow, Tiger, Triumph, Turkey Merchant*, Unicorn, Unity, Vanguard, Victory, Virgin, Warspite, Welcome, Yarmouth, York, Zealand.

* *hired*

BUGIA 1671   8 May 1671

Advice, Dragon, Garland, Little Victory, Mary, Portsmouth, Revenge.

SOLE BAY 1672   28 May 1672

Adventure, Advice, Alice and Francis, Ann and Judith, Anne, Antelope, Bantam, Bonaventure, Bristol, Cambridge, Charles, Crown, Dartmouth, Diamond, Dover, Dreadnought, Dunkirk, Edgar, Fairfax, Forester, Fountain, French Ruby, Gloucester, Greenwich, Henry, Katherine, Leopard, London, Mary, Mary Rose, Monck, Monmouth, Mountague, Old James, Phoenix, Plymouth, Prince, Princess, Rachel, Rainbow, Resolution, Robert, Royal James, Royal Katherine, Ruby, Rupert, St. Andrew, St. George, St. Michael, Sovereign, Success, Sweepstakes, Thomas and Edward, Tiger, Triumph, Unicorn, Victory, Warspite, Yarmouth, York.

SCHOONEVELD 1673
28 May and 4 June 1673

Advice, Anne, Assurance, Bonaventure, Cambridge*,Charles, Constant Warwick, Crown, Diamond, Dreadnought, Dunkirk, Edgar, Falcon, Foresight, French Ruby, Gloucester, Greenwich, Hampshire, Happy Return, Henrietta, Henry, Lion, London, Mary, Mary Rose, Monck, Newcastle, Old James, Prince, Princess, Providence*, Rachel*, Rainbow, Resolution*, Revenge, Royal Charles, Royal Katherine, Ruby, Rupert, St. Andrew, St. George, St. Michael, Samuel and Anne*, Sovereign, Stavoreen, Sweepstakes, Swiftsure**, Triumph, Unicorn, Victory, Warspite, Welcome**, Yarmouth, York.

* *First action only.*   ** *Second action only.*

TEXEL 1673   11 August 1673

Advice, Anne, Assurance, Blessing, Bonaventure, Bristol, Cambridge, Charles, Crown, Diamond, Dolphin, Dreadnought, Dunkirk, Edgar, Fairfax, Falcon, Foresight, French Ruby, Friendship, Gloucester, Greenwich, Guernsey, Hampshire, Happy Return, Hard Bargain, Henrietta (bis), Henry, Hopewell, Katherine(bis), Leopard(bis), Lion, Lizard, London, Mary, Mary Rose, Monck, Monmouth, Newcastle, Nonsuch, Old James, Pearl(bis), Plymouth, Portsmouth, Prince, Princess, Prudent Mary, Rainbow, Resolution, Roe, Rose, Royal Charles, Royal Katherine, Ruby, Rupert, St. Andrew, St. George, St. Michael, Society, Sovereign, Stavoreen, Success, Swallow, Sweepstakes, Swiftsure, Triumph, Truelove, Unicorn, Victory, Warspite, Yarmouth, York.

BARFLEUR 1692   19-24 May 1692

Adventure, Advice, Aetna, Albemarle, Berwick, Blaze, Bonaventure, Britannia, Burford, Cadiz Merchant, Cambridge, Captain, Centurion, Charles Galley, Chester, Crown, Defiance, Deptford, Dragon, Dreadnought, Duchess, Duke, Eagle, Edgar, Elizabeth, Essex, Expedition, Extravagant, Falcon, Flame, Fox, Grafton, Greenwich, Greyhound, Griffin, Half-Moon, Hampton Court, Hawk, Hope, Hopewell, Hound, Hunter, Kent, Lenox, Lightning, Lion, London, Mary Galley, Monck, Monmouth, Mountague, Neptune, Northumberland, Ossory, Owner's Love, Oxford, Phaeton, Portsmouth, Resolution, Restoration, Roebuck, Royal Katherine, Royal William, Ruby, Rupert, St. Albans, St. Andrew, St. Michael, Sandwich, Sovereign, Speedwell, Spy, Stirling Castle, Strombolo, Suffolk, Swiftsure, Thomas and Elizabeth, Tiger Prize, Vanguard, Vesuvius, Victory, Vulcan, Vulture, Warspite, Windsor Castle, Wolf, Woolwich.

VIGO 1702   12 October 1702

Association, Barfleur, Bedford, Berwick, Cambridge, Essex, Grafton, Griffin, Hawk, Hunter, Kent, Lightning, Mary, Monmouth, Northumberland, Orford, Pembroke, Phoenix, Ranelagh, Royal Sovereign*, Somerset, Swiftsure, Terrible, Torbay, Vulture.

* *Not engaged*

GIBRALTAR 1704   24 July 1704

Berwick, Burford, Dorsetshire, Eagle, Essex, Grafton, Kingston, Lenox, Monck, Monmouth, Mountague, Nassau, Nottingham, Ranelagh, Royal Katherine, Suffolk, Swiftsure, Yarmouth.

VELEZ MALAGA 1704   13 August 1704

Assurance, Barfleur, Bedford, Berwick, Boyne, Burford, Cambridge, Centurion, Charles galley, Dorsetshire, Eagle, Essex, Firebrand, Firme, Garland, Grafton, Griffin, Hare, Hunter, Jefferies, Kent, Kingston, Lark, Lenox, Lightning, Monck, Monmouth, Mountague, Namur, Nassau, Newark, Newport, Norfolk, Nottingham, Orford, Panther, Phoenix, Prince George, Princess Anne, Ranelagh, Roebuck, Royal Katherine, Royal Oak, St. George, Shrewsbury, Somerset, Suffolk, Swallow, Swiftsure, Tartar, Terror, Tilbury, Torbay, Triton, Vulcan, Vulture, Warspite, William and Mary, Yarmouth.

MARBELLA 1705   10 March 1705

Antelope, Bedford, Canterbury, Expedition, Greenwich, Hampton Court, Lark, Leopard, Newcastle, Nottingham, Pembroke, Revenge, Swallow, Tiger, Warspite.

(List incomplete)

PASSERO 1718   31 July 1718 (Old Style)
                                    11 August 1718 (New Style)

Argyll, Barfleur, Breda, Burford, Canterbury, Captain, Dorsetshire, Dreadnought, Dunkirk, Essex, Garland, Grafton, Griffin, Kent, Lenox, Loo, Mountague, Orford, Ripon, Rochester, Royal Oak, Rupert, Shrewsbury, Superb.

PUERTO BELLO 1739   22 November 1739

Burford, Hampton Court, Norwich, Princess Louisa, Strafford, Worcester.

FINISTERRE 1747   3 May 1747

Ambuscade, Bristol, Centurion, Defiance, Devonshire, Falcon, Falkland, Monmouth, Namur, Nottingham, Pembroke, Prince Frederick, Prince George, Princess Louisa, Vulcan, Windsor, Yarmouth.

USHANT 1747   14 October 1747

Defiance, Devonshire, Eagle, Edinburgh, Gloucester, Kent, Lion, Monmouth, Nottingham, Portland, Princess Louisa, Tilbury, Weazle, Windsor, Yarmouth.

CAPE FRANÇOIS 1757   21 October 1757

Augusta, Dreadnought, Edinburgh.

SADRAS 1758   29 April 1758

Cumberland, Elizabeth, Newcastle, Protector, Queenborough, Salisbury, Tiger, Weymouth, Yarmouth.

LOUISBURG 1758   8 June – 26 July 1758

Aetna, Beaver, Bedford, Boreas, Burford, Captain, Centurion, Defiance, Devonshire, Diana, Dublin, Gramont, Halifax, Hawke, Hunter, Juno, Kennington, Kingston, Lancaster, Lightning, Namur, Nightingale, Northumberland, Nottingham, Orford, Pembroke, Port Mahon, Prince Frederick, Prince of Orange, Princess Amelia, Royal William, Scarborough, Shannon, Somerset, Squirrel, Sutherland, Terrible, Trent, Vanguard, York.

NEGAPATAM 1758   3 August 1758

Cumberland, Elizabeth, Newcastle, Protector, Queenborough, Salisbury, Tiger, Weymouth, Yarmouth.

LAGOS 1759   17-18 August 1759

Active, Ambuscade, America, Conqueror, Culloden, Edgar, Etna, Favourite, Gibraltar, Glasgow, Gramont, Guernsey, Intrepid, Jersey, Lyme, Namur, Newark, Portland, Prince, Rainbow, St. Albans, Salamander, Shannon, Sheerness, Swiftsure, Tartar's Prize, Thetis, Warspite.

PORTO NOVO 1759   10 September 1759

Cumberland, Elizabeth, Grafton, Newcastle, Queenborough, Salisbury, Sunderland, Tiger, Weymouth, Yarmouth.

QUEBEC 1759   July - 13 September 1759

Alcide, Baltimore, Bedford, Boscawen, Captain, Centurion, Cormorant, Crown, Devonshire, Diana, Dublin, Echo, Eurus, Fowey, Halifax, Hind, Hunter, Lizard, Lowestoffe, Medway, Neptune, Nightingale, Nothumberland, Orford, Pelican, Pembroke, Porcupine, Prince Frederick, Prince of Orange, Princess Amelia, Racehorse, Richmond, Rodney, Royal William, Scarborough, Scorpion, Seahorse, Shrewsbury, Somerset, Squirrel, Stirling Castle, Strombolo, Sutherland, Terrible, Trent, Trident, Vanguard, Vesuvius, Zephyr.

QUIBERON BAY 1759   20 November 1759

In this action Admiral Sir Edward Hawke led his fleet into hazardous waters in a rising gale to defeat a French fleet under Admiral Comte de Conflans. It was a bold tactic and required superb seamanship. Coming so soon after the victory at Quebec, it gave rise to the toast:'May our officers have the eye of a Hawke and the heart of a Wolfe.'

Burford, Chatham, Chichester, Coventry, Defiance, Dorsetshire, Duke, Dunkirk, Essex, Falkland, Hercules, Hero, Intrepid, Kingston, Magnanime, Maidstone, Mars, Minerva, Mountague, Namur, Portland, Resolution, Revenge, Rochester, Royal George, Sapphire, Swiftsure, Temple, Torbay, Union, Vengeance, Venus, Warspite.

BELLE ISLE 1761   7 June 1761

Achilles, Actaeon, Adventure, Aetna, Aldborough, Blast, Buckingham, Burford, Chichester, Dragon, Druid, Escort, Essex, Firedrake, Flamborough, Fly, Furnace, Hampton Court, Hero, Infernal, Launceston, Lynn, Melampe, Monmouth, Prince of Orange, Sandwich, Southampton, Swiftsure, Temeraire, Torbay, Valiant, Vesuvius.

MARTINIQUE 1762
7 January - 16 February 1762

Alcide, Amazon, Antigua, Barbados, Basilisk, Crescent, Crown, Culloden, Devonshire, Dover, Dragon, Dublin, Echo, Falkland, Foudroyant, Granado, Greyhound, Levant, Lizard, Marlborough, Modeste, Nightingale, Norwich, Nottingham, Penzance, Raisonnable, Repulse, Rochester, Rose, Stag, Stirling Castle, Sutherland, Temeraire, Temple, Thunder, Vanguard, Virgin, Woolwich, Zephyr.

HAVANA 1762   6 June - 13 August 1762

Alarm, Alcide, Basilisk, Belleisle, Bonetta, Boreas, Cambridge, Centaur, Centurion, Cerberus, Culloden, Cygnet, Defiance, Devonshire, Dover, Dragon, Dublin, Echo, Edgar, Enterprize, Ferret, Glasgow, Granado, Hampton Court, Intrepid, Lizard, Lurcher, Marlborough, Mercury, Namur, Nottingham, Orford, Pembroke, Porcupine, Richmond, Ripon, Stirling Castle, Sutherland, Temeraire, Temple, Thunder, Trent, Viper, Valiant.

LAKE CHAMPLAIN 1776
11 and 13 October 1776

These two actions were part of the American War of Independence (1775-1783), and by the end of the second action, all but four of the American ships on the Lake had either been sunk or captured.

Carleton, Inflexible, Loyal Convert, Maria, Thunderer.

ST. LUCIA 1778   15 December 1778

Ariadne, Aurora, Barbados, Boyne, Carcass, Centurion, Ceres, Isis, Nonsuch, Pelican, Preston, Prince of Wales, St. Albans, Snake, Venus, Weazle.

ST. VINCENT 1780   16 January 1780

Admiral Sir George Rodney captured a Spanish convoy and then fought a Spanish Fleet under Admiral Don Juan de Langara. The battle continued overnight, earning it the nickname 'The Moonlight Battle'. It gave rise to the Barbadian native song 'Nebba see de day, dat Rodney run away; Nebba see um night, dat Rodney cannot fight.'

Ajax, Alcide, Alfred, Andromeda, Apollo, Bedford, Bienfaisant, Culloden, Cumberland, Defence, Edgar, Hyena, Invincible, Marlborough, Monarch, Montagu, Pegasus, Prince George, Resolution, Royal George, Sandwich, Terrible, Triton.

CHESAPEAKE 1781   16 March 1781

Adamant, America, Bedford, Europe, Guadeloupe, Iris, London, Pearl, Prudente, Robust, Royal Oak.

DOGGER BANK 1781   5 August 1781

Artois, Belle Poule, Berwick, Bienfaisant, Buffalo, Cleopatra, Dolphin, Fortitude, Latona, Preston, Princess Amelia, Surprise.

USHANT 1781   12 December 1781

Agamemnon, Alexander, Arethusa, Britannia, Courageux, Duke, Edgar, Medway, Monsieur, Ocean, Prudente, Queen, Renown, Tartar, Tisiphone, Union, Valiant, Victory.

ST. KITTS 1782   25-26 January 1782

Ajax, Alcide, Alfred, America, Barfleur, Bedford, Belliqueux, Canada, Centaur, Champion, Eurydice, Expedition, Gros Islet, Intrepid, Invincible, Monarch, Montagu, Nymphe, Prince George, Prince William, Princesssa, Prudent, Resolution, Russell, St. Albans, Shrewsbury, Sibyl, Solebay, Torbay.

SADRAS 1782   17 February 1782

Burford, Combustion, Eagle, Exeter, Hero, Isis, Monarca, Monmouth, Seahorse, Superb, Worcester.

THE SAINTS 1782   12 April 1782

Agamemnon, Ajax, Alarm, Alcide, Alecto, Alert, Alfred, America, Andromache, Anson, Arrogant, Barfleur, Bedford, Belliqueux, Canada, Centaur, Champion, Conqueror, Duke, Endymion, Eurydice, Fame, Flora, Formidable, Hercules, Magnificent, Marlborough, Monarch, Montagu, Namur, Nonsuch, Prince George, Prince William, Princessa, Prothée, Repulse, Resolution, Royal Oak, Russell, St. Albans, Torbay, Triton, Valiant, Warrior, Yarmouth, Zebra.

PROVIDIEN 1782   12 April 1782

Burford, Combustion, Eagle, Exeter, Hero, Isis, Magnanime, Monarca, Monmouth, Seahorse, Sultan, Superb, Worcester.

NEGAPATAM 1782   6 July 1782

Burford, Eagle, Exeter, Hero, Isis, Magnanime, Monarca, Monmouth, Seahorse, Sultan, Superb, Worcester.

TRINCOMALEE 1782   3 September 1782

Active, Burford, Combustion, Coventry, Eagle, Exeter, Hero, Isis, Magnanime, Medea, Monarca, Monmouth, San Carlos, Sceptre, Seahorse, Sultan, Superb, Worcester.

MARTINIQUE 1794 5-22 March 1794

Asia, Assurance, Avenger, Beaulieu, Blonde, Boyne, Dromedary, Experiment, Irresistible, Nautilus, Quebec, Rattlesnake, Roebuck, Rose, Santa Margarita, Seaflower, Spiteful, Tormentor, Ulysses, Vengeance, Venom, Vesuvius, Veteran, Winchelsea, Woolwich, Zebra.

FIRST OF JUNE 1794
                28-29 May and 1 June 1794

Admiral Lord Howe's glorious action against the French Admiral Villaret de Joyeuse in the North Atlantic.

Alfred, Aquilon, Audacious, Barfleur, Bellerophon, Brunswick, Caesar, Charon, Comet, Culloden, Defence, Gibraltar, Glory, Impregnable, Incendiary, Invincible, Latona, Leviathan, Majestic, Marlborough, Montagu, Niger, Orion, Pegasus, Phaeton, Queen, Queen Charlotte, Ramillies, Ranger, Rattler, Royal George, Royal Sovereign, Russell, Southampton, Thunderer, Tremendous, Valiant, Venus.

GENOA 1795   13-14 March 1795

Agamemnon, Bedford, Britannia, Captain, Courageux, Diadem, Egmont, Fortitude, Fox, Illustrious, Inconstant, Lowestoffe, Meleager, Moselle, Poulette, Princess Royal, Romulus, St. George, Tarleton, Terrible, Windsor Castle.

CORNWALLIS' RETREAT 1795
17 June 1795

Bellerophon, Brunswick, Mars, Pallas, Phaeton, Royal Sovereign, Triumph.

GROIX ISLAND 1795   23 June 1795

Aquilon, Argus, Astraea, Babet, Barfleur, Charon, Colossus, Dolly, Galatea, Incendiary, Irresistible, London, Megaera, Nymphe, Orion, Prince, Prince George, Prince of Wales, Queen, Queen Charlotte, Revolutionnaire, Royal George, Russell, Sans Pareil, Thalia, Valiant.

CAPE OF GOOD HOPE 1795
14 July - 16 September 1795

America, Crescent, Echo, Hope, Jupiter, Monarch, Moselle, Rattlesnake, Ruby, Sceptre, Sphinx, Stately, Tremendous, Trident.

ST. LUCIA 1796   27 April – 24 May 1796

Alfred, Arethusa, Astraea, Beaulieu, Bulldog, Fury, Ganges, Hebe, Madras, Pelican, Thunderer, Vengeance, Victorieuse, Woolwich.

ST. VINCENT 1797   14 February 1797

Barfleur, Blenheim, Bonne Citoyenne, Britannia, Captain, Colossus, Culloden, Diadem, Egmont, Excellent, Fox, Goliath, Irresistible, Lively, Minerve, Namur, Niger, Orion, Prince George, Raven, Southampton, Victory.

CAMPERDOWN 1797   11 October 1797

Active, Adamant, Agincourt, Ardent, Beaulieu, Bedford, Belliqueux, Brackel, Circe, Diligent, Director, Isis, King George, Lancaster, Martin,

Monarch, Monmouth, Montagu, Powerful, Rose, Russell, Speculator, Triumph, Venerable, Veteran.

NILE 1798   1 August 1798

Alexander, Audacious, Bellerophon, Culloden, Defence, Goliath, Leander, Majestic, Minotaur, Mutine, Orion, Swiftsure, Theseus, Vanguard, Zealous.

DONEGAL 1798   12 October 1798

Amelia, Anson, Canada, Ethalion, Foudroyant, Magnanime, Melampus, Robust.

MINORCA 1798   7-15 November 1798

Argo, Aurora, Centaur, Constitution, Comorant, Leviathan, Peterel.

ACRE 1799   17 March - 20 May 1799

Alliance, Theseus, Tigre.

COPENHAGEN 1801   2 April 1801

Agamemnon, Alcmene, Amazon, Ardent, Arrow, Bellona, Blanche, Cruizer, Dart, Defence*, Defiance, Desirée, Discovery, Edgar, Elephant, Explosion, Ganges, Glatton, Harpy, Hecla, Isis, Jamaica, London*, Monarch, Otter, Polythemus, Raisonnable*, Ramillies*, Russell, St. George*, Saturn*, Suphur, Terror, Veteran*, Volcano, Warrior*, Zebra, Zephyr.

*Support ships, not engaged.

GUT OF GIBRALTAR 1801
12-13 July 1801

Audacious, Caesar, Calpe, Louisa, Spencer, Superb, Thames, Venerable.

EGYPT 1801   8 March - 2 September 1801

Active, Agincourt, Ajax, Alexander, Alligator, Asp, Astraea, Athenien, Babelmandeb, Ballahou, Blonde, Bonne Citoyenne, Brackel, Cameleon, Ceres, Charon, Chichester, Cruelle,

Cyclops, Cynthia, Dangereuse, Delft, Determinée, Diadem, Diane, Dictator, Dido, Dolphin, Dover, Dragon, Druid, El Carmen, Entreprenante, Espiegle, Europa, Eurus, Expedition, Experiment, Flora, Florentina, Foudroyant, Fox, Fulminante, Fury, Gibraltar, Good Design, Gorgon, Gozo, Greyhound, Haerlem, Hebe, Hector, Heroine, Inconstant, Inflexible, Iphigenia, Janissary, Kangaroo, Kent, Leda, Leopard, Madras, Malta, Minerve, Minorca, Minotaur, Modeste, Mondovi, Monmouth, Negresse, Niger, Northumberland, Pallas, Pearl, Pegasus, Penelope, Peterel, Phoenix, Pigmy, Pique, Port Mahon, Regulus, Renommée, Renown, Resource, Roebuck, Romney, Romulus, Rosa, Salamine, Santa Dorothea, Santa Teresa, Scampavia, Sensible, Sheerness, Sir Sidney Smith, Spider, Stately, Sultana, Swiftsure, Tartarus, Termagant, Thetis, Thisbe, Tigre, Tourterelle, Transfer, Trusty, Ulysses, Urchin, Vestal, Victor, Victorieuse, Vincejo, Wilhelmina, Winchelsea, Woolwich.

CAPE TENEZ 1805   4 February 1805

Acheron, Arrow. (*see Single Ship Actions*)

TRAFALGAR 1805   21 October 1805

This action marked the end of a long campaign at sea against the French and Spanish Fleets, and was the last major Fleet encounter under sail (apart from Navarino). The major victory was overshadowed by the death of Admiral Lord Nelson.

Achilles, Africa, Agamemnon, Ajax, Belleisle, Bellerophon, Britannia, Colossus, Conqueror, Defence, Defiance, Dreadnought, Entreprenante, Euryalus, Leviathan, Mars, Minotaur, Naiad, Neptune, Orion, Phoebe, Pickle, Polyphemus, Prince, Revenge, Royal Sovereign, Sirius, Spartiate, Swiftsure, Temeraire, Thunderer, Tonnant, Victory.

BAY OF BISCAY 1805   4 November 1805

Aeolus, Caesar, Courageux, Hero, Namur, Phoenix, Revolutionnaire, Santa Margarita.

CAPE OF GOOD HOPE 1806
8-18 January 1806

Belliqueux, Diadem, Diomede, Encounter,

Espoir, Leda, Protector, Raisonnable.

SAN DOMINGO 1806   6 February 1806

Acasta, Agamemnon, Atlas, Canopus, Donegal, Epervier, Kingfisher, Magicienne, Northumberland, Spencer, Superb.

CURAÇOA 1807   1 January 1807

Anson, Arethusa, Fisgard, Latona, Morne Fortunée.

CAYENNE 1809   14 January 1809

Confiance.

MARTINIQUE 1809
30 January – 24 February 1809

This is the third Honour with this name(the others being 1762 and 1794) indicating the strategic importance of the island. In this action Rear Admiral The Hon. Alexander Cochrane's fleet escorted 10,000 troops and captured the island in an operation lasting just over three weeks.

Acasta, Aeolus, Amaranthe, Bacchus, Belleisle, Bellette, Captain, Cherub, Circe, Cleopatra, Cuttle, Demerara, Dominica, Eclair, Ethalion, Eurydice, Express, Fawn, Forester, Frolic, Gloire, Gorée, Haughty, Hazard, Intrepid, Liberty, Mosambique, Neptune, Pelorus, Penelope, Pompée, Port d'Espagne, Pultusk, Recruit, Ringdove, St. Pierre, Snap, Star, Stork, Subtle, Superieure, Surinam, Swinger, Ulysses, Wolverine, York.

BASQUE ROADS 1809   11 April 1809

Aetna, Aigle, Beagle, Bellona, Caesar, Caledonia, Conflict, Contest, Donegal, Doterel, Emerald, Encounter, Fervent, Foxhound, Gibraltar, Growler, Hero, Illustrious, Imperieuse, Indefatigable, Insolent, King George, Lyra, Martial, Mediator, Nimrod, Pallas, Redpole, Resolution, Revenge, Theseus, Thunder, Unicorn, Valiant, Whiting.

GUADELOUPE 1810
28 January - 5 February 1810

Abercrombie, Achates, Alcmene, Alfred, Amaranthe, Asp, Attentive, Aurora, Bacchus, Ballahou, Bellette, Blonde, Castor, Cherub, Cygnet, Elizabeth, Fawn, Forester, Freija, Frolic, Gloire, Grenada, Guadeloupe, Hazard, Laura, Loire, Melampus, Morne Fortunée, Netley, Observateur, Orpheus, Pelorus, Perlen, Plumper, Pompée, Pultusk, Ringdove, Rosamond, Savage, Sceptre, Scorpion, Snap, Star, Statira, Subtle, Superieure, Surinam, Thetis, Vimiera, Wanderer.

AMBOINA 1810
17 February 1810

Cornwallis, Dover, Samarang.

BAY OF NAPLES 1810
3 May 1810

Spartan.

BANDA NEIRA 1810
9 August 1810

Barracouta, Caroline, Piedmontaise.

TERNATE 1810
29 August 1810

Dover.

LISSA 1811
13 March 1811

Active, Amphion, Cerberus, Volage.

TAMATAVE 1811
20 May 1811

Astraea, Galatea, Phoebe, Racehorse.

JAVA 1811
July – 18 September 1811

Akbar, Barracouta, Bucephalus, Caroline, Cornelia, Dasher, Doris, Harpy, Hecate, Hesper, Hussar, Illustrious, Leda, Lion, Minden, Modeste, Nisus, Phaeton, Phoebe, President, Procris, Psyche, Samarang, Scipion, Sir Francis Drake.

PELAGOSA 1811
29 November 1811

Active, Alceste, Unité.

SAN SEBASTIAN 1813
August - 8 September 1813

Ajax, Andromache, Arrow, Beagle, Challenger, Constant, Despatch, Freija, Holly, Juniper, Lyra, Magicienne, President, Revolutionnaire, Sparrow, Surveillante.

GLÜCKSTADT 1814
5 January 1814

Blazer, Desiree, Hearty, Piercer, Redbreast, Shamrock, and gunboats.

CATTARO 1814
5 January 1814

Bacchante, Saracen.

ALGIERS 1816
27 August 1816

Albion, Belzebub, Britomart, Cordelia, Fury, Glasgow, Granicus, Hebrus, Hecla, Heron, Impregnable, Infernal, Leander, Minden, Mutine, Prometheus, Queen Charlotte, Severn, Superb and rocket boats. Gunboats No 1, 5, 19, 23, and 24.

Note: A Falmouth was also present, but this vessel was a sailing dockyard lighter. The Falmouth frigate was not present, being one of the ships guarding St. Helena. The name does not therefore qualify for the Battle Honour.

BURMA 1824-26
5 March 1824 - 24 February 1826

Alligator, Arachne, Boadicea, Champion, Diana (hired steamer), Larne, Liffey, Slaney, Sophia, Tamar, Tees.

NAVARINO 1827
20 October 1827

Albion, Asia, Brisk, Cambrian, Dartmouth, Genoa, Glasgow, Hind, Mosquito, Philomel, Rose, Talbot.

ADEN 1839
19 January 1839

Coote (Indian Navy), Cruizer, Mahé (Indian Navy), Volage.

SYRIA 1840
10 September - 9 December 1840

Asia, Bellerophon, Benbow, Cambridge, Carysfort, Castor, Cyclops, Daphne, Dido, Edinburgh, Ganges, Gorgon, Hastings, Hazard, Hydra, Implacable, Magicienne, Medea, Phoenix, Pique, Powerful, Princess Charlotte, Revenge, Rodney, Stromboli, Talbot, Thunderer, Vanguard, Vesuvius, Wasp, Zebra.

Note: Hecate was awarded the medal, but as she arrived out only just in time to qualify for the medal, she is NOT entitled to the Battle Honour.

CHINA 1841-42
7 January 1841 - 21 July 1842

1841 - Alligator, Blenheim, Conway, Cruizer, Druid, Herald, Larne, Melville, Nimrod, Pylades, Samarang Sulphur, Wellesley

1841-42 - Algerine, Blonde, Calliope, Columbine, Hyacinth, Jupiter, Modeste, Rattlesnake, Starling.

1842 - Apollo, Belleisle, Childers, Clio, Cornwallis, Dido, Endymion, Harlequin, Hazard, North Star, Plover, Sapphire, Vixen, Wanderer, Young Hebe (tender to Cornwallis)

NEW ZEALAND 1845-47   1845-7

Calliope (1846-7), Castor, Driver, Elphinstone (Indian Navy), Hazard, Inflexible, North Star, Osprey, Racehorse.

KUA KAM 1849   20 October 1849

Columbine, Fury, Phelgethon. (*see Single Ship Actions*)

BURMA 1852-53
10 January 1852 - 30 June 1853

1852 - Hastings, Hermes, Rattler, Salamander, Serpent.

1852-53 - Fox, Spartan, Sphinx, Winchester.

1853 - Bittern, Cleopatra, Contest, Styx.

BALTIC 1854-55
28 March - 20 September 1854
17 April - 10 December 1855

1854 - Alban, Algiers, Boscawen, Cumberland, Dauntless, Gladiator, Hannibal, Hecla, Janus, Leopard, Miranda, Monarch, Neptune, Odin, Penelope, Pigmy, Prince Regent, Princess Royal, Resistance, Rhadamanthus, Rosamund, Royal William, St. George, St. Jean d'Acre, St. Vincent, Sphinx, Stromboli, Termagant, Tribune, Tyne, Valorous, Wrangler, Zephyr.

1854 -55 - Ajax, Amphion, Archer, Arrogant, Basilisk, Belleisle, Blenheim, Bulldog, Caesar, Conflict, Cressy, Cruizer, Cuckoo, Desperate, Dragon, Driver, Duke of Wellington, Edinburgh, Euryalus, Gorgon, Hogue, Imperieuse, James Watt, Lightning, Locust, Magicienne, Majestic, Nile, Otter, Porcupine, Royal George, Snap, Volcano, Vulture.

1855 - Aeolus, Badger, Beacon, Biter, Blazer, Calcutta, Carron, Centaur, Colossus, Cornwallis, Cossack, Dapper, Drake, Eask, Exmouth, Falcon, Firefly, Geyser, Gleaner, Grappler, Growler, Harrier, Hastings, Havock, Hawke, Hind, Jackdaw, Lark, Magpie, Manly, Mastiff, Merlin, Orion, Pelter, Pembroke, Pickle, Pincher, Porpoise, Princess Alice, Prompt, Pylades, Redbreast, Redwing, Retribution, Rocket, Ruby, Russell, Sinbad, Skylark, Snapper, Starling, Stork, Surly, Swinger, Tartar, Thistle, Volage, Weazel.

CRIMEA 1854-55
17 September 1854 - 9 September 1855
(Sea of Azov to 22 November 1855)

1854 - Apollo, Arethusa, Bellerophon, Brenda, Britannia, Circassia, Fury, Minna, Modeste, Pigmy, Retribution, Sampson, Sans Pareil, Shark, Trafalgar, Varna, Vengeance.

1854-55 - Agamemnon, Albion, Algiers, Ardent, Arrow, Banshee, Beagle, Caradoc, Curlew, Cyclops, Danube, Dauntless, Diamond, Firebrand, Furious, Gladiator, Harpy, Highflyer, Industry, Inflexible, Leander, London, Lynx, Medina, Megaera, Miranda, Niger, Queen, Rodney, Royal Albert, Sidon, Simoom, Sphinx, Spiteful, Spitfire, Stromboli, Swallow, Terrible, Tribune, Triton, Valorous, Vesuvius, Viper, Vulcan, Wasp.

1855 - Boxer, Camel, Clinker, Cracker,

Curacoa, Fancy, Firm, Flamer, Glatton, Grinder, Hannibal, Hardy, Jasper, Leopard, Magnet, Meteor, Moslem, Oberon, Odin, Oneida, Princess Royal, Raven, Recruit, St. Jean d'Acre, Snake, Sulina, Weser, Wrangler.

CHINA 1856-60
1 October 1856 - 26 June 1858
1 August - 24 October 1860

1856-60 - Acorn, Actaeon, Adventure, Algerine, Amethyst, Assistance, Auckland (Indian Navy), Banterer, Barracouta, Beagle, Belleisle, Bittern, Bustard, Calcutta, Camilla, Clown, Comus, Cormorant (1856-59), Coromandel, Cruiser, Drake, Elk, Encounter, Esk, Firm, Forester, Furious, Fury, Haughty, Hesper, Highflyer, Hong Kong, Hornet, Inflexible, Insolent, Janus, Kestrel, Lee (1856-59), Leven, Nankin, Niger, Nimrod, Opossum, Pioneer, Pique, Plover (1856-59), Racehorse, Sampson, Sans Pareil, Sir Charles Forbes, Slaney, Spartan (1856-57), Starling, Staunch, Surprise, Sybille, Tribune, Volcano, Watchful, Winchester, Woodcock.

1860 - Bouncer, Cambrian, Centaur, Chesapeake, Cockchafer, Flamer, Grasshopper, Hardy, Havock, Imperieuse, Magicienne, Odin, Pearl, Retribution, Reynard, Ringdove, Roebuck, Scout, Simoom, Snake, Snap, Sparrowhawk, Sphinx, Urgent, Vulcan, Watchman, Weazel.

LUCKNOW 1857-58
(Indian Mutiny 1857-58)

Shannon. *(See Single Ship Actions)*

AMORHA 1858
5 March 1858
(Indian Mutiny 1857-8)

Pearl. *(See Single Ship Actions)*

NEW ZEALAND 1860-66
1860-66

1860-61 - Cordelia, Iris, Niger, Pelorus.

1863-66 - Curacoa, Eclipse, Esk, Falcon, Harrier, Himalaya, Miranda.

1865 - Brisk.

ABYSSINIA 1868
13 April 1868

Dryad, Octavia, Satellite.

Note: The following ships also took part in the campaign, but as they did not land a Naval brigade they are NOT eligible for the Battle Honour:

Argus, Daphne, Nymphe, Spiteful, Star, Vigilant.

ASHANTEE 1873-74
9 June 1873 - 4 February 1874

1873 - Rattlesnake, Seagull.

1873-74 - Active, Amethyst, Argus, Barracouta, Beacon, Bittern, Coquette, Decoy, Dromedary, Druid, Encounter, Himalaya, Merlin, Simoom, Tamar.

1874 - Victor Emmanuel.

ALEXANDRIA 1882
11 July 1882

Alexandra, Beacon, Bittern, Condor, Cygnet, Decoy, Hecla, Helicon, Inflexible, Invincible, Monarch, Penelope, Sultan, Superb, Temeraire.

BENIN 1897
8 - 28 February 1897

Alecto, Barrosa, Forte, Magpie, Philomel, Phoebe, St. George, Theseus, Widgeon.

SOUTH AFRICA 1899-1900
1899-1900

Barrosa, Doris, Forte, Monarch, Philomel, Powerful, Tartar, Terrible.

Note: The following ships also qualified for the medal, but as they did not land a Naval brigade they are NOT eligible for the Battle Honour:

Barracouta, Beagle, Blanche, Dwarf, Fearless, Gibraltar, Magicienne, Magpie, Naiad, Niobe, Partridge, Pearl, Pelorus, Penelope, Racoon, Rambler, Rattler, Redbreast, Sappho, Sybille, Terpsichore, Thetis, Thrush, Widgeon.

CHINA 1900   10 June - 31 December 1900

Alacrity, Algerine, Aurora, Barfleur, Centurion, Endymion, Fame, Orlando, Phoenix, Terrible, Whiting.

Note: The following ships were also entitled to the medal, but did not land a Naval Brigade nor did they take part in the capture of the Taku forts. They are therefore ineligible for the Battle Honour:

Arethusa, Bonaventure, Canning (RIM), Clive (RIM), Dalhousie(RIM), Daphne, Dido, Esk, Goliath, Hart, Hermione, Humber, Isis, Linnet, Marathon, Peacock, Pigmy, Pique, Plover, Protector, Redpole, Rosario, Snipe, Undaunted, Wallaroo, Waterwitch, Woodcock, Woodlark.

HELIGOLAND 1914   28 August 1914

Aboukir, Acheron, Amethyst, Archer, Arethusa, Ariel, Attack, Bacchante, Badger, Beaver, Birmingham, Cressy, Defender, Druid, Euryalus, Falmouth, Fearless, Ferret, Firedrake, Forester, Goshawk, Hind, Hogue, Invincible, Jackal, Laertes, Laforey, Lance, Landrail, Lapwing, Lark, Laurel, Lawford, Legion, Lennox, Leonidas, Liberty, Linnet, Lion, Liverpool, Lizard, Llewellyn, Lookout, Louis, Lowestoft, Lucifer, Lurcher, Lydiard, Lysander, New Zealand, Nottingham, Phoenix, Princess Royal, Queen Mary, Sandfly, Southampton, Submarines: - D.2, D.8, E.4, E.5, E.6, E.7, E.8 & E.9.

FALKLAND ISLANDS 1914
8 December 1914

A fast Squadron of battlecruisers was sent south from Britain to counter a German raiding force which had defeated a British force off Coronel. The British Squadron engaged the German Squadron off the Falkland Islands, only the Dresden escaping, to be sunk later. The action showed the flexibility of British seapower.

Bristol, Carnarvon, Cornwall, Glasgow, Inflexible, Invincible, Kent, Macedonia.

CAMEROONS 1914   1914

Astraea, Challenger, Cumberland, Dwarf.

MESOPOTAMIA 1914-17   1914-17

1914 - Ocean.
1914-15 - Comet, Lawrence, Lewis Pelly, Shaitan.
1914-16 - Espiegle, Miner.
1914-17 - Odin.
1915 - Bahrein, Clio, Massoudieh, Shushan.
1915-16 - Muzaffri, Sumana.
1915-17 - Butterfly, Cranefly, Dragonfly, Flycatcher, Gadfly,
1915 & 1917 - Firefly.
1916 - Julnar,
1916-17 - Gnat, Grayfly, Greenfly, Mantis, Mayfly, Moth, Sawfly, Snakefly, Stonefly, Tarantula, Waterfly.
1917 - Bee, Blackfly, Caddisfly, Hoverfly, Scarab, Sedgefly,

BELGIAN COAST 1914-18
4 August 1914 - 19 October 1918

1914 - Ariel, Brilliant, Exmouth, Foresight, Hazard, Humber, Irresistible, Lapwing, Lizard, Rinaldo, Russell, Sapphire, Severn, Sirius, Vestal.
1914-15 - Columbia, Flirt, Maori, Mersey, Nubian, Revenge, Venerable, Viking.
1914-16 - Amazon, Bustard, Cossack, Crusader, Excellent, Gurkha, Kangaroo, Laurel, Myrmidon, Tartar.
1914-17 - Crane, Falcon, Gipsy, Mermaid, Syren.
1914-18 - Attentive, Fawn,
1915 - Brighton Queen, Cambridge, Curran, Devonia, Duchess of Montrose, Glen Avon, Gransha, Lady Ismay, Marmion II, Marshal Ney, Menelaus, Peary, Queen Victoria, Ravenswood, Redoubtable, Riviera, Saracen, Sargetta, Westward Ho. TBs 4, 24.
1915-16 - Albyn, Jupiter II, Leven, Lysander, Mohawk, Prince Rupert, Racehorse, Ure, Zulu.
1915-18 - General Craufurd, Greyhound, Lord Clive, Marshal Soult, Prince Eugene, Sir John Moore, Monitor M.25.
1916 - Carysfort, Cleopatra, Lightfoot, Lucifer, Medea, Milne, Murray, P.11, Undaunted.
1916-17 - Afridi, Centaur, Lochinvar.
1916-18 - Erebus, General Wolfe, Manly, Mansfield, Mastiff, Matchless, Melpomene, Miranda, Terror.
1917 - Ferret, Kempton, Lance, Nimrod, Nugent, Radiant, Recruit, Retriever, Satyr, Sharpshooter, Skilful, Springbok, Starfish, Surprise, Taurus, Thruster, Truculent. Monitor M.24. CMBs 1, 3, 8, 9, 13, 15A.

1917-18 - Botha, Broke, Faulknor, Mentor, Moorsom, Morris, Phoebe, Swift. Monitor M.23, M.26, M.27. CMBs 2, 4, 5, 7, 10, 12.
1918 - Gorgon, Iris, Termagant, Velox. CMBs 14A, 16A, 19A, 20A, 21B, 22B, 23B, 24A, 25BD, 28A, 30B, 33A, 38B, 63BD, 64BD, 66BD, 68B, 70A, 71A, 73BD, 74BD, 76A, 86BD, 89BD. (List incomplete)
MLs 103, 105, 110, 239, 252, 272, 276, 279, 280, 282, 283, 532.

DOGGER BANK 1915　　　24 January 1915

Acheron, Arethusa, Ariel, Attack, Aurora, Birmingham, Defender, Druid, Ferret, Forester, Goshawk, Hornet, Hydra, Indomitable, Jackal, Laertes, Laforey, Landrail, Lapwing, Lark, Laurel, Lawford, Legion, Liberty, Lion, Lookout, Louis, Lowestoft, Lucifer, Lydiard, Lysander, Mastiff, Mentor, Meteor, Milne, Minos, Miranda, Morris, New Zealand, Nottingham, Phoenix, Princess Royal, Sandfly, Southampton, Tiger, Tigress, Undaunted.

SUEZ CANAL 1915　　　2 - 4 February 1915

Clio, Dufferin (RIM), Hardinge (RIM), Himalaya, Minerva, Ocean, Proserpine, Swiftsure.
TB 043.

DARDANELLES 1915-16
19 February 1915 - 8 January 1916

1915-16 - Abercrombie, Agamemnon, Anemone, Arno, Aster, Bacchante, Basilisk, Beagle, Ben-my-Chree, Blenheim, Bulldog, Canopus, Chatham, Chelmer, Colne, Doris, Earl of Peterborough, Edgar, Endymion, Foresight, Fury, Gazelle, Grafton, Grasshopper, Havelock, Hector, Heliotrope, Hibernia, Honeysuckle, Hussar, Jed, Kennet, Laforey, Lawford, Lord Nelson, Lydiard, Mars, Osiris II, Peony, Prince Edward, Prince George, Queen Victoria, Racoon, Raglan, Rattlesnake, Ribble, Roberts, Russell, Scorpion, Sir Thomas Picton, Staunch, Swiftsure, Talbot, Theseus, Usk, Wear, Welland, Wolverine.
Monitors: M.15, M.16, M.17, M.29, M.31, M.32.
Submarine: E.14.
1915 - Adamant, Albion, Amethyst, Ark Royal, Canning, Cornwall, Cornwallis, Dartmouth,

Dublin, Euryalus, Exmouth, Foxhound, Glory, Goliath, Grampus, Harpy, Humber, Implacable, Inflexible, Irrestistible, Jonquil, London, Louis, Magnificent, Majestic, Manica, Minerva, Mosquito, Ocean, Prince of Wales, Queen, Queen Elizabeth, Renard, River Clyde, Sapphire, Scourge, Triad, Triumph, Venerable, Vengeance.
Monitors: M. 18, M.19, M.21, M33.
Submarines: AE.2, B.6, B.11, E.2, E.7, E.11, E.12, E.15, E.20.
TB 064.

JUTLAND 1916　　　31 May 1916

Abdiel, Acasta, Achates, Acheron, Active, Agincourt, Ajax, Ambuscade, Ardent, Ariel, Attack, Badger, Barham, Bellerophon, Bellona, Benbow, Birkenhead, Birmingham, Black Prince, Blanche, Boadicea, Broke, Calliope, Canada, Canterbury, Caroline, Castor, Centurion, Champion, Chester, Christopher, Cochrane, Collingwood, Colossus, Comus, Conqueror, Constance, Contest, Cordelia, Defence, Defender, Dublin, Duke of Edinburgh, Engadine, Erin, Falmouth, Faulknor, Fearless, Fortune, Galatea, Garland, Gloucester, Goshawk, Hampshire, Hardy, Hercules, Hydra, Inconstant, Indefatigable, Indomitable, Inflexible, Invincible, Iron Duke, Kempenfelt, King George V, Landrail, Lapwing, Laurel, Liberty, Lion, Lizard, Lydiard, Maenad, Magic, Malaya, Mandate, Manners, Marksman, Marlborough, Marne, Martial, Marvel, Mary Rose, Menace, Michael, Midge, Milbrook, Mindful, Minion, Minotaur, Mischief, Monarch, Mons, Moon, Moorsom, Moresby, Morning Star, Morris, Mounsey, Munster, Mystic, Narbrough, Narwhal, Neptune, Nerissa, Nessus, Nestor, New Zealand, Nicator, Noble, Nomad, Nonsuch, Nottingham, Oak, Obdurate, Obedient, Onslaught, Onslow, Opal, Ophelia, Orion, Ossory, Owl, Pelican, Petard, Phaeton, Porpoise, Princess Royal, Queen Mary, Revenge, Royal Oak, Royalist, St. Vincent, Shannon, Shark, Southampton, Sparrowhawk, Spitfire, Superb, Temeraire, Termagant, Thunderer, Tiger, Tipperary, Turbulent, Unity, Valiant, Vanguard, Warrior, Warspite, Yarmouth.

DOVER 1917　　　21 April 1917

Broke, Swift. *(See Single Ship Actions)*

SCANDINAVIAN CONVOYS 1917
17 October and 12 December 1917

Mary Rose, Partridge, Pellew, Strongbow.

ZEEBRUGGE 1918　　　　23 April 1918

Zeebrugge: - Attentive, Daffodil, Erebus, Intrepid, Iphigenia, Iris II, Lingfield, Manly, Mansfield, Melpomene, Moorsom, Morris, Myngs, North Star, Phoebe, Scott, Stork, Teazer, Termagant, Terror, Thetis, Trident, Truculent, Ulleswater, Velox, Vindictive, Warwick, Whirlwind.
Submarines: C.1, C.3.
CMBs 5,7,15A, 16A, 17A, 21B, 22B, 23B, 24A, 25BD, 26B, 27A, 28A, 29A, 30B, 32A, 34A, 35A.
MLs: 79, 110, 121, 128, 223, 239, 241, 252, 258, 262, 272, 280, 282, 308, 314, 345, 397, 416, 420, 422, 424, 513, 525, 526, 533, 549, 552, 555, 557, 558, 560, 561, 562.

Ostend: - Afridi, Brilliant, Faulknor, General Craufurd, Lightfoot, Lord Clive, Marshal Soult, Mastiff, Matchless, Mentor, Prince Eugene, Sirius, Swift, Tempest, Tetrarch, Zubian.
Monitors: M.21, M.24, M.26.
CMBs 2, 4, 10, 12, 19A, 20A.
MLs: 11, 16, 17, 22, 23, 30, 60, 105, 254, 274, 276, 279, 283, 429, 512, 532, 551, 556.

OSTEND 1918　　　　　　10 May 1918

Faulknor, Prince Eugene, Trident, Velox, Vindictive, Warwick, Whirlwind.
CMBs: 22B, 23B, 24A, 25BD, 26B, 30B.
MLs: 254, 276.

ATLANTIC 1939-45　　　　　　1939-45

This major Area Battle Honour reflects the long, six-year struggle to maintain the supply chain of food and other material to Britain in World War II and which resulted in the defeat of the U-boats.

Abelia 41-45, Aberdeen 39-45, Acanthus 41-45, Acasta 39-40, Achates 40/42, Active 39-44, Activity 44, Acute 43, Affleck 43-44, Agassiz 41-45, Ailsa Craig 44, Aire 43-45, Alaunia 39-41, Albatross 42-43, Alberni 41-44, Alca 42, Alcantara 40, Aldenham 42, Algoma 41-44, Alisma 41-43/45, Allington Castle 44-45,

Alnwick Castle 45, Alynbank 40/42-43, Amaranthus 41-45, Amazon 39-43, Amberley Castle 45, Ambuscade 40-41/44, America 41, Amethyst 45, Amherst 41-45, Anchusa 41-45, Anemone 40-43, Angle 40-43, Anguilla 44, Annan 44, Annapolis 41-44, Antares 43-44, Antelope 39-44, Anthony 40-41/43-44, Antigonish 45, Antigua 44, Antwerp 41, Aquamarine 42-43, Arab 40-43, Arabis 40-42, Arawa 40, Arbiter 44, Arbutus 40-42, Archer 43-44, Arctic Explorer 42, Arctic Pioneer 40, Arctic Ranger 40/42, Arcturus 43, Ardent 39-40, Argus 41-42, Ariguani 41, Armeria 42-45, Arnprior 44-45, Arran 43, Arrow 40/43, Arrowhead 41-45, Arsenal 40, Arvida 41-45, Asbestos 44-45, Ascania 39-41*, Ascension 44, Ashanti 40, Asphodel 40-44, Assiniboine 39-45, Aster 41, Asturias 39-40, Atherstone 43, Atholl 44-45, Atmah 42, Attacker 43-44, Aubretia 41-45, Auckland 39, Audacity 41, Aurania 40-41, Auricula 41-42, Ausonia 39-41, Australia 40-41, Avon 43-44, Avon Vale 41-43, Awe 44, Aylmer 44-45, Ayrshire 41/43-45, Azalea 41-43,

Bachaquero 43, Baddeck 41-45, Badsworth 41-43, Baffin 44, Bahamas 44-45, Balfour 44, Ballinderry　　43-45,　　Balsam　　43-45, Bamborough Castle 44, Banff 41-43, Barberry 45, Barcliff 42, Barle 43, Barnwell 45, Barrie 41-45, Barthorpe 45, Bartizan 45, Bath 41, Battleford 41-45, Battler 42-45, Bayfield 43-44, Bayntun 43-44, Bazely 43/45, Beacon Hill 44, Beagle 40-43/45, Beauharnois 44-45, Beaumaris 45, Beaver 42, Bedouin 40-41, Begonia 41, Belleville 45, Bellwort 41-45, Belmont 41-42, Bentinck 43-45, Bentley 44, Bergamot 41-45, Berkeley Castle 44, Berkshire 40, Bermuda 43, Berry 43-44, Berwick 39, Betony 43, Beverley 40-43, Bickerton 44, Bideford 39-45, Birdlip 42-43, Biter 43-44, Bittersweet 41-45, Black Swan 41-43, Blackfly 40/42-44, Blackmore 43, Blackwood 43-44, Blairmore 43/45, Blankney 41-43, Bleasdale 44, Bligh 44-45, Bluebell 40-44, Boadicea 41-43, Bombardier 43-45, Borage 42-45, Border Cities 44-45, Boreas 41-42, Boston 42, Bowmanville 44-45, Bradford 41-43, Braithwaite 44, Brandon 41-45, Brantford 42-44, Brecon 45, Breda 40, Bredon 42, Bridgewater 42-43, Brilliant 41-43, Brimnes 44, Brissenden 43, Broadwater 41, Broadway 41-43, Brocklesby 43, Brockville 43-45, Broke 39-42, Bruiser 44, Bryony 43, Buckingham 45, Buctouche 41-45, Bude 43, Bugloss 44, Bulldog 41/43-45, Bullen 44, Bulolo 40, Burdock 41-44, Burges 43-44, Burke 41, Burlington 42-44, Burnham 41-43,

Burra 41, Burwell 41-43, Bush 42-43, Bushwood 42, Bute 41/43, Butser 42-44, Buttercup 42-45, Buttermere 41-42/44, Buxton 41-43, Byard 43-44, Byron 44-45,

Cachalot 39, Caicos 44, Cairo 40-41, Calder 43-45, Caldwell 40-43, Calendula 40-41, Calgary 42-45, California 41, Cam 44, Camellia 40-42/45, Camito 40, Campania 44, Campanula 40-44, Campbell 40/42-43, Campbeltown 41-42, Campeador V 40, Campion 41-45, Camrose 41-45, Candytuft 40-41, Canso 44, Canton 40, Cap-de-la-Madelaine 45, Cape Argona 40-45, Cape Breton 44-45, Cape Clear 42, Cape Comorin 43-44, Cape Mariato 42-45, Cape Palliser 42-44, Cape Portland 42-45, Cape Warwick 41-42, Capel 44, Capilano 44-45, Caradoc 40, Caraquet 43-44, Carisbrooke Castle 44, Carlplace 45, Carnarvon Castle 39-40/42, Carnation 41-42, Carnoustie 43, Carthage 42-43, Castleton 40-42, Cathay 40-41, Catherine 43, Cato 43, Cauvery 43-44, Cava 42, Cavina 42, Cayman 44, Celandine 41-45, Celia 41-42, Ceres 39, Chambly 41-45, Chamois 44, Chance 44, Chanticleer 43, Charlestown 41-42, Charlock 44-45, Charlottetown 42, Charybdis 43, Chaser 43, Chaudiere 44, Chebogue 44, Chedabucto 42-43, Chelmer 43-45, Chelsea 40-43, Cheshire 40-42, Chesterfield 41-43, Chicoutimi 41-44, Chilliwack 41-45, Chitral 41, Churchill 41-44, Cilicia 39-42, Clare 40-43, Clarkia 40-41/43-44, Clayoquot 42/44, Clematis 40-45, Clevela 43-44, Cleveland 41-44, Clinton 43, Clover 41-45, Coaticook 44-45, Cobalt 41-45, Cobourg 44-45, Coldstreamer 43-45, Coll 43, Collingwood 41-44, Colombo 39/42/44, Coltsfoot 41-43/45, Colombia 40-44, Columbine 40-44, Combatant 44, Comorin 40-41, Conn 44-45, Conqueror 44-45, Convolvulus 41-44, Cooke 44, Copinsay 43-44, Copper Cliff 44-45, Coreopsis 40-43, Corfu 40/42, Corinthian 41-43, Cosby 44-45, Cossack 40-41, Cotillion 43-44, Cotton 44, Coventry 40, Coventry City 41, Cowdray 43, Cowichan 41-43, Cowslip 41-45, Crane 43-44, Cranstoun 45, Crispin 41, Crocus 40-45, Croome 41-42, Cubitt 44-45, Cuckmere 43, Culver 41-42, Cumbrae 43, Curacoa 40, Cutty Sark 40, Cyclamen 40-45, Cygnet 43-44,

Dacres 43, Dahlia 41-44, Dainty 40, Daneman 40-43, Dangay 40, Dart 44, Dasher 42, Dauntless 39, Dauphin 41-45, Davy 44, Dawson 44-45, Deane 45, Decoy 42, Delhi 40, Delphinium 40-41/44-45, Deptford 39-43, Derby County 40, Derbyshire 40-42*,

Derwent 42, Despatch 39, Deveron 43-44, Devon City 45, Dianella 41-42/44-45, Dianthus 41-44, Digby 42-44, Dittany 43-45, Dochet 43, Domett 43-45, Dominica 44-45, Dorade II 41, Dornoch 43, Dorothy Gray 42-43, Dorsetshire 41, Douglas 40-44, Dovey 44, Drumheller 41-45, Drummondville 42-45, Drury 43-45, Duckworth 43-44, Dumbarton Castle 44-45, Duncan 41-45, Duncton 42-44, Dundas 42-45, Dundee 40, Dunedin 41, Dunkery 42-43, Dunnottar Castle 39-42, Dunvegan 41-44, Dunvegan Castle 40, Dunver 43-45,

Earl Kitchener 42, East View 44-45, Ebor Wyke 42-44, Echo 39, Eclipse 43, Eday 42, Edinburgh 41, Edmunston 42-45, Effingham 39-40, Eglantine 41-44, Eglinton 40, Egret 39/41-42, Ekins 44, Electra 39-40, Ellesmere 40/44, Elm 42/44, Emerald 39-40, Emperor 43-44, Empress 44, Enchantress 39-45, Encounter 39, Engadine 43, Enterprise 39-40, Erebus 43, Erica 40-41, Erin 40, Eriskay 43/45, Erne 42-45, Erraid 45, Escapade 39/43/45, Escort 39-40, Esk 39, Esperance Bay 40-41, Esquimalt 43-44, Essington 43-45, Ettrick 43-45, Evadne 42/45, Evenlode 43-44, Exe 42-45, Exmoor 41-42, Exmouth 39, Eyebright 41-45,

Fairfax 44, Fal 43-45, Fame 42-44, Fandango 40/42-43, Fantome 43, Farndale 41, Faulknor 39/41/43, Fearless 41, Fencer 43-44, Fennel 41-45, Fergus 45, Fetlar 43-44, Fidelity 42, Findhorn 43-44, Firedrake 39-40/42, Fishguard 41-43, Fitzroy 44-45, Flatholm 44, Fleetwood 40-44, Fleur de Lys 40-41, Flint 43, Flint Castle 44-45, Foley 43-44, Folkestone 40-44, Foresight 41, Forest Hill 44, Forester 39/41/43-44, Fort Frances 45, Fort William 43, Fort York 43, Fortune 39, Fowey 39-45, Foxhound 39/41, Foxtrot 40/42-43, Fraser 39, Fredericton 42-45, Freesia 41-42, Friendship 43/45, Fritillary 41-42/45, Frontenac 44-45, Fury 41-43, Fusilier 43-45,

Gallant 39, Galt 41-45, Gananoque 42-45, Gardenia 40-42, Gardiner 43-45, Garland 40-43, Garlies 43-44, Gateshead 43, Gatineau 43-44, Gavotte 42-43, Gazelle 43-44, Genista 42, Gentian 40-44, Georgetown 40-43, Georgian 41-42/44, Geranium 40-45, Giffard 44, Gipsy 39, Glace Bay 44-45, Gladiolus 40-41,Gleaner 40-41, Glenarm 43-44, Glowworm 39, Gloxinia 40/44, Goathland 43, Godavari 43, Goderich 42-45, Godetia 40/42-43, Goodall 44, Goodson 44, Gore 43-44, Gorgon 43, Gorleston 41-43, Gossamer 40-41, Gould 43-

44, Gozo 43, Grafton 39, Granby 42-44, Grandmere 43/45, Great Admiral 43, Grecian 43-44, Grenade 39, Grenadier 43-45, Grenville 39, Greyhound 39, Griffin 42, Grindall 43-45, Grou 44, Grove 42, Gruinard 43, Guardsman 44-45, Guelph 44-45, Gurkha 41, Guysborough 43-44,

Haarlem 40/42-44, Hadleigh Castle 43-44, Halifax 42-45, Hallowell 44-45, Hamilton 42-43, Hamlet 41-42/44, Hardy 40, Hargood 44, Hart 44-45, Hartland 41-42, Harvester 40-43, Hascosay 44, Hastings 40-43, Hasty 39, Havant 40, Havelock 40-45, Havock 39, Hawkesbury (RCN) 44-45, Hazard 43-44, Hazel 42-44, Heartsease 40-41, Heather 40-45, Heliotrope 40-42, Helmsdale 43-44, Hepatica 40-45, Hereward 40, Hermes 40, Heron 40, Herschell 43, Hertfordshire 43, Hespeler 44-45, Hesperus 40-45, Heythrop 41, Hibiscus 40-42, Highlander 40-45, Hilary 41-42, Hollyhock 40-41, Holmes 44-45, Homeguard 44-45, Honesty 43, Honeysuckle 40-45, Hornpipe 40, Hoste 44, Hostile 39-40, Hotspur 40/43-44, Huddersfield Town 40, Hugh Walpole 41-43, Humberstone 44-45, Hunter 39-40 and 43-44, Huntsville 44-45, Hurricane 40-44, Hurst Castle 44, Hurworth 41, Husky 40, Hussar 43, Hyderabad 42-43/45, Hydrangea 41-44, Hyperion 39,

Ibis 41-42, Icarus 39/41/43-44, Ilex 39, Ilfracombe 43/45, Imogen 39, Imperial 39, Imperialist 41/43, Impulsive 42-43, Inchkeith 42, Inchmarnock 42, Inconstant 43-44, Indian Star 40/42, Inglefield 39-41/43, Inglis 44-45, Ingonish 44, Inkpen 42, Inman 44-45, Intrepid 39/41, Inver 43-45, Iroquois 43, Isis 39-43, Itchen 43, Ithuriel 42, Ivanhoe 39,

Jacinth 40, Jackal 39/41, Jaguar 40, Janus 39, Jaseur 45, Jasmine 41-42, Jason 40, Jasper 40, Javelin 40, Jed 43-44, Jervis Bay 40, Joliette 44, Jonquiere 44, Jonquil 41-45, Juliet 42, Jumna 41, Juno 39,

Kale 43, Kamloops 41/43-45, Kamsack 42-45, Kapuskasing 44-45, Keats 44-45, Keith 39-40, Kelly 39, Kelvin 40, Kempenfelt 39, Kempthorne 44-45, Kenilworth Castle 44, Kenogami 41-45, Kenora 42-45, Kent 40, Kentville 44-45, Kenya 41, Keppel 40-43, Kerrera 42, Khyber 42, Kilburnie 44-45, Kilbride 44, Killegray 42, Kilmarnock 44-45, Kilmartin 44-45, Kilmelford 44-45, Kilmington 45, Kilmore 45, Kincardine 44-45, King George V 41, King Sol 40-43, Kingcup 41-45, Kingston 39, Kingston Agate 44,

Kingston Amber 43-44, Kingston Beryl 42, Kingston Chrysolite 40/43, Kipling 40, Kirkella 42-44, Kistna 43, Kitchener 42-43, Kite 43-44, Kiwi 42, Knaresborough Castle 44-45, Kokanee 44-45, Konkan 42, Kootenay 43-45,

La Hulloise 45, La Malbaie 42-45, La Malouine 40-43, Lacennia 41/43/45, Lachine 42-45, Lachute 45, Laconia 40-41, Lady Beryl 43-44, Lady Elsa 40-42, Lady Hogarth 41-43/45, Lady Lilian 40, Lady Madeleine 40-45, Lady Shirley 41, Laforey 42, Lagan 43, Lamerton 41-42, Lanark 44-45, Lancaster 41, Lancer 43-45, Landguard 41-43, Largs 42, Larkspur 41, Lasalle 45, Lauderdale 42, Launceston Castle 44, Lauzon 44-45, Lavender 41-45, Lawson 44, Leamington 41-43, Leaside 44-45, Leda 39/41, Leeds Castle 45, Leeds United 40, Legion 41, Leith 39-44, Lethbridge 41-45, Letitia 39-40, Levis 41/44/45, Leyland 42, Liddesdale 43, Lightfoot 43, Linaria 43, Lincoln 41-43, Lincoln City 40, Lindsay 44-45, Lively 41, Lobelia 41-44, Loch Achray 45, Loch Craggie 45, Loch Eck 45, Loch Fada 45, Loch Fyne 45, Loch Glendhu 45, Loch Insh 44, Loch Killin 44, Loch More 45, Loch Oskaig 43, Loch Quoich 45, Loch Ruthven 45, Loch Scavaig 45, Loch Shin 45, Loch Tulla 44, Lockeport 43, London 41, Londonderry 39-45, Long Branch 44-45, Longueuil 44-45, Loosestrife 42-45, Lord Hotham 40/42, Lord Middleton 42-44, Lord Nuffield 42-44, Lord Stanhope 43, Loring 45, Lossie 43-44, Lotus 44-45, Louis 44, Louisburg 41-42/44-45, Lowestoft 40/42/44-45, Ludlow 41-42, Lulworth 41-43, Lunenburg 42-45,

Macbeth 41-42-44, Mackay 39-40, Magnolia 42, Magpie 43-44, Mahone 42/44-45, Malaya 40-41, Malcolm 40-42/44-45, Malines 41, Mallow 40-43, Maloja 40-41, Malpeque 41-42, Man-o-war 40-43/45, Manners 44-45, Mansfield 41-44, Maori 41, Maplin 41-42, Margaree 40, Marguerite 41, Marigold 41-42, Maron 41-42, Marsdale 41-42, Martin 42, Matane 41, Matapedia 41-45, Mauritius 41, Mayflower 41-43, Mazurka 42-44, Meadowsweet 42-44, Medicine Hat 43, Melbreak 44-45, Melita 45, Melville 42-45, Menestheus 41, Meon 44-45, Merceditta 40, Merrittonia 45, Meteor 42-43, Middlesex 44-45, Middleton 44, Midland 42-45, Mignonette 41-45, Mildenhall 39, Milford 40-41/43-44, Milltown 42-44, Milne 42-43, Mimico 45, Mimosa 41-42, Minas 41-44, Minna 43, Miscou 44, Moa 41, Moncton 42-43,

Monkshood 41-44, Monnow 44-45, Montbretia 41-42, Montclare 39-41, Montgomery 41-43, Montreal 44-45, Montrose 39-40, Mooltan 40, Moorsman 45, Moorsom 44, Moosejaw 41-43, Morden 41-45, Moreton Bay 40, Morpeth Castle 44-45, Morris Dance 43, Mounsey 44, Mourne 43-44, Moyola 43-44, Mulgrave 43-44, Musketeer 43, Myosotis 41-43,

Nab Wyke 41-44, Nairana 44, Nanaimo 41-44, Napanee 41-45, Narbrough 45, Narcissus 41-45, Narwhal 39, Nasturtium 40-45, Nene 43-44, Neptune 39, Ness 43-44, Nestor 41, New Glasgow 44-45, New Waterford 44, New Westminster 42-45, New York City 44, Newark 41-42, Newmarket 41-42, Newport 41, Niagara 40-44, Nigella 41-42, Niger 41, Nigeria 41, Nipigon 41-45, Noranda 43-45, Norfolk 41, Norsyd 44-45, North Bay 44-45, Northern Dawn 40-42, Northern Foam 43-45, Northern Gem 40-45, Northern Gift 43-45, Northern Pride 40-45, Northern Reward 43-45, Northern Sky 43-45, Northern Spray 40-45, Northern Sun 42-45, Northern Wave 39/41-45, Norwich City 40-42, Notts County 40-42, Nyasaland 44-45,

Oakham Castle 45, Oakville 42-45, Oasis 43, Obdurate 43, Obedient 43, Odzani 43-45, Offa 43, Onslaught 43, Onslow 42, Ophelia 42, Opportune 43, Orangeville 44-45, Orchis 41-44, Orduna 42, Orfasy 42-43, Oribi 42-43, Orient Star 39, Orillia 41-45, Orion 39, Orissa 42, Orwell 43, Oshawa 44-45, Ottawa 39-45, Otway 40, Outremont 44, Owen Sound 44-45, Oxford Castle 44-45, Oxlip 42-45, Oxna 43,

PC 74 (43), Palomares 42, Panther 42-43, Papua 44-45, Parrett 43, Parrsboro 43, Parry Sound 44-45, Pasley 44, Pathfinder 42-43, Patroller 44-45, Paynter 42-44, Peacock 45, Pegasus 40-41, Pelican 42-44, Pelorus 45, Penetang 45, Penn 42-43, Pennywort 42-45, Pentland Firth 40, Pentstemon 41-42, Penzance 40, Peony 40, Perim 44-45, Periwinkle 40-41, Perth 39, Peterborough 44-45, Peterhead 43, Petrolia 44-45, Petunia 41-45, Pevensey Castle 44, Pheasant 43-44, Philante 40-42, Picotee 40-41, Pict 42-43, Pictou 41-45, Pimpernel 41-45, Pincher 45, Pink 42-44, Pirouette 42, Plym 43, Polruan 43, Polyanthus 41-43, Poppy 43-45, Porcher 43, Porpoise 40-41, Port Arthus 42-44, Port Colborne 44-45, Port Hope 43-45, Portage 44-45, Portchester Castle 44, Portsdown 42-44, Postillion 44-45, Potentilla 42-43, Poundmaker 44-45, Pozarica 42, Premier 44,

Prescott 41-45, Pretoria Castle 40/42, Primrose 40-43/45, Primula 40/44, Prince David 41, Prince Robert 43-44, Prince Rupert 44, Prodigal 43, Prompt 45, Prospect 43, Protea 43-44, Puffin 40, Puncher 44, Punjabi 40/42, Pursuer 43-45, Pylades 44,

Qu'Appelle 44, Quadrille 42-44, Qualicum 43, Quantock 43, Queen 44, Queen Emma 43, Quentin 42, Quesnel 42-45, Quiberon 43, Quickmatch 43, Quinte 42,

Racehorse 43, Rajah 44, Rajputana (AMC) 40-41, Rajputana(m/s) 42, Ramillies 41, Ramsey 41-42, Ranee 45, Ranpura 40-41/43, Rapid 43, Ravager 43, Reading 41-42, Reaper 44, Recruit 45, Reculver 42, Red Deer 42-45, Redmill 45, Redoubt 43, Redpole 43-44, Redshank 43, Regina 42-44, Registan 41, Reighton Wyke 42-43, Reindeer 40, Renown 40, Repulse 39-40, Resolution 39-40, Restigouche 39-45, Retalick 44, Retriever 42, Revenge 39-41, Rhododendron 40-42/44-45, Richmond 41/43, Rimouski 42-45, Ringdove 43, Ripley 41-42, Riviere du Loup 44-45, Rochester 39-44, Rockcliffe 45, Rockingham 41-43, Rockrose 41-42, Rockwood 44, Rodney 40-41, Rorqual 44, Rosaura 40, Rose 41-44, Rosebay 43, Rosemary 40, Rosthern 41-45, Rother 42-44, Rowley 45, Roxborough 41-43, Royal Marine 44-45, Royal Mount 44-45, Royal Scotsman 44, Royal Sovereign 40-41, Ruler 44, Runnymede 44-45, Rupert 45, Rushen Castle 44-45, Rutherford 44, Rye 42,

Sabina 42, Sable 40, Sabre 40-43, Sackville 42-44, Sagitta 40, Saguenay 39-42, St. Albans 41-43, St. Apollo 40-41, St. Boniface 44-45, St. Cathan 41, St. Catherines 43-44, St. Clair 40-43, St. Croix 40-43, St. Elstan 40-44, St. Francis 41-43, St. John 44, St.Kenan 44, St. Lambert 44-45, St. Laurent 39-45, St. Loman 40, St. Mary's 42, St. Nectan 42-44, St. Pierre 45, St. Stephen 44-45, St. Thomas 44-45, St. Wistan 44, St. Zeno 40-41, Sainte Therese 45, Saladin 40-44, Salisbury 41-43, Salopian 39-40, Salvia 40, Samphire 41-42, Sanda 42, Sandwich 39-44, Saon 45, Sapper 43-45, Sarawak 44, Sardonyx 40-42, Sarnia 42-43, Saskatchewan 43-44, Saskatoon 42-45, Saulte Sainte Marie 44-45, Saxifrage 42-43, Scarba 42, Scarborough 39-44, Sceptre 44, Scimitar 40-42/44, Scottish 43, Scylla 43, Scythian 44, Sea Cliff 44-45, Sea Rover 45, Seadog 44, Seaford 44, Seaham 42, Seal 39, Sealyham 42/44/45, Seanymph 45, Searcher 43-44, Seascout 44, Selkirk 39, Sennen 41-43, Setter 42-43, Severn 40-41, Seychelles 45,

Shakespeare 44, Shalimar 44, Sharpshooter 42-44, Shawinigan 42-44, Shediac 41-44, Sheffield 41-43, Sheldrake 42, Sherbrooke 41-45, Sherwood 41-43, Shiant 42, Shiel 44, Shikari 40-43, Shippigan 43, Shropshire 41, Sidon 45, Sikh 40-41, Sioux 45, Skagi 43, Skate 40-42/44, Skeena 39-44, Skomer 45, Smilax 44, Smiter 44, Smiths Falls 45, Snakefly 40, Snapper 40, Snowberry 41-44, Snowdrop 41-44, Snowflake 41-44, Somaliland 44, Sorel 41-45, Southern Flower 42-44, Southern Gem 40/43-44, Southern Isle 43, Southern Pride 41/43-44, Southern Prince 40-41, Southern Sea 44, Southern Shore 40/42-44, Spark 44, Spartan 43, Speaker 44, Spearhead 45, Speedwell 41/43, Spey 42-44, Sphene 40/42/43, Spikenard 41-42, Spirea 42-45, Sportsman 45, Sposa 42-44, Staffa 43, Stafnes 42-44, Stalker 43-44, Stanley 41, Starling 43-45, Starwort 41-45, Statice 44-45, Steadfast 44, Stella Capella 40-41, Stella Carina 41-43, Stella Pagasi 44, Stellarton 45, Stoic 45, Stoke City 40, Stonecrop 41-45, Stonetown 44-45, Stora 42-44, Stork 40-44, Storm 45, Stormont 44-45, Stratford 42-44, Strathadam 45, Strathella 43-44, Strathroy 45, Striker 43-44, Stroma 42, Strongbow 44, Strule 44, Stuart Prince 44, Stubborn 45, Sturdy 40, Stygian 44, Sudbury 41-44, Summerside 41-44, Sunflower 41-45, Supreme 44, Surf 44, Surprise 41, Sussexvale 45, Swale 42-44, Swansea 43-44, Sweetbriar 41-45, Swift Current 43-44, Sybil 45, Symbol 43,

Taciturn 45, Tadoussac 43/45, Tamarisk 42-43, Tanatside 43, Tango 42-43, Tantivy 45, Tarantella 40, Tattoo 44, Taurus 44-45, Tavy 43-44, Tay 42-45, Tedworth 39, Tees 43-45, Test 43, Texada 43, Thalassa 43-44, Thane 44, The Pass 42-44, Thetford Mines 45, Thirlmere 41-44, Thorlock 45, Thornborough 45, Thrasher 44, Three Rivers 42-44, Thule 44, Thunder 41/42/44, Thyme 41-42, Tillsonburg 44-45, Timmins 42-45, Tintagel Castle 44-45, Tiree 43-44, Tobago 44, Torbay 44, Torrington 44, Tortola 44-45, Totland 41-44, Tourmaline 43, Towy 43-45, Tracker 43-44, Trail 41-45, Transcona 43-45, Trent 43, Trentonian 44, Trident 44, Trillium 40-45, Tritellia 43, Trondra 43-44, Trouncer 44, Truant 44, Truculent 44, Trumpeter 43-44, Truro 42-45, Tui 42, Tumult 43, Tunsberg Castle 44, Turcoman 42, Tweed 43-44, Tyler 45, Tyrian 43,

Uganda 43, Ullswater 40, Ulster Queen 44, Ultimatum 44, Ultor 44, Ungava 42/44,

Universal 44, Unruly 44, Unsparing 44, Unst 43, Unswerving 45, Untiring 44, Upstart 44, Usk 43-44,

Valentine 39, Valleyfield 44, Vancouver 44-45, Vanessa 39-40/42-43, Vanoc 40-42/44, Vanquisher 39-45, Vansittart 39-43, Varanga 42-44, Vascama 41-45, Vegreville 44, Veleta 43-44, Velox 40-43, Venetia 39-40, Vengeful 45, Venomous 40-43, Verbena 41, Verity 39-42/44-45, Veronica 41, Versatile 39-40/43-45, Vervain 41-45, Vesper 39-40/43-45, Vetch 41-43, Veteran 39-42, Victoriaville 45, Victrix 40/43-44, Vidette 40-44, Ville de Quebec 42-44, Vimy 39-45, Vindex 44, Violet 41-44, Viscount 39-44, Visenda 41/43/45, Visigoth 44, Viva II 40, Vivacious 39-40, Viviana 42-43, Vizalma 40-45, Voltaire 40-41, Volunteer 39-45, Voracious 44, Vortigern 39-40, Vulcan 40,

Wakeful 39-40, Walker 39-43, Wallaceburg 44-45, Wallflower 41-45, Walney 41-42, Walpole 39-40/43, Wanderer 39-44, Warspite 39, Warwick 39-40/42-44, Wasaga 44, Waskesiu 43-45, Watchman 40-44, Waveney 42-43, Wear 40-44, Wedgeport 43, Wellard 41-42, Wellington 39-45, Wells 41-42, Wensleydale 43-44, Wentworth 44-45, Wessex 39-40, West York 45, Westcott 40-43, Westmount 44, Weston 40-44, Wetaskiwin 41-45, Weyburn 42, Whimbrel 43-44, Whirlwind 39-40, Whitaker 44, Whitby 44-45, Whitehall 39-43, Whitehaven 42, Whitehorn 42-43, Whitethroat 45, Whitshed 40, Wild Goose 43-44, Wild Swan 40-42, Wildflower 40, William Scoresby 40, Willowherb 43-45, Winnchelsea 39-44, Winchester 44, Windermere 41-45, Windflower 41, Windrush 43-44, Windsor 39-40, Winnipeg 43-45, Wishart 39/41-44, Wistaria 42-44, Witch 39-43, Witherington 39-40/42-44, Wivern 39-43, Wolborough 44, Wolfe 41-43, Wolsey 40/42, Wolverine 39-42/44-45, Woodcock 43-45, Woodpecker 43-44, Woodruff 41-45, Woodstock 42-44, Woolston 41, Worcester 40, Worcestershire 40-41, Worthing 43, Wren 39-45, Wrestler 40/42-43,

Yes Tor 42-44, York 39, York City 40, Yorkshireman 44, Zanzibar 44, Zetland 42-45, Zinnia 41, Zulu 41.

FAA Sqn: 700 (40-41), 801 (40), 802 (41), 804 (41), 807 (40), 808 (43), 810 (41), 811 (43-44), 813 (42, 44), 814 (40), 816 (43), 818 (41), 820 (41), 824 (42), 825 (44), 826 (40), 833 (44), 835 (43-44), 836 (43-45), 837 (43), 838 (43),

840 (43), 842 (43-44), 846 (44), 850 (44), 860 (44-45), 881 (44), 882 (43-44), 892 (43), 896 (44), 898 (44), 1832 (44).

M.L.s: 170 (43), M.L. 172 (43), M.L.175 (43), MMS. 80 (43), MMS. 81 (43), MMS. 303 (44), MMS 1066 (45),

* Red Ensign

NORTH SEA 1939-45   1939-45

Acanthus 44, Acute 42, Adonis 43, Aigon 41, Ailsa Craig 44, Alarm 42, Alberni 44, Albrighton 45, Ampulla 42, Angle 43-44, Annan 44, Aquilla 42, Arab 43-45, Ardrossan 42, Arrow 42, Ascension 44, Aster 44, Atherstone 42-43, Atmah 42, Ayrshire 42,

Baluchistan 42, Bassett 42, Bayntun 45, Begonia 41, Berkeley 42, Berkshire 42-44, Betony 43, Black Swan 40, Blean 42, Bleasdale 43-45, Blencathra 41-45, Blyth 42, Bonito 42, Borage 44, Bournemouth Queen 42, Braithwaite 45, Bressay 42, Bridgewater 42, Broadway 44, Broke 39, Brontes 44, Burges 44, Bute 44, Byron 44-45,

Cadmus 42, Caistor Castle 45, Calgary 45, Camellia 44, Campbell 41-45, Camrose 44, Cape Comorin 42, Cape Palliser 42, Cape Portland 42-43, Cape Sable 42, Carnatic 42, Castlenau 43, Castleton 42-44, Cattistock 41-45, Charlestown 43-44, Charlock 44, Chelmer 44, Cleveland 43, Clover 44, Coll 42, Congre 42, Conn 44-45, Conqueror 42-43, Copper Cliff 44, Corinthian 42-43, Cosby 44, Cotillion 41-42, Cotswold 41-45, Cottesmore 41-45, Coverley 41-43, Cowdray 44-45, Cranstoun 44, Cubitt 44-45, Culver 41, Curacoa 40-42, Curzon 44-45,

Daffodil 44, Dahlia 44, Dakins 44, Damsay 42, Daniel Clowden 42, Davy 44, Deane 44, Doon 43, Dudgeon 44, Dunavon 42, Dunbar 42, Duncton 42, Dunkery 42,

Easton 45, Ebor Wyke 43, Eglinton 41-44, Ekins 44-45, Else Rykens 41, Erebus 41, Eroican 42, Escort 40, Estrella D'Alva 42, Estrella Do Norte 42, Evelyn Rose 42, Exmoor 41,

Farndale 45, Fencer 44, Fernie 41-45, Filla 42, Fitzroy 44-45, Flamingo 39-40, Flores 42-43, Fortune 40, Foxtrot 41-42,

Garth 41-45, Gavotte 41, Gleaner 41-42, Goatfell 42, Goathland 44, Godetia 44, Goldcock 43, Goodwin 42, Gossamer 42, Graph 43, Grayling 42, Greenfly 44, Grenadier 43, Guillemot 42/43/45, Gunner 42, Gurkha 40,

H.49 (40), Halstead 44, Hambledon 41-44, Haydon 45, Holderness 42-45, Holmes 44, Hornbeam 43, Hornpipe 41-43, Hyderabad 42, Hydra 43,

Icarus 39, Imogen 40, Indian Star 41-42, Inglefield 40, Invercauld 42, Jason 41-42, Jasper 45, Jura 42,

Kashmir 39, Kellett 43, Kenilworth Castle 45, Kennet 41, Killegray 42, Kingcup 44, Kings Grey 42, Kingston 39, Kingston Agate 42, Kingston Amber 42, Kingston Olivina 42, Kintyre 42, Kittiwake 41-44,

Lacerta 42, Lady Estella 42, Lady Madeleine 42, Lancaster 43-45, Lapwing 44, Lark 44, Lauderdale 42, Leeds 41-45, Leicester City 43-44, Lewes 42, Liddesdale 41-43, Limbourne 43, Lincoln 42/44, Loch Dunvegan 45, Loch Eck 45, Londonderry 40, Loosestrife 44, Lord Austin 42, Lord Howe 42, Lord Plender 44, Lowestoft 40-42/45, Ludlow 42-45, Lydd 42, Lynton 42,

Macbeth 44, Mackay 42-45, Magnolia 42, Malcolm 40, Mallard 41-43, Mallow 42, Man-o-war 41, Maron 42, Mazurka 41-42, Melbreak 45, Mendip 41-43/45, Meynell 41-45, Middleton 44-45, Mignonette 44, Millet 42, Minster 42, Minuet 41-43, Mona's Isle 42-43, Monnow 45, Montrose 42-44, Moorsom 44,

Narwhal 40, Natal 45, Neil Mackay 41, Nene 45, Newark 43-44, Northern Foam 42, Northern Sun 42,

Oakley 45, Ocean Brine 42, Ogano 42, Olive 42, Onyx 43, Ophelia 42, Orchis 42, Oresay 42, Orkney 45, Othello 42,

P.247 (42), Pearl 42, Pennywort 43-44, Pentland Firth 42, Peterhead 43, Phrontis 42, Pink 42, Pintail 40-41, Pirouette 41-42, Pitstruan 42, Polka 41-45, Polo Norte 42, Poppy 42/44, Port Colborne 45, Portsdown 42, Potentilla 44, Preston North End 43-44, Primrose 42, Prince Charles 42, Puffin 41-45, Pytchley 42-45,

Quadrille 41-42, Qualicum 42, Quantock 41-45, Quorn 41-44,

Rattlesnake 42, Rayon 42, Redmill 44-45, Regardo 42, Reighton Wyke 42, Restigouche 40, Retako 42, Retalick 45, Retriever 42, Rinaldo 42, Ringwood 42, Riou 45, Rosalind 41, Ross 42, Rousay 42, Rowena 44, Rupert 45, Ruskholm 42, Rutherford 44-45,

St. Albans 43, St. Elstan 42, St. John 45, St. Kilda 42, St. Mary's 43, Sainte Therese 45, Salmon 39-40, Salterelo 41-43, Sapphire 41-42, Scalpay 42, Scarborough 43, Sealion 40, Selkirk 42, Seymour 44-45, Shark 40, Shearwater 40-43/45, Sheldon 42, Sheldrake 41-45, Sheppey 42, Sherwood 43, Shippigan 42, Sir Galahad 42, Sir Geraint 42, Snowflake 41, Sorel 42, Southdown 41-45, Southern Gem 43, Spearfish 40, Speedy 42, Spirea 43, Spry 43, Spurs 42-45, Staffa 42, Starwort 42/44, Stayner 44, Stella 44, Stella Canopus 44, Stella Polaris 42, Stella Rigel 43, Stevenstone 44, Stoke City 43-45, Stork 40, Stornoway 42, Sturgeon 40, Sturton 42, Sunfish 40, Sunflower 44, Surface 42, Switha 42-43, Sword Dance 41-42,

Tadoussac 43, Talybont 43-44, Tango 41-42, Tarantella 41-43, Tartan 42, Thames Queen 42, Thetford Mines 45, Thirlmere 42, Thornborough 45, Thyme 41, Tiree 42, Torrington 44-45, Trident 42, Tumby 42, Turquoise 42-43, Typhoon 42,

Ursula 39, Valorous 40-45, Valse 41-45, Vanity 39-45, Vascama 41-42, Vega 40/42-45, Veleta 41-42, Verdun 40-45, Verity 40, Versatile 41-42/45, Vesper 41-42, Veteran 40, Viceroy 42-45, Vimiera 41-42, Vimy 44-45, Violet 43-44, Visenda 42, Vivacious 42-45, Vivien 40-45, Vizalma 42, Volunteer 45, Vortigern 41-42,

Wakeful 44, Wallace 41-45, Wallflower 42, Walpole 42-44, Wedgeport 42, Wellard 41, Wells 43-44, Wensleydale 43-44, Westminster 40-45, Weston 40, Westray 42, Whaddon 41-43, Whiting 42, Whitshed 41-45, Widgeon 41-45, Wilton 45, Winchelsea 42, Winchester 40-44, Windsor 42-45, Witch 44, Wivern 44-45, Wolfhound 43-45, Wolsey 41-45, Wolves 42-45, Woolston 41-45, Worcester 40-43, Worcestershire 43, Worthing 42, Wye 44,

Yes Tor 42,

FAA Sqn: 803 (39), 811 (42), 812 (40), 826 (40-44).

MGBs (all 1943) – 17, 20, 21, 38, 39, 59, 61, 64, 67, 74, 75, 86, 87, 89, 111, 112.
MTBs (all 1943) – 32, 34, 69, 70, 88, 93, 224, 230, 233, 234, 241, 617, 622, 624, 628.

ENGLISH CHANNEL 1939-45   1939-45

Abelia 44, Acacia 42, Acanthus 43, Affleck 44, Albrighton 42-44, Algoma 45, Alisma 45, Amarose 42, Ambrose Pare 42, Anchusa 45, Anthony 44-45, Aristocrat 42, Armana 42, Armeria 44-45, Ashanti 43-44, Assiniboine 44-45, Atalanta 42, Athabaskan 44, Atherstone 40-42, Avon Vale 43-44, Azalea 44-45,

Bachaquero 42, Baddeck 44-45, Balfour 44, Balsam 44-45, Bangor 44, Barrie 42, Bay 43, Beagle 43, Ben Urie 42, Berkeley 42, Berkshire 42, Bickerton 44, Bideford 45, Bilsdean 42, Birch 42-43, Black Prince 44, Blackpool 42, Blackthorn 40/42-44, Blackwood 44, Bleasdale 42-44, Blencathra 42-44, Bligh 45, Blyth 43, Borage 43, Boreas 40, Boston 45, Bradford 43, Brazen 40, Brecon 43, Brilliant 40/43, Brissenden 43-45, Brocklesby 42-43, Bude 42, Bulldog 40/45, Burdock 44-45, Burges 45, Burke 43, Byron 44,

Calgary 44-45, Calpe 42, Cambridgeshire 42-43, Campanula 44-45, Campbell 42-44, Camrose 45, Canalside 43, Cape Comorin 42-43, Capel 44, Capstone 42, Cattistock 42-44, Cayton Wyke 39, Celandine 44, Charles Henri 42, Charybdis 43, Chelmer 44, Chiddingfold 45, Clarkia 44-45, Clematis 44-45, Cleveland 42-43, Clyne Castle 43, Commander Evans 42, Conn 44, Conqueror 43-45, Convolvulus 45, Cooke 44-45, Corinthian 42, Coriolanus 42, Cornelian 42-43, Cosby 44, Cotswold 43, Cottesmore 42-44, Cowdray 44, Crane 44, Cranstoun 44-45, Curzon 44, Cyclamen 43,

Daffodil 42-43, Dahlia 44-45, Dakins 44, Daneman 40, Deane 44, Delphinium 45, Deodar 40/42, Deptford 45, Deveron 44, Dianella 43, Dianthus 44, Domett 45, Dominica 45, Doon 42, Dornoch 43, Drumheller 44-45, Duckworth 45, Duff 44,

Eastbourne 42/44, Easton 42, Egilsay 42, Eglinton 40-44, Ekins 44, Elgin 42, Ellesmere 42/43/45, Ennerdale 42**, Ensay 42, Erebus 40/44, Eskdale 42-43, Eskimo 44, Essington 44-45,

Felixstowe 42, Fernie 40-44, Fidelity 42, Fir

42-45, Fitzroy 44, Fleetwood 45, Fluellen 42, Forester 44,

Ganilly 43, Garth 42-44, Gaston Riviere 42, Gentian 44-45, Geranium 44, Glaisdale 42-44, Gloxinia 45, Goathland 43, Godetia 45, Good Hope 45, Goodson 44, Grenville 43, Grey Fox 43, Grey Goose 42-43, Grey Owl 43-44, Grey Seal 43, Grey Shark 43, Grey Wolf 43, Griffin 43, Grimsby Town 42-43, Grimstead 42, Gweal 43-44,

Haida 44, Halsted 44, Hambledon 43, Hart 44, Hartland 42, Hatsuse 42, Havelock 44, Heather 44-45, Herschell 43, Hesperus 45, Holmes 44-45, Honeysuckle 44, Horatio 42, Hornbeam 42, Huron 44, Hyderabad 43, Hydrangea 45,

Icarus 45, Ideshire 42, Ijuin 42, Ilfracombe 42, Impulsive 44, Inchgower 42, Inconstant 44, Iris 42, Istria 45, Jackal 40, Jasper 42, Javelin 44, Juliet 42,

Kalan 42, Keppel 44, Kingcup 44-45, Kingsmill 44, Kingston Andalusite 42, Kingston Chrysoberyl 40/42/43, Kitchener 44-45, Kittiwake 42, Kootenay 44,

Labuan 45, Lark 44, Lavender 44, Leeds United 42, Leith 45, Lerwick 42, Limbourne 42-43, Lincolnshire 42-43, Lindsay 44, Lioness 45, Loch Achanalt 45, Loch Alvie 45, Loch Fada 45, Loch Fyne 45, Loch Killin 45, Loch Ruthven 45, Locust 42-44, Londonderry 44-45, Longa 45, Loosestrife 44-45, Lord Essenden 42-43, Lord Hailsham 42-43, Lord Howe 42, Lord Plender 45, Lord Snowden 42, Lord Stanhope 42-44, Lord Stonehaven 42, Lord Wakefield 43-44, Louisburg 44-45, Lundy 43, Lunenburg 44,

Mackay 42-44, Malaya 44, Malcolm 43, Mangrove 42, Manor 42, Mayflower 45, Melbreak 43-44, Mendip 42-43, Meon 44, Meynell 41-43, Middleton 44, Mignonette 45, Milford Duchess 42, Mimico 45, Montrose 43-44, Moosejaw 44-45, Morris Dance 42, Mourne 44, Mousa 42, Myosotis 45,

Narbada 43, Narbrough 44, Nasturtium 44-45, Ness 45, Newport 42, Night Hawk 42, Northward Ho 42, Notre Dame de France 42-43,

Ocean View 42, Offa 44, Olive 42-44, Olvina 42-44, Ommering 42, Orchis 44, Ottawa 44,

P.511 (43), PC 74 (44), Pangbourne 44, Parrsboro 42, Patti 42, Pearl 42-44, Pelican 44, Penylan 42, Perim 45, Peterhead 42, Petunia 44-45, Pine 42-44, Pink 44, Pointer 42, Poppy 44, Port Arthur 45, Port Colborne 44, Prescott 44-45, Primrose 44, Prince Charles 42, Prince Leopold 44, Prince Robert 44, Princess Iris 42-44, Prins Albert 42, Prospect 45, Puckeridge 42,Puffin 39, Pytchley 42-44,

Quadrille 43, Qualicum 44, Quickmatch 42, Quorn 42-44,

Radnor Castle 42, Reboundo 42, Redmill 44, Redwood 44, Regina 44, Retalick 44, Revenge 40, Rhododendron 42, Rhyl 42, Righto 42, Rimouski 44-45, Rocket 43, Rockwood 44, Rodney 44, Romsey 42, Rosevean 44-45, Rothesay 42, Rousay 42, Rowan 42/43/45, Rowley 44-45, Royal Eagle 42, Ruby 42-43, Rupert 44, Ruskholm 42, Rutherford 44,

St. Albans 42, St. Helena 45, St John 44, St. Kilda 42-43, Saladin 44, Sasebo 42, Scalpay 43, Scarborough 44, Scarron 42, Scimitar 43-44, Shakespeare 43, Shippigan 44, Skate 44, Snowberry 45, Spragge 44, Staffa 42, Star of India 42, Starwort 44, Stata 42, Statice 44-45, Stayner 44, Stevenstone 43-44, Stockham 44, Stonecrop 45, Stormont 44, Stornoway 42, Stratagem 44, Stronsay 42, Sulist 42, Summerside 44-45, Sunflower 44-45, Sussexvale 45, Sutton 42-43, Swansea 44, Swansea Castle 42, Swordfish 40,

Talybont 43-44, Tantaside 43-45, Tartar 44, Tavy 44, Thornborough 44, Torbay 44, Torrington 44, Towy 45, Trentonian 44-45, Trollope 44, Tyler 44-45, Tynedale 42-43,

Ullswater 42, Ulster 43, Ulster Monarch 44, United Boys 42, Unseen 44,

Vanity 43, Vanoc 43-44, Vanquisher 43-44, Vatersay 45, Versatile 44-45, Vesper 40/42/44/45, Victrix 42-43, Vidette 44, Ville de Quebec 44-45, Vimy 44-45, Vivacious 43-44, Volunteer 40/44-45,

Waldegrave 44, Walker 44, Walnut 42-44, Walpole 42-44, Wanderer 44, Warspite 44, Watchman 44-45, Waterfly 42, Wedgeport 42/44, Wensleydale 43-44, Westcott 43, Westminster 43, Weston 45, Whalsey 42, Whimbrel 44, Whitaker 44, Whitehall 44, Whitshed 42-44, Wild Goose 45, Winchester 43, Windsor 42-43, Witherington 40, Wolsey 43, Woodcock 44, Woodstock 44, Worcester

42-43, Wrestler 44,

Zanzibar 45.

FAA Sqn: 811 (42), 812 (40-42), 819 (42), 825 (40-42), 841 (43).

ML.s: 163 (42), ML.291 (42), ML.1231 (42), MGBs: 608 (43), MGB 615 (43), MTB. 15 (40), MTB. 17 (40), MTB. 22 (40), MTB. 31 (40), MTB. 32 (40), MTB.49 (42), MTB. 52 (42), MTB.55 (42), MTB. 56 (42), MTB.69 (40), MTB. 84 (42), MTB.86 (42), MTB.95 (42), MTB.229 (42), MTB. 236 (42),

**RFA*

RIVER PLATE 1939   13 December 1939

In this action Commodore Harwood's Squadron of three cruisers engaged the German pocket battleship Admiral Graf Spee which had been preying on British merchant vessels. The battleship was forced to retire and finally scuttled herself.

Achilles, Ajax, Exeter.
FAA Sqn: 700.

NARVIK 1940   10 and 13 April 1940

Bedouin, Cossack, Eskimo, Forester, Foxhound, Furious, Hardy, Havock, Hero, Hostile, Hotspur, Hunter, Icarus, Kimberley, Punjabi, Warspite.

NORWAY 1940-45
8 April - 8 June 1940; and later years

1940 - Acasta, Acheron, Afridi, Amazon, Angle, Arab, Ardent, Ark Royal, Arrow, Ashanti, Aston Villa, Auckland, Aurora, Basilisk, Beagle, Berwick, Birmingham, Bittern, Black Swan, Bradman, Brazen, Cairo, Calcutta, Campbell, Cape Chelyuskin, Cape Passero, Cape Siretoko, Carlisle, Clyde, Codrington, Cossack, Coventry, Curacoa, Curlew, Delight, Devonshire, Diana, Echo, Eclipse, Effingham, Electra, Ellesmere, Encounter, Enterprise, Escapade, Esk, Fame, Faulknor, Fearless, Firedrake, Forester, Foxhound, Flamingo, Fleetwood, Galatea, Gaul, Glasgow, Glorious, Glowworm, Grenade, Greyhound, Griffin, Guardian, Gurkha, Hammond, Hasty, Havelock, Havock,

Hero, Hesperus, Highlander, Hostile, Imperial, Impulsive, Isis, Ivanhoe, Jackal, Janus, Jardine, Javelin, Juniper, Kelly, Kimberley, Kipling, Larwood, Loch Shin, Manchester, Maori, Margaret, Mashona, Matabele, Melbourne, Mohawk, Narwhal, Northern Gem, Nubian, Pelican, Penelope, Porpoise, Protector, Ranen, Renown, Repulse, Resolution, Rhine, Rodney, Rutlandshire, St. Goran, St. Magnus, St. Sunniva, Severn, Sheffield, Sikh, Snapper, Southampton, Spearfish, Stork, Suffolk, Sussex, Tarpon, Tetrarch, Thirlmere, Thistle, Triad, Triton, Truant, Ursula, Valiant, Vandyck, Vanoc, Vansittart, Veteran, Vindictive, Walker, Wanderer, Warspite, Warwickshire, Westcott, Whirlwind, Wisteria, Witch, Witherington, Wolverine, Wren, York, Zulu.
FAA Sqn: 700, 701, 802, 803, 806, 810, 816, 818, 821, 823, 825.
1940-41 & 44 - Furious.
1940-41 - Arethusa, Bedouin, Edinburgh, Eskimo, Icarus, Sealion, Seawolf, Somali, Sunfish, Tartar, Trident,
1940-42 - Inglefield,
1940 & 44 Taku
1940-44 - FAA Sqn: 800, 801, 804, 820.
1941 - Acanthus, Cachalot, Chiddingfold, Eglantine, Kenya, Legion, Mansfield, Nigeria, Offa, Oribi, Prince Charles, Prince Leopold, Prins Albert, Prinses Beatrix, Punjabi, Queen Emma, Scott, Tigris, Tuna. FAA Sqn: 817,
1941-42 - Intrepid,
1941-44 - Victorious,
1941 & 45 - Onslow
1944 - Algonquin, Emperor, Fencer, Formidable, Implacable, Kent, Myngs, Pursuer, Satyr, Sceptre, Striker, Stubborn, Terrapin, Verulam, X 24, Zambesi.
FAA Sqn: 827, 828, 829, 830, 831, 841, 842, 852, 880, 881, 887, 894, 896, 898, 1770, 1771, 1832, 1834, 1836, 1840, 1841, 1842.
1944-45 - Bellona, Campania, Searcher, Trumpeter, Venturer, FAA Sqn: 846, 856, 882.
1945 - Diadem, Iroquois, Mauritius, Nairana, Norfolk, Onslaught, Orwell, Premier, Queen, Tapir, Zealous, Zest.
FAA Sqn: 853.
MTBs: 711, 722.

DUNKIRK 1940   26 May - 4 June 1940

Albury, Amulree*, Anthony, Archangel*, Argyllshire, Arley, Autocarrier*, Basilisk, Ben-my-Chree*, Biarritz*, Bideford, Blackburn Rovers, Boy Roy, Brighton Belle, Brighton Queen, Brock, Calcutta, Calvi,

Canterbury*, Cape Argona, Cayton Wyke, Chico, Codrington, Comfort, Conidaw, Crested Eagle, Devonia, Dinard**, Duchess of Fife, Dundalk, Eileen Emma, Emperor of India, Esk, Express, Fenella*, Fidget, Fisher Boy, Fitzroy, Fyldea, Forecast, Gallant, Gervais Rentoul, Girl Gladys, Girl Pamela, Glen Avon, Glen Gower, Golden Eagle, Golden Gift, Golden Sunbeam, Gossamer, Gracie Fields, Grafton, Grenade, Greyhound, Grive*, Grimsby Town, Guillemot, Gulzar, Halcyon, Harvester, Havant, Hebe, Icarus, Impulsive, Intrepid, Inverforth, Isle of Guernsey**, Isle of Thanet**, Ivanhoe, Jacketa, Jaguar, Javelin, John Cattling, Keith, Kellett, Killarney*, King George V*, King Orry, Kingfisher, Kingston Alalite, Kingston Andalusite, Kingston Olivine, Lady of Mann*, Lady Philomena, Leda, Llanthony, Loch Garry*, Locust, Lord Cavan, Lord Howard, Lord Howe, Lord Inchcape, Lorina*, Lydd, Mackay, Maid of Orleans*, Malcolm, Malines*, Manxman*, Marmion, Medway Queen, Midas, Mona's Isle, Mona's Queen*, Montrose, Mosquito, Nautilus, Netsukis, Niger, Normania*, Olvina, Oriole, Our Bairns, Pangbourne, Paris**, Paxton, Plinlimmon, Polly Johnson, Prague*, Princess Elizabeth, Princess Maud*, Queen of the Channel*, Queen of Thanet, Ross, Royal Daffodil*, Royal Eagle, Royal Sovereign*, Sabre, St. Andrew**, St. Helier*, St. Julien**, St. Seiriol*, Saladin, Salamander, Saltash, Sandown, Saon, Sargasso, Scimitar, Scotia*, Sharpshooter, Shikari, Shipmates, Silver Dawn, Skipjack, Snaefell, Speedwell, Spurs, Stella Dorado, Sutton, The Boys, Thomas Bartlett, Thuringia, Torbay II, Tynwald*, Ut Prosim,, Vanquisher, Venomous, Verity, Vimy, Vivacious, Wakeful, Waverley, Westella, Westward Ho, Whitehall, Whitshed, Wild Swan, Winchelsea, Windsor, Wolfhound, Wolsey, Wolves, Worcester, Worthing**, Yorkshire Lass, Young Mum.
MASB 6, 7, 10. MTBs 16, 67, 68, 102, 107.
FAA Sqn: 801, 806, 825, 826.

Note: * *Personnel and mercantile ships and ** hospital carriers – Red Ensign ships not entitled to Battle Honours for HM Ships.*

BISCAY 1940-45   1940-45

Abdiel 41, Albrighton 44, Archer 43, Ashanti 44, Assiniboine 44, Bellona 44, Berry 43, Bideford 43, Borage 43, Brissenden 44,

Cachalot 40-41, Calgary 43, Charybdis 43, Chaudiere 44, Conqueror 44, Crane 43, Dahlia 43, Diadem 44, Dominica 44, Duckworth 44, Edmunston 43, Egret 43, Enterprise 43, Essington 44,

Glasgow 43, Godetia 43, Graph 42, Haida 44, Hastings 43, Havelock 43, Hurricane 43, Iroquois 43-44, Kite 43, Kootenay 44, Landguard 43, Loch Killin 44, Louis 44,

Mauritius 44, Monkshood 43, Nene 43, Onslow 44, Ottawa 44, Pimpernel 43, Qu'Appelle 44, Restigouche 44, Rockingham 43,

Saskatchewan 44, Saxifrage 43, Sceptre 44, Scylla 43, Seanymph 43, Sheffield 43, Skeena 44, Snowberry 43, Starling 43-44, Stubborn 43,

Tally-Ho 43, Tanatside 44, Tartar 44, Thunderbolt 40, Tuna 40/43, Tweed 43, Unbeaten 42, Unique 42, Ursa 44,

Victorious 42, Vimy 43, Viscount 43, Volunteer 43, Warspite 44, Warwick 43, Waveney 43, Wear 43, Wild Goose 43, Woodpecker 43, Wren 43-44,

FAA Sqn: 817 (42).

MEDITERRANEAN 1940-45   1940-45

Abercrombie 43, Ajax 40-41, Alynbank 43, Aphis 40/41/43, Argonaut 42, Ark Royal 40-41, Atherstone 43, Aubretia 44, Aurora 41-43,

Barham 41, Beaufort 42, Bicester 43-44, Blackfly 44, Blankney 44, Blencathra 44, Bluebell 44, Brecon 44,

Calcutta 41, Caledon 40, Calpe 43, Capetown 40, Chiddingfold 43-44, Clyde 41, Cockchafer 44, Coventry 41, Croome 42, Cuckmere 43,

Dainty 40-41, Decoy 40, Deptford 44, Diamond 41, Dido 42-44, Dulverton 42, Duncan 41,

Eagle 40, Easton 43, Enchantress 42, Encounter 41, Erebus 43, Eridge 42, Euryalus 41-43, Exmoor 44,

Farndale 41, Faulknor 43-44, Fearless 41, Firedrake 40-41, Fleetwood 44, Foresight 41, Formidable 41, Foxhound 41, Fury 41,

Galatea 41, Gallant 40-41, Garland 44,

Glenearn 41, Glengyle 41, Gloucester 41, Gloxinia 43, Gnat 41, Grenville 43-44, Greyhound 41, Griffin 40-41, Gurkha 41,

Haarlem 43, Hambledon 44, Hasty 40-41, Havock 40-41, Hereward 40-41, Hermione 41, Hero 41, Hobart 41, Holcombe 43, Hotspur 40-41, Hursley 42-43, Hurworth 42, Hyacinth 41-43, Hyperion 40,

Ilex 40/41/43, Illustrious 40-41, Imperial 41, Inglefield 44, Isis 41-43, Islay 42,

Jackal 41, Jade 41, Jaguar 41, Janus 40-42/44, Javelin 42-43, Jersey 41, Jervis 40-44, Juno 40-41, Jupiter 41,

Kandahar 41, Kashmir 41, Kelly 41, Kelvin 41-43, Kent 40, Kilmarnock 44, Kipling 41,

Ladybird 40-41, Laforey 43-44, Lamerton 43, Lance 41, Largs 43, Lauderdale 43, Legion 41, Liddesdale 44, Lively 41, Liverpool 40, Lookout 43/45, Lotus 42, Loyal 43,

Malaya 40-41, Marigold 41, Mauritius 43-44, Mendip 43, Meteor 45, Misoa 43, Mohawk 40-41, Mull 44,

Naiad 41, Nelson 43, Neptune 40, Newfoundland 43, Nubian 40/41/43,

Offa 43, Orion 40/43-44, Osiris 40,

P.31 (41-42), P.33 (41), P.34 (42), P.35 (42), P.37 (42), P.42 (42), P.46 (42), P.228 (42), P.247 (42), Pakenham 42-43, Paladin 43, Pandora 40-41, Panther 43, Parthian 40/41/43, Penelope 41/43, Penn 43, Petard 42-43, Phoebe 44, Poppy 42/44, Porpoise 42, Port Arthur 43, Prinses Beatrix 43, Protea 42-44, Proteus 41-42,

Quail 43, Queen Emma 43, Queenborough 43, Quentin 42, Quiberon 42, Quilliam 43,

Raider 43, Ramillies 40, Regent 40-41, Regina 43, Renown 41, Restigouche 43, Roberts 43, Rodney 43, Rorqual 40/41/43, Rover 41, Royal Ulsterman 43, Rysa 40,

Safari 43, Sahib (P.212) 43, Saltarelo 44, Saracen (P.247) 42, Saxifrage 43, Scarab 43-44, Seraph 43, Shakespeare 43, Sheffield 41, Shoreham 43, Sickle 43, Sikh 42, Simoom 43, Sirius 42, Southern Isle 44, Southern Maid 42/44, Southern Sea 44, Spartan 44, Splendid (P.228) 42, Sportsman 44, Starwort 42, Stuart

40, Sydney 40,
Tactician 43, Taku 41, Talisman 41, Tartar 43, Taurus 43, Teazer 43, Tenacious 44, Termagant 43-44, Terror 41, Tetcott 42, Tetrarch 40-41, Thorn 41-42, Thrasher 41-42, Thunderbolt 42, Tigris 42, Torbay 41-43, Triad 40, Trident 43, Triton 40, Triumph 41, Trooper 43, Troubridge 43, Truant 40-41, Tumult 43-44, Turbulent 42, Tyrian 43,

Uganda 43, Ulster 44, Ultimatum (P.34) 42-44, Ultor 43-44, Umbra (P.35) 42, Unbeaten 41-42, Unbending (P.37) 42, Undine 44, Unique 41, United 43, Universal 44, Unrivalled 43, Unseen 43, Unshaken 43, Untiring 43-44, Upholder 41-42, Upright 41, Uproar 43-44, Upstart 44, Urchin 44, Urge 41-42, Ursula 41, Utmost 41,

Valiant 40/41/43, Vendetta 41, Vetch 43, Ville de Quebec 43, Voyager 41,

Warspite 40/41/43, Whaddon 43, Wilton 44, Wishart 42, Wollongong 43, Wrestler 40/42, Wryneck 41,

York 40-41, Zetland 43-44, Zulu 42.

FAA Sqn: 700 (42), 767 (40), 800 (40-41), 803(41), 806 (40-41), 810 (40-41), 812 (41), 813 (40-41), 815 (40-41), 816 (41), 818 (40-41), 819 (40-41), 820 (40), 821 (42-43), 824 (40), 826 (41-43), 828 (41-43), 829 (41), 830 (40-42).

MTBs (all 1943) - 311, 633, 634, 635, 637, 639, 656.

EAST INDIES 1940-45
June 1940-August 1945

Falmouth, Kandahar, Khartoum, Kimberley, Kingston, Moonstone, Shoreham

1941 - Formidable, Shropshire. FAA Sqn 700, 813, 824, 826, 829

1943 - Haarlem, Hyacinth, Wollongong (RAN)

1944 - Battler, Begum, Cauvery (RIN), Findhorn, Godavari (RIN), Illustrious, Ipswich (RAN), Jumna (RIN), Launceston (RAN), Nadder, Norman (RAN), Paladin, Parret, Petard, Phoebe, Queenborough, Quiberon (RAN), Quilliam, Raider, Renown, Shah, Shakespeare, Storm, Taff, (Van Galen-

RNethN), Wager, Wakeful, Wessex, Whelp, FAA Sqn 810, 815, 817, 822, 831, 832, 834, 847, 851, 1830, 1833, 1837.

1945 - Ameer, Emperor, Eskimo, Gozo, Imersay, Indefatigable, Khedive, Lennox, Lightfoot, Lingay, Melita, Nigeria, Pelorus, Persian, Postillion, Queen Elizabeth, Racehorse, Rapid, Redoubt, Rocket, Rotherham, Royalist, Saumarez, Stalker, Venus, Verulam, Vigilant, Virago, Volage, FAA Sqn 800, 804, 808, 809, 820, 849, 857, 887, 888, 894, 896, 1770.

1944-45 - Cumberland, Indomitable, London, Relentless, Roebuck, Suffolk, Victorious, FAA Sqn 845, 1834, 1836, 1839, 1844.

CALABRIA 1940   9 July 1940

Dainty, Decoy, Defender, Eagle, Gloucester, Hasty, Hereward, Hero, Hostile, Hyperion, Ilex, Janus, Juno, Liverpool, Malaya, Mohawk, Neptune, Nubian, Orion, Royal Sovereign, Stuart, Sydney, Vampire, Voyager, Warspite.
FAA Sqn: 813, 824.

SPADA 1940   19 July 1940

Hasty, Havock, Hero, Hyperion, Ilex, Sydney.

LIBYA 1940-42 September 1940 - June 1942

The Royal Navy operated in support of the Army in the Western Desert between Port Said and Benghazi.

1940 - Herward, Hyperion, Janus, Juno, Mohawk, Nubian. FAA Sqn: 819.

1940-41 - Chakla, Dainty, Fiona, Ladybird, Protector, Stuart (RAN), Terror, Vampire (RAN), Vendetta (RAN), Voyager (RAN), Waterhen (RAN). FAA Sqn: 803, 806, 813, 815, 824.

1940-42 - Aphis, Jervis.

1941 - Abdiel, Arthur Cavanagh, Auckland, Aurora II, Bagshot, Calcutta, Calm, Chakdina, Chantala, Coventry, Cricket, Defender, Encounter, Fareham, Flamingo, Glenearn, Glengyle, Glenroy, Gnat, Greyhound,

Grimsby, Hailstorm, Huntley, Kai, Kandahar, Kingston, Kos 21, Latona, May, Milford Countess, Muroto, Napier, Nebb, Nizam (RAN), Ouse, Parramatta (RAN), Rosaura, Salvia, Sikh, Sindonis, Siona, Skudd III, Skudd IV, Soira, Southern Floe (SANF), Stoke, Svana, Thorbryn, Thorgrim, Wryneck, Yana, Yarra (RAN).
MLs: 1012, 1023.
MTBs: 68, 215.

1941-42 - Aberdare, Avon Vale, Burgonet, Carlisle, Cocker (ex Kos 19), Decoy, Eridge, Falk, Farndale, Gloxinia, Griffin, Hasty, Havock, Hero, Heythrop, Hotspur, Hyacinth, Jackal, Jaguar, Kimberley, Kipling, Klo, Legion, Moy, Peony, Protea (SANF), Skudd V, Soika, Sotra, Southern Isle (SANF), Southern Maid (SANF), Southern Sea (SANF), Toneline, Wolborough.
FAA Sqn: 805 (RAN), 826.
MLs: 1048, 1051.

1942 - Airedale, Aldenham, Antwerp, Arrow, Beaufort, Bever (SANF), Boksburg (SANF), Croome, Delphinium, Dulverton, Erica, Exmoor, Farnham, Firmament, Gribb (SANF), Grove, Hurworth, Imhoff (SANF), Kingston Coral, Kingston Crystal, Langlaate (SANF), Lively, Malines, Parktown (SANF), Primula, Seksern (SANF), Snapdragon, Southwold, Tetcott, Treern (SANF), Victoria I, Vulcan, Zulu.
MLs: 266, 267, 348, 355, 1004, 1005, 1039, 1046, 1069.
MTBs: 61, 259, 260, 261, 262, 263, 266, 267, 309, 311, 312.
FAA Sqn: 821

TARANTO 1940   11 November 1940

Illustrious.
FAA Sqn: 813, 815, 819, 824.

SPARTIVENTO 1940   27 November 1940

Ark Royal, Berwick, Coventry, Defender, Despatch, Diamond, Duncan, Encounter, Faulknor, Firedrake, Forester, Fury, Gallant, Gloxinia, Greyhound, Hereward, Hotspur, Hyacinth, Jaguar, Kelvin, Manchester, Newcastle, Peony, Ramillies, Renown, Salvia, Sheffield, Southampton, Vidette, Wishart.
FAA Sqn: 700, 800, 808, 810, 818, 820.

MALTA CONVOYS 1941-42   1941-42

This award is in recognition of the successful convoys fought through to bring much needed supplies to the beleaguered island of Malta.

Ajax 41, Amazon 42, Antelope 42, Arethusa 41-42, Argus 42, Ark Royal 41, Arrow 42, Ashanti 42, Aurora 41, Avon Vale 41-42,

Badsworth 42, Beaufort 42, Bedouin 42, Beverley 41, Bicester 42, Blankney 42, Bonaventure 41, Boston 42, Bramham 42, Breconshire 41-42, Cachalot 41, Cairo 42, Calcutta 41, Carlisle 41-42, Charybdis 42, Cleopatra 42, Clyde 42, Coltsfoot 42, Cossack 41, Dainty 41, Decoy 41-42, Defender 41, Derwent 42, Diamond 41, Dido 42, Dulverton 42, Duncan 41,

Eagle 42, Echo 42, Edinburgh 41, Encounter 41, Eridge 41-42, Escapade 42, Eskimo 42, Euryalus 41-42, Farndale 41, Faulknor 41, Fearless 41, Firedrake 41, Fleur de Lys 41, Foresight 41-42, Forester 41, Fortune 41-42, Foxhound 41, Furious 42, Fury 41-42, Gallant 41, Geranium 42, Gloucester 41, Gloxinia 41, Greyhound 41, Griffin 41-42, Gurkha 41-42,

Hasty 41-42, Havock 41-42, Hebe 42, Hereward 41, Hermione 41-42, Hero 41-42, Heythrop 41-42, Hurworth 42, Hyacinth 41, Hythe 42, Icarus 42, Ilex 41, Illustrious 41, Indomitable 42, Inglefield 42, Intrepid 42, Ithuriel 42, Jaguar 41-42, Janus 41, Jervis 41-42, Jonquil 42, Juno 41, Kandahar 41, Kelvin 42, Kenya 41-42, Keppel 42, Kimberley 41, Kingston 41-42, Kipling 41-42,

Laforey 41-42, Lance 41-42, Ledbury 42, Legion 41-42, Lightning 41-42, Lively 41-42, Liverpool 42, Lookout 42, Malaya 41-42, Malcolm 42, Manchester 41-42, Manxman 41-42, Maori 41-42, Marne 42, Matchless 42, Middleton 42, Mohawk 41, Naiad 41-42, Nelson 41-42, Neptune 41, Nestor 41-42, Nigeria 42, Nizam 41, Nubian 41,

Olympus 41-42, Onslow 42, Oribi 41, Orion 41, Osiris 41, Otus 41, P.31 (42), P.32 (41), P.34 (42), P.36 (41), P.42 (42), P.43 (42), P.44 (42), P.46 (42), P.211 (42), P.222 (42), Pandora 41-42, Parthian 42, Partridge 42, Pathfinder 42, Penelope 41-42, Penn 42, Peony 41, Perth 41, Phoebe 42, Porpoise 42, Prince of Wales 41, Proteus 42, Quentin 42, Renown 41-42, Rodney 41-42, Rorqual 41-42, Rye 42,

Salvia 41, Sheffield 41, Sikh 41-42, Sirius 42, Somali 42, Southampton 41, Southwold 42, Speedy 42, Spirea 42, Talisman 41, Tartar 42, Thunderbolt 41-42, Triumph 41, Trusty 41,

Unbeaten 41-42, Unique 41, Upholder 41-42, Upright 41, Urge 41, Ursula 41, Utmost 41-42, Valiant 41, Vansittart 42, Venomous 42, Victorious 42, Vidette 42, Warspite 41, Welshman 42, Westcott 42, Wilton 42, Wishart 42, Wolverine 42, Wrestler 42, York 41, Zetland 42, Zulu 41-42.

FAA Sqn: - 800 (41-42), 801 (42), 806 (42), 807 (41-42), 808 (41), 809 (42), 812 (41), 813 (42), 816 (41), 820 (41), 824 (42), 825 (41), 827 (42), 831 (42), 832 (42), 884 (42), 885 (42).

MLs:- 121, 134, 135, 168, 459, 462. (all 1942)

ARCTIC 1941-45   1941-45

Acanthus 43, Achates 42, Active 44, Activity 44, Airedale 42, Algonquin 44-45, Allington Castle 44-45, Alnwick Castle 45, Alynbank 42, Amazon 42, Ambuscade 42, Angle 42, Anguilla 45, Anson 42-43, Arab 42, Argonaut 42, Argus 41, Ashanti 42-43, Athabaskan 43-44, Avenger 42, Ayrshire 42,

Badsworth 42, Bahamas 44, Bamborough Castle 44-45, Bazeley 45, Beagle 42-44, Bedouin 41-42, Belfast 43, Bellona 44-445, Belvoir 42, Bentinck 45, Bergamot 42-43, Bermuda 43, Berwick 41-44, Beverley 42, Bickerton 44, Black Prince 44, Blackfly 42, Blankney 42-43, Bluebell 42/44/45, Boadicea 42-44, Borage 43-44, Bramble 42, Bramham 42, Brissenden 43, Britomart 41-43, Broke 42, Bryony 42-43, Bulldog 42/44, Burdock 44, Bute 42, Byron 44,

Caesar 44, Cambrian 44, Camellia 42-45, Campania 44-45, Campanula 42, Campbell 42, Cape Argona 42-43, Cape Breton 44, Cape Mariato 42-43, Cape Palliser 42, Caprice 44, Cassandra 44, Cavalier 45, Celia 42, Charlock 44, Chaser 44, Chiltern 42, Cockatrice 43-44, Conn 44, Cotton 45, Cowdray 42, Cumberland 42-43, Curacoa 42, Cygnet 44-45,

Daneman 42-43, Dasher 43, Deane 44, Denbigh Castle 45, Devonshire 41, Diadem 44-45, Dianella 42-44, Dido 44, Douglas 42, Dragon 44, Drury 45, Duckworth 44, Duke of York 42-43, Duncton 42,

Echo 41-43, Eclipse 41-43, Edinburgh 41-42, Eglantine 43-45, Electra 41, Elm 44, Escapade 41-42, Eskdale 42, Eskimo 42, Essington 44,

Farndale 42, Farnham Castle 45, Faulknor 42-43, Fencer 44, Fitzroy 44, Foresight 42, Forester 42-43, Fury 42-43,

Garland 42, Glasgow 43, Gleaner 42-44, Goodall 45, Gossamer 41-42, Graph 42-43, Grou 44, Grove 42,

Haida 43-45, Halcyon 41-44, Hamlet 41, Hardy 43-44, Harrier 41-43, Hazard 41-42, Heather 43, Hebe 41-42, Honeysuckle 42-45, Hound 43-44, Howe 42-43, Hugh Walpole 41-42, Huron 43-45, Hussar 41-44, Hyderabad 42-43, Hydra 43-44,

Icarus 41-43, Impulsive 41-44, Inconstant 42-44, Indian Star 42, Inglefield 42-43, Intrepid 41-43, Iroquois 43-45, Jamaica 42-44, Jason 43, Javelin 42,

Kent 42-43, Kenya 41-42, Keppel 42/44/45, King George V 42-43, King Sol 42, Kite 44,

La Malouine 42, Lady Madeleine 42-43, Lamerton 42, Lancaster 42, Lancaster Castle 45, Lapwing 44-45, Lark 44-45, Leamington 42, Leda 41-42, Ledbury 42-43, Liverpool 42, Loch Alvie 44-45, Loch Dunvegan 44, Loch Insh 45, Loch Shin 45, London 41-43, Lookout 42, Lord Austin 42-43, Lord Middleton 42, Lotus 42-45, Louis 44, Loyalty 44,

Macbeth 41, Mackay 42, Magpie 44, Mahratta 43-44, Majesty 42, Malcolm 42, Manchester 42, Marne 42-44, Martin 42, Matabele 41-42, Matane 45, Matchless 42-44, Mermaid 44, Meteor 42-44, Meynell 43, Middleton 42-43, Milne 42-44, Monnow 44-45, Montrose 42-43, Mounsey 44, Musketeer 42-44, Myngs 44-45,

Nairana 44-45, Nene 44-45, Newmarket 42, Newport 42, Niger 41-42, Nigeria 42, Norfolk 41-43, Northern Gem 42-43, Northern Pride 42-43, Northern Spray 42, Northern Wave 42-43, Notts County 42, Nubian 44,

Oakley 42, Obdurate 42-45, Obedient 42-44, Offa 41-45, Onslaught 42-45, Onslow 41-45, Onyx 44, Ophelia 41-42, Opportune 42-45, Orestes 44, Oribi 42-44, Orwell 42-45, Outremont 44, Oxlip 42-45,

P.45 (42), P.54 (42), P.212 (42), P.221 (42), P.247 (42), P.614 (42), P.615 (42), Palomares

42, Pasley 45, Paynter 42, Peacock 44, Poppy 42-44, Port Colborne 44, Pozarica 42, Premier 45, Punjabi 41-42, Pytchley 43,

Quadrant 42-43, Queen 45, Queenborough 42-43,

Raider 42-43, Rattlesnake 44, Ready 44, Redmill 44, Renown 42, Retriever 42, Rhododendron 42-45, Richmond 42, Rodney 44, Rupert 44,

St. Albans 42, St. Elstan 42-43, St. John 44, St. Kenan 42-43, St. Pierre 45, Saladin 42-43, Salamander 41-42, Sardonyx 42, Saumarez 43-44, Savage 43-45, Saxifrage 42, Scimitar 42, Scorpion 43-45, Scourge 43-45, Scylla 42-43, Seadog 42-43, Seagull 41-44, Sealion 41-42, Seanymph 42-43, Seawolf 41-42, Serapis 44-45, Sharpshooter 41-43, Sheffield 41-43, Shropshire 41, Shusa 42, Silja 42, Sioux 44-45, Sirius 42, Skate 43, Snowflake 42, Somali 41-42, Somaliland 44, Speedwell 42-44, Speedy 42, Starling 44, Starwort 42-44, Stella Capella 42, Stormont4 4, Striker 44, Strule 44, Sturgeon 42, Suffolk 41-42, Sulla 42, Sumba 42, Sweetbriar 42, Swift 44,

Tango 42, Tartar 42, Taurus 42-43, Tavy 44, Termagant 43, Tigris 41-442, Torbay 42-43, Tortola 44, Tracker 44, Tribune 42, Trident 41-42, Trinidad 42, Truculent 43, Trumpeter 44, Tuna 43, Tunsberg Castle 44,

Ulster Queen 42, Ulysses 44, Unique 42, Unruly 42-43, Ursula 42, Venomous 42, Venus 42-44, Verdun 42, Verulam 44, Victorious 41-42, Vigilant 43-44, Vindex 44-45, Virago 43-44, Vivacious 43, Viviana 42, Vizalma 42-43, Volage 44, Volunteer 42,

Walker 44-45, Wallflower 43-44, Wanderer 44, Waskesiu 44, Wastwater 42, Watchman 44, Wells 42, Westcott 43-45, Wheatland 42, Whimbrel 44, Whitehall 43-45, Wild Goose 44, Wilton 42, Windsor 42, Woolston 42, Worcester 42-43, Wren 44, Wrestler 43-44, Zambesi 45, Zealous 45, Zebra 45, Zephyr 45, Zest 45, Zodiac 45,

FAA Sqn:- 802 (42), 809 (41), 811 (44), 813 (44-45), 816 (44), 819 (44), 822 (43), 824 (44), 825 (42-45), 832 (42), 833 (44), 835 (44-45), 842 (44), 846 (44-45), 853 (44-45), 856 (45), 882 (45), 883 (42), 893 (43), 1832 (44).

MMS 90 (42), MMS.203 (42), MMS 212 (42),

MATAPAN 1941   28-29 March 1941

Ajax, Barham, Defender, Formidable, Gloucester, Greyhound, Griffin, Hasty, Havock, Hereward, Hotspur, Ilex, Jaguar, Janus, Jervis, Juno, Mohawk, Nubian, Orion, Perth, Stuart, Valiant, Vendetta, Warspite.
FAA Sqn: 700, 803, 806, 815, 826, 829.

SFAX 1941   15-16 April 1941

Janus, Jervis, Mohawk, Nubian.

GREECE 1941   24 - 29 April 1941

Ajax, Auckland, Calcutta, Carlisle, Coventry, Decoy, Defender, Diamond, Flamingo, Glenearn, Glengyle, Griffin, Grimsby, Hasty. Havock, Hereward, Hero, Hotspur, Hyacinth, Isis, Kandahar, Kimberley, Kingston, Muroto, Nubian, Orion, Perth, Phoebe, Salvia, Stuart, Ulster Prince, Vampire, Vendetta, Voyager, Waterhen, Wryneck.

CRETE 1941   20 May - 1 June 1941

Abdiel, Ajax, Auckland, Barham, Calcutta, Carlisle, Coventry, Decoy, Defender, Dido, Fiji, Flamingo, Formidable, Glengyle, Glenroy, Gloucester, Greyhound, Griffin, Grimsby, Hasty, Havock, Herward, Hero, Hotspur, Ilex, Imperial, Isis, Jackal, Jaguar, Janus, Jervis, Juno, Kandahar, Kashmir, Kelly, Kelvin, Kimberley, Kingston, Kipling, Kos 21, Kos 22, Kos 23, Lanner, Naiad, Napier, Nizam, Nubian, Orion, Perth, Phoebe, Queen Elizabeth, Rorqual, Salvia, Stuart, Syvern, Valiant, Vampire, Vendetta, Voyager, Warspite, Waterhen, Widnes.
MLs: 1011, 1030, 1032. MTBs 67, 213, 216, 217, 314.
FAA Sqn: 805.

'Bismarck' 1941   23-27 May 1941

Achates, Active, Antelope, Anthony, Ark Royal, Aurora, Cossack, Dorsetshire, Echo, Edinburgh, Electra, Galatea, Hermione, Hood, Icarus, Inglefield, Intrepid, Kenya, King George V, Maori, Mashona, Neptune, Nestor, Norfolk, Prince of Wales, Punjabi, Renown, Repulse, Rodney, Sheffield, Sikh, Somali, Suffolk, Tartar, Victorious, Zulu.
FAA Sqn: 800, 808. 810, 818, 820, 825.

CAPE BON 1941   13 December 1941

Legion, Maori, Sikh.

NEW GUINEA 1942-44   1942-44

1942 - Warrego.
1942-44 - Arunta, Australia, Ballarat, Bendigo, Broome, Colac, Deloraine, Katoomba, Lithgow, Stuart, Swan, Whyalla.
1943 - Ararat.
1943-44 - Benalla, Bunbury, Bundaburg, Echuca, Gladstone, Glenelg, Kapunda, Latrobe, Pirie, Reserve, Shepparton, Shropshire, Stawell, Vendetta, Wagga, Warramunga.
1944 - Cootamunda, Cowra, Gascoyne, Geelong, Goulburn, Gympie, Hawkesbury, Kiama, Mildura, Parkes, Rockhampton, Strahan, Townsville.

PACIFIC 1941-45   1941-45

1942: Armidale, Deloraine, Kalgoorlie, Voyager, Warrnambool.
1942-45: Arunta
1945: Barcoo, Burdekin, Colac, Diamantina, Dubbo, Gascoyne, Hawkesbury, Hobart, Kiama, Lachlan, Latrobe, Lithgow, Shropshire, Stawell, Warramunga, Warrego.

MALAYA 1942-45   1942-45

1942 - Electra, Encounter, Exeter, Jupiter,
1943 - (O-21 (RNLN)),
1943-44 - Tally Ho, Taurus,
1944 - Porpoise, Sea Rover, Stoic, Stonehenge, Storm, Stratagem, Strongbow, Tantalus, Tantivy, Telemachus, Templar, Trespasser, Truculent, (Zwaardfisch (RNLN)),
1944-45 - Subtle, Terrapin, Thorough, Thule, Tradewind, Trenchant, Tudor,
1945 - Cumberland, Emperor, (O-19 (RNLN)), Saumarez, Scythian, Seascout, Selene, Sleuth, Solent, Statesman, Stubborn, Sturdy, Stygian, Taciturn, Tartar, Tiptoe, Torbay, Trump, Venus, Verulam, Vigilant, Virago, XE.4, XE.5..
FAA Sqn - 1945 - 800, 807, 851.

SUNDA STRAIT 1942
28 February - 1 March 1942

Encounter, Exeter, Perth.(*See Single Ship Actions*)

49

SIRTE 1942   22 March 1942

Avon Vale, Beaufort, Breconshire, Carlisle, Cleopatra, Dido, Dulverton, Eridge, Euryalus, Hasty, Havock, Hero, Hurworth, Jervis, Kelvin, Kingston, Kipling, Legion, Lively, Penelope, Sikh, Southwold, Zulu.

ST. NAZAIRE 1942   28 March 1942

Atherstone, Campbeltown, Tynedale.
MLs: 156, 160, 177, 192, 262, 267, 268, 270, 298, 306, 307, 443, 446, 447, 457.
MGB 314
MTB 74

DIEGO SUAREZ 1942   5 - 7 May 1942

Active, Anthony, Auricula, Bachaquero, Cromarty, Cromer, Cyclamen, Devonshire, Duncan, Freesia, Fritillary, Genista, Hermione, Illustrious, Inconstant, Indomitable, Jasmine, Javelin, Karanja, Keren, Laforey, Lightning, Lookout, Nigella, Pakenham, Paladin, Panther, Poole, Ramillies, Romney, Royal Ulsterman, Thyme, Winchester Castle*.
FAA Sqn: 800, 806, 810, 827, 829, 831, 880, 881, 882.

Red Ensign

CORAL SEA 1942   7 May 1942

Australia, Hobart.

SAVO ISLAND 1942   9 August 1942

Australia, Canberra, Hobart.

DIEPPE 1942   19 August 1942

Albrighton, Alresford, Bangor, Berkeley, Blackpool, Bleasdale, Blyth, Bridlington, Bridport, Brocklesby, Calpe, Clacton, Duke of Wellington, Eastbourne, Felixstowe, Fernie, Garth, Glengyle, Ilfracombe, Invicta, Locust, Polruan, Prince Charles, Prince Leopold, Prins Albert, Prinses Astrid, Prinses Beatrix, Queen Emma, Rhyl, Sidmouth, Stornoway, Tenby.
MLs: 114, 120, 123, 171, 187, 189, 190, 191, 193, 194, 208, 214, 230, 246, 291, 292, 309, 343, 344, 346.
MGBs: 50, 51, 52, 57, 312, 315, 316, 317, 320,

321, 323, 326
SGBs: 5, 8, 9.

BARENTS SEA 1942   31 December 1942

Achates, Hyderabad, Jamaica, Northern Gem, Obdurate, Obedient, Onslow, Orwell, Rhododendron, Sheffield.

GUADALCANAL 1942-43
                        August 1942 - February 1943

Achilles, Arunta, Australia, Canberra (1942), Hobart, Kiwi, Moa, Tui.

ALEUTIANS 1942-43
RCN Battle Honour

Dawson, Vancouver.

1942 - Prince David, Prince Henry, Prince Robert.

Awarded to eligible units of the Royal Canadian Navy by the Canadian ND Headquarters 8.1994:

GULF OF ST. LAWRENCE 1942/1944
RCN Battle Honour

Proposed in Canada in 1991.

NORTH AFRICA 1942-43
          8 November 1942 – 20 February 1943

In this operation, the Royal Navy supported the major landings in North Africa, which opened the way for further landings in Sicily and Italy, and helped relieve the siege of Malta.

1942 - Abbeydale**, Aberdeen, Achates, Algerine, Alynbank, Argonaut, Argus, Avenger, Beagle, Bermuda, Bideford, Biter, Blean, Boadicea, Bradford, Bramham, Broke, Brown Ranger**, Bulldog, Bulolo, Burke, Charybdis, Clyne Castle, Coltsfoot, Coreopsis, Cowdray, Cumberland, Dasher, Delhi, Deptford, Derwentdale**, Dianella, Duke of York, Eastbourne, Empyrean, Ennerdale**, Erne, Exe, Fluellen, Gardenia, Geranium, Glengyle, Hartland, Horatio, Hoy, Ibis, Ilfracombe, Imperialist, Ithurial, Jamaica, Jonquil, Karanja,

Keren, Kingston Chrysolite, Landguard, Largs, Laurel, Leith, Leyland, Lord Hotham, Lulworth, Malcolm, Marigold, Martin, Meteor, Milne, Misoa, Nasprite**, Norfolk, Opportune, Onslow, Oribi, Othello, P.45, P.46, P.48, P.54, P.221, P.222, P.228, Palmomares, Partridge, Pelican, Philante, Poppy, Porcupine, Quentin, Roberts, Renown, Returno, Rhododendron, Rochester, Ronaldsay, Rousay, Rysa, St. Nectan, Sandwich, Scarborough, Scottish, Scylla, Sheffield, Spirea, Starwort, Stork, Swale, Tribune, Tynwald, Ulster Monarch, Ursula, Vansittart, Victorious, Viscol**, Walney, Wrestler.
FAA Sqn: 800, 802, 804, 809, 817, 832, 833, 880, 882, 883, 884, 891.

1942-3 - Acute, Alarm, Albacore, Amazon, Antelope, Arctic Ranger, Ashanti, Aubretia, Aurora, Avon Vale, Bachaquero, Banff, Bicester, Boreas, Brilliant, Brixham, Bude, Cadmus, Calpe, Cava, Clacton, Clare, Convolvulus, Coriolanus, Dewdale**, Dingledale**, Eday, Egret, Elbury, Enchantress, Eskimo, Farndale, Felixstowe, Filey Bay, Fleetwood, Formidable, Foula, Furious, Goth, Hengist, Hunda, Hussar, Inchcolm, Inchmarnock, Jaunty, Juliet, Jura, Kerrera, Kintyre, Lamerton, Linnet, Loch Oskaig, Londonderry, Lookout, Lord Nuffield, Lotus, Lunenburg, Maidstone, Mull, Negro, Nelson, Offa, P.51, P.217, Panther, Pathfinder, Penn, Penstemon, Polruan, Pozarica, Prescott, Prinses Beatrix, Puckeridge, Quality, Queen Emma, Quiberon, Restive, Rhyl, Rodney, Rother, Rothesay, Royal Scotsman, Royal Ulsterman, Ruskholm, St. Day, St. Mellons, Samphire, Sennen, P219 (Seraph), Shiant, Sirius, Speedwell, Spey, Storoway, Stroma, Stronsay, Sturgeon, Tartar, Tasajera, Vanoc, Velox, Venomous, Verity, Vetch, Vienna, Violet, Westcott, Westray, Weyburn, Wheatland, Wilton, Wishart, Wivern, Woodstock, Zetland.
FAA Sqn: 700, 807, 820, 822, 885, 888, 893.
ML: 238, 273, 280, 283, 295, 307, 336, 338, 433, 444, 458, 463, 469, 471, 480, 483.
HDML: 1127, 1128, 1139.

1943 - Easton.

** *RFAs*

SICILY 1943   10 July - 17 August 1943

Abdiel, Abercrombie, Acute, Albacore, Aldenham, Alynbank, Antwerp, Aphis, Arrow,

Atherstone, Aurora, Banff, Bann, Beaufort, Belvoir, Bergamot, Blankney, Blencathra, Bluebell, Bonito, Boston, Boxer, Brecon, Brissenden, Brittany, Brixham, Brocklesby, Bruiser, Bryony, Bulolo, Burra, Cadmus, Cairns, Calpe, Camellia, Carlisle, Cava, Cedardale**, Cessnock, Chanticleer, Circe, Clacton, Clare, Cleopatra, Cleveland, Cockchafer, Colombo, Convolvulus, Coriolanus, Crane, Cromarty, Cygnet, Dart, Delhi, Delphinium, Derwentdale**, Dianella, Dido, Dulverton, Easton, Echo, Eclipse, Eday, Eggesford, Ennerdale**, Erebus, Erne, Eskimo, Espiegle, Euryalus, Exmoor, Farndale, Faulknor, Felixstowe, Fishguard, Fly, Formidable, Foxtrot, Fury, Gavotte, Gawler, Geraldton, Glengyle, Grayling, Guardian, Hambledon, Haydon, Hazard, Hebe, Hilary, Holcombe, Honeysuckle, Howe, Hursley, Hurworth, Hyacinth, Hyderabad, Hythe, Ilex, Inchmarnock, Inconstant, Indomitable, Inglefield, Intrepid, Ipswich, Isis, Islay, Jervis, Juliet, Jumna, Keren, Kerrara, King George V, King Sol, Laforey, Lamerton, Largs, Lauderdale, Ledbury, Liddesdale, Lismore, Lookout, Lotus, Loyal, Man-o-war, Maryborough, Mauritius, Mendip, Mullet, Mutine, Nelson, Newfoundland, Nubian, Oakley, Offa, Orion, Osiris, Oxlip, Paladin, Panther, Parthian, Pathfinder, Pearleaf**, Penelope, Penn, Penstemon, Petard, Pheasant, Pirouette, Plym, Polruan, Poole, Poppy, Primula, Prince Charles, Prince Leopold, Prins Albert, Prinses Astrid, Prinses Beatrix, Prinses Josephine Charlotte, Protea, Puckeridge, Quail,, Quantock, Queen Emma, Queenborough, Quilliam, Raider, Reighton Wyke, Rhododendron, Rhyl, Roberts, Rockwood, Rodney, Romeo, Romney, Rorqual, Rothesay, Royal Scotsman, Royal Ulsterman, Rye, Safari, Saracen, Scarab, Seaham, Seraph, Severn, Shakespeare, Sharpshooter, Shiant, Shoreham, Sibyl, Simoom, Sirius, Southern Isle, Southern Sea, Sportsman, Starwort, Stella Carina, Stornoway, Stroma, Sutlej, Tactician, Tango, Tartar, Taurus, Templar, Test, Tetcott, Teviot, Thruster, Torbay, Trent, Trespasser, Tribune, Trident, Trooper, Troubridge, Tumult, Tynedale, Tyrian, Uganda, Ulster Monarch, Ulster Queen, Ultor, Unbroken, Unison, United, Universal, Unrivalled, Unnruffled, Unruly, Unseen, Unshaken, Unsparing, Uproar, Usurper, Valiant, Venomous, Vetch, Viceroy, Visenda, Wallace, Wanderer, Warspite, Whaddon,Wheatland, Whimbrel, Whitehaven, Whiting, Wilton, Wishart, Wolborough, Wollongong, Woolston, Wrestler.
FAA Sqn: 807, 817, 820, 880, 885, 888, 893, 899.
MLs: 125, 126, 565, 1158, 1252.

51

MGBs: 641, 657, 659, 660.
MTBs: 57, 62, 63, 75, 77, 81, 82, 84, 85, 260, 265, 288, 289, 290, 295, 313, 315, 316, 633, 640, 665, 670.

**RFAs*

KULA GULF 1943   13 July 1943

Leander.

SALERNO 1943
                    9 September - 6 October 1943

Abercrombie, Acute, Albacore, Alynbank, Antwerp, Atherstone, Attacker, Aurora, Battler, Beaufort, Belvoir, Blackmore, Blankney, Blencathra, Boxer, Brecon, Brittany, Brixham, Brocklesby, Bruiser, Bude, Cadmus, Calpe, Catterick, Charybdis, Circe, Clacton, Cleveland, Coverley, Delhi, Derwentdale**, Dido, Dulverton, Echo, Eclipse, Eggesford, Ensay, Espiegle, Eurylaus, Exmoor, Farndale, Faulknor, Felixstowe, Fly, Formidable, Fury, Gavotte, Glengyle, Hambledon, Haydon, Hengist, Hilary, Holcombe, Hunter, Ilex, Illustrious, Inglefield, Intrepid, Jervis, Laforey, Lamerton, Ledbury, Liddesdale, Lookout, Loyal, Mauritius, Mendip, Minuet, Mousa, Mutine, Nelson, Nubian, Offa, Orion, Palomares, Panther, Pathfinder, Penelope, Penn, Petard, Pirouette, Polruan, Prince Charles, Prince Leopold, Prinses Astrid, Prinses Beatrix, Prinses Josephine Charlotte, Quail, Quantock, Queenborough, Quilliam, Raider, Reighton Wyke, Rhyl, Roberts, Rodney, Rothesay, Royal Scotsman, Royal Ulsterman, St. Kilda, Scylla, Shakespeare, Sheffield, Sheppey, Sirius, Stalker, Stella Carina, Stornoway, Tango, Tartar, Tetcott, Thruster, Troubridge, Tumult, Tyrian, Uganda, Ulster Monarch, Ulster Queen, Unicorn, Valiant, Visenda, Warspite, Whaddon, Wheatland.
FAA Sqn: 807, 808, 809, 810, 820, 834, 878, 879, 880, 886, 887, 888, 890, 893, 894, 897, 899.
MLs: 121, 126, 134, 135, 238, 273, 280, 283, 336, 554, 555, 556, 557, 559, 560, 561, 562, 564, 566.
HMDLs: 1242, 1246, 1247, 1253, 1254, 1258, 1270, 1271, 1297, 1301.
BYMS: 11, 14, 24, 209.
MMS: 5, 133, 134.

**RFA*

AEGEAN 1943-44
7 September - 28 November 1943: and 1944

1943 - Aldenham, Belvoir, Blencathra, Carlisle, Croome, Dido, Dulverton, Echo, Eclipse, Faulknor, Fury, Hambledon, Haydon, Hedgehog, Hursley, Hurworth, Intrepid, Jervis, Lamerton, Panther, Pathfinder, Penelope, Penn, Petard, Phoebe, Rockwood, Rorqual, Seraph, Severn, Shakespeare, Simoom, Surf, Torbay, Trespasser, Trooper, Unrivalled, Wilton.

1943-44 - Aurora, Beaufort, Exmoor, Sibyl, Sickle, Sirius, Sportsman, Tetcott, Tumult, Unruly, Unsparing.

1944 - Ajax, Argonaut, Attacker, Bever, Bicester, Black Prince, Boksburg, Brecon, Bruiser, Caledon, Calpe, Catterick, Cleveland, Clinton, Colombo, Easton, Emperor, Farndale, Gribb, Hunter, Kelvin, Khedive, Kimberley, Langlaate, Larne, Ledbury, Liddesdale, Marne, Meteor, Musketeer, Orion, Prince David, Prince Henry, Protea, Pursuer, Rinaldo, Royalist, Saxifrage, Searcher, Seksern, Southern Maid, Stalker, Teazer, Termagant, Terpsichore, Thruster, Treern, Troubridge, Tuscan, Tyrian, Ulster Queen, Ultimatum, Ultor, Unswerving, Vampire, Vigorous, Virtue, Vivid, Vox, Whaddon, Zetland.
FAA Sqn: 800, 807, 809, 879, 881, 899.

NORTH CAPE 1943   26 December 1943

This action led to the destruction of the German battle cruiser Scharnhorst by gunfire and torpedo attacks from the battleship Duke of York, cruisers and destroyers.

Belfast, Duke of York, Jamaica, Matchless, Musketeer, Norfolk, Opportune, Saumarez, Savage, Scorpion, Sheffield, Virago.

ADRIATIC 1944   1944

Aldenham, Aphis, Atherstone, Avon Vale, Belvoir, Bicester, Blackmore, Brocklesby, Cleveland, Colombo, Delhi, Eggesford, Grenville, Janus, Jervis, Kimberley, Lamerton, Lauderdale, Ledbury, Loyal, Quantock, Scarab, Teazer, Tenacious, Termagant, Terpsichore, Tetcott, Troubridge, Tumult, Tuscan, Tyrian, Ulster, Undine, Urchin, Whaddon, Wheatland, Wilton, Zetland.

ANZIO 1944   22-31 January 1944

Albacore, Barmond, Barndale, Beaufort, Boxer, Bruiser, Bude, Bulolo, Cadmus, Cava, Circe, Crete, Delhi, Dido, Espiegle, Faulknor, Fly, Glengyle, Grenville, Hornpipe, Inglefield, Janus, Jervis, Kempenfelt, Laforey, Loyal, Mauritius, Orion, Palomares, Penelope, Prinses Beatrix, Rinaldo, Rothesay, Royal Ulsterman, St. Kilda, Sheppey, Spartan, Tetcott, Thruster, Twostep, Ulster Queen, Ultor, Urchin, Waterwitch.
ML: 121, 134, 295, 307, 338, 443, 462, 554, 558, 565, 567, 569, 575, 581.

NORMANDY 1944   6 June - 3 July 1944

Although there is a substantial list of ships awarded this Honour, it should be remembered that large numbers of Royal Naval personnel formed Naval Parties (COPPs, Landing Craft Obstruction Clearance Units, Naval Beach Commando, Naval Beach Signal Sections etc), which landed ahead of the soldiery, who were brought ashore by naval manned landing craft.

Abelia, Adventure, Affleck, Ajax, Albatross, Alberni, Albrighton, Albury, Algonquin, Apollo, Ardrossan, Arethusa, Argonaut, Aristocrat, Armeria, Ashanti, Aylmer, Azalea, Bachaquero, Baddeck, Balfour, Balsam, Bangor, Beagle, Beaumaris, Belfast, Bellona, Bentley, Bickerton, Black Prince, Blackpool, Blackwood, Blairmore, Blankney, Bleasdale, Blencathra, Bligh, Bluebell, Boadicea, Bootle, Borage, Boston, Braithwaite, Bridlington, Bridport, Brigadier, Brissenden, Britomart, Bulolo, Burdock, Buttercup,
Calgary, Cam, Camellia, Campanula, Campbell, Camrose, Cape Breton, Capel, Capetown, Caraquet, Catherine, Cato, Cattistock, Celandine, Ceres, Charlock, Chaudiere, Chelmer, Clarkia, Clematis, Clover, Cockatrice, Cooke, Cotswold, Cottesmore, Cowichan, Crane,
Dacres, Dahlia, Dakins, Danae, Despatch, Deveron, Diadem, Dianella, Dianthus, Domett, Dominica, Dornoch, Douwe Aukes, Drumheller, Duckworth, Duff, Duke of Wellington, Dunbar,
Eastbourne, Eglinton, Elgin, Emerald, Emperor, Enterprise, Erebus, Eskimo, Essington,
Fame, Fancy, Faulknor, Fernie, Forester, Fort William, Fort York, Fraserburgh, Friendship, Frobisher, Fury,
Garlies, Garth, Gatineau, Gazelle, Gentian,
Geranium, Glasgow, Gleaner, Glenearn, Glenroy, Goatfell, Godetia, Golden Eagle, Goodson, Gore, Gorgon, Gozo, Grecian, Grenville, Grey Fox, Grey Goose, Grey Owl, Grey Seal, Grey Shark, Grey Wolf, Grou, Guysborough,
Haida, Halcyon, Halsted, Hambledon, Hargood, Harrier, Hart, Havelock, Hawkins, Heather, Hilary, Hind, Holmes, Honeysuckle, Hotham, Hotspur, Hound, Huron, Hussar, Hydra,
Icarus, Ilfracombe, Impulsive, Inconstant, Inglis, Invicta, Isis,
Jason, Javelin, Jervis,
Keats, Kellett, Kelvin, Kempenfelt, Kenora, Keppel, Kingcup, Kingsmill, Kitchener, Kite, Kootenay, Lapwing, Largs, Lark, Larne, Lavender, Lawford, Lawson, Lennox, Lightfoot, Lindsay, Llandudno, Loch Fada, Loch Killin, Lochy, Locust, Londonderry, Loosestrife, Louisburg, Loyalty, Lunenburg, Lydd, Lyme Regis,
Mackay, Magpie, Malpeque, Matane, Mauritius, Mayflower, Melbreak, Melita, Mendip, Meon, Meynell, Middleton, Mignonette, Milltown, Mimico, Minas, Misoa, Montrose, Moorsom, Moosejaw, Mounsey, Mourne,
Narbrough, Narcissus, Nasturtium, Nelson, Nith, Northway,
Obedient, Offa, Onslaught, Onslow, Onyx, Opportune, Orchis, Orestes, Oribi, Orion, Orwell, Ottawa, Outremont, Oxlip,
Pangbourne, Parrsboro, Pelican, Pelorus, Pennywort, Persian, Petunia, Pickle, Pincher, Pink, Pique, Plover, Plucky, Poole, Poppy, Port Arthur, Port Colborne, Postillion, Potentilla, Prrescott, Primrose, Prince Baudouin, Prince Charles, Prince David, Prince Leopold, Prins Albert, Prises Astrid, Prinses Josephine Charlotte, Pursuer, Pytchley,
Qu'Appelle, Qualicum, Queen Emma, Quorn, Ramillies, Rattlesnake, Ready, Recruit, Redpole, Regina, Restigouche, Retalick, Rhododendron, Rifleman, Rimouski, Riou, Roberts, Rochester, Rodney, Romney, Ross, Rowley, Royal Ulsterman, Rupert, Ryde, Rye,
St. Helier, St. John, St. Laurent, Salamander, Saltash, Sandown, Saskatchewan, Saumarez, Savage, Scarborough, Scawfell, Scorpion, Scott, Scourge, Scylla, Seagull, Seaham, Selkirk, Serapis, Seymour, Shippigan, Sidmouth, Sioux, Sirius, Skeene, Southdown, Southern Prinnce, Speedwell, Spragge, Starling, Starwort, Statice, Stayner, Steadfast, Stevenstone, Stockham, Stork, Stormont, Strule, Summerside, Sunflower, Sutton, Swansea, Sweetbriar, Swift,

Tadoussac, Talybont, Tanatside, Tartar, Tasajera, Tavy, Teme, Tenby, Thames Queen, Thornborough, Torrington, Tracker, Trentonian, Trollope, Tyler, Ulster, Ulster Monarch, Ulysses, Undaunted, Undine, Urania, Urchin, Ursa, Vanquisher, Vegreville, Venus, Versatile, Verulam, Vervain, Vesper, Vestal, Vidette, Vigilant, Vimy, Virago, Vivacious, Volunteer, Waldegrave, Walker, Wallflower, Walpole, Wanderer, Warspite, Wasaga, Waskesiu, Watchman, Waveney, Wedgeport, Wensleydale, Westcott, Whimbrel, Whippingham, Whitaker, Whitehall, Whitehaven, Whitshed, Wild Goose, Windsor, Woodstock, Worthing, Wren, Wrestler, X.20, X.23.

FAA Sqn: 700, 800, 804, 808, 816, 819, 838, 846, 848, 849, 850, 854, 855, 881, 885, 886, 896, 897.

Small craft and auxiliaries:

Surveying: - Astral, Franklin, Gulnare

A/S Trawlers: - Annet, Asie, Bern, Bombardier, Bressay, Caldy, Cambridgeshire, Coll, Cornelian, Damsay, Ellesmere, Fiaray, Flint, Foulness, Fusilier, Gairsay, Ganilly, Gateshead, Grassholm, Grenadier, Grimsby Town, Gweal, Herschell, Hugh Walpole, Kingston Andalusite, Kingston Chrysoberyl, La Nantaise, Lancer, Lincolnshire, Lindisfarne, Lord Austin, Lord Essenden, Lord Middleton, Lord Stanhope, Lord Wakefield, Neave, Northern Foam, Northern Gem, Northern Gift, Northern Pride, Northern Reward, Northern Sky, Northern Spray, Northern Sun, Northern Wave, Notre Dame de France, Olivina, Pearl, Quadrille, Ruby, Sapper, Scalpay, Skomer, Skye, Steepholm, Switha, Texada, Ulva, Veleta, Victrix.

LL Trawlers: - Conway Castle, Courtier, Georgette, Northcoates, Perdrant, Probe, Proctor, Proof, Prowess, Sir Agravaine, Sir Gareth, Sir Geraint, Sir Kaye, Sir Lamorak, Sir Tristram.

Danlayers: - Alexander Scott, Bayfield, Blyth, Bryher, Calvay, Canso, Chamois, Chance, Colsay, Commander Evans, Craftsman, Dalmatia, Doon, Dorothy Lambert, Fairway, Farne, Fuday, Georgian, Gilsay, Green Howard, Gunner, Hanna Ray, Hornbeam, Ijuin, James Lay, Jude, Kings Grey, Lord Ashfield, Lord Melchett, Mulgrave, Neil Smith, Niblick, Peterhead, Righto, St. Barbe,

Sigma, Sir Galahad, Sir Lancelot, Stella Leonis, Stella Rigel, Sylvana, Thunder.

Mulberries:- Adelphi, All Hallows, Ambition, Andanes, Ann Melville, Arabesque, Atalanta, Avondee, Barbain, Barberry, Barcock, Barcombe, Barlow, Barnes Ness, Barnwell, Barova, Barrage, Barthorpe, Bartizan, Ben Glas, Benjamin Coleman, Bervie Braes, Bona, Braes O'Mar, Brittany, Bucephalus, Caverock, Cherwell, Choice, Cloughstone, Controller, Coronatia, Coryphene, Crevette, Dandolo, Dragonet, East Coast, Eridanes, Eroican, Etruscan, Fernmoor, Fossbeck, Fratton, General Birdwood, Haslemere, Heroine, Ibis II, Isobel, Jacqueline Clasine, Kernevel, Laverock, Leonian, Lephreto, Marie Jose Rosette, Martinet, Mikasa, Minster, Mirabelle, Muroto, North Lynn, Peggy Nutten, Pitstruan, Plantagenet, Prince Victor, Queen of Kent, Queen of Thanet, Riano, Rigoletto, Ringwood, River Lenn, River Spey, Roxano, St. Minver, Salvini, Scomber, Settsu, Shielburn, Sonnet, Southward Ho, Staunch, Strathalladale, Strathfina, Strathmartin, Sturton, Taipo, The Way, Tocsin, Ugiebank, Viking Deeps, War Star, William Stroud, Witham.

Pluto: - Algerian, Bustler, Cedar, Coronia, Danube V, Grampian, Holdfast, Latimer, Lilac, Marauder, Persephone, Sancroft.

Blockships: - Centurion, Durban.

Flotillas (Numbers of vessels)

MGB: 1st (6)

MTB: 1st(8), 5th (7), 13th (8), 14th (12), 21st (7), 22nd (7), 29th (8), 35th (10), 51st (7), 52nd (9), 53rd (7), 55th (12), 59th (8), 63rd(8), 64th (7), 65th (9).

MLs: 1st (8), 2nd(9), 4th (4), 5th (12), 7th (14), 10th (10), 11th (13), 13th (8), 14th(13), 15th (6), 19th(4), 20th (14), 21st(9), 23rd(8), 33rd (7), 50th(5), 51st(4), 103rd(8), 150th(9), 151(9). Unattached (2).

MMS: 101st(10), 102nd(10), 104th(10), 115th(10), 132nd(10), 143rd(10), 205th(11).

BYMS: 150th (10), 159th(10), 165th(10), 167th(10).

SABANG 1944   25 July 1944

Ceylon, Cumberland, Gambia, Illustrious, Kenya, Nigeria, Phoebe, Quality, Queen Elizabeth, Quickmatch, Quilliam, Racehorse, Raider, Rapid, Relentless, Renown, Rocket,

Roebuck, Rotherham, Tantalus, Templar, Valiant, Victorious.
FAA Sqn: 831, 1830, 1833, 1834, 1836, 1837, 1838.

SOUTH FRANCE 1944   15-27 August 1944

Ailsa Craig, Ajax, Aldenham, Antares, Antwerp, Aphis, Arcturus, Argonaut, Aries, Atherstone, Attacker, Aubretia, Aurora, Bardolf, Barford, Barholm, Barmond, Beaufort, Belvoir, Bicester, Black Prince, Blackmore, Borealis, Brave, Brecon, Brixham, Bruiser, Bude, Caledon, Calm, Calpe, Catterick, Cleveland, Clinton, Colombo, Columbine, Crowlin, Delhi, Dido, Eastway, Eggesford, Emperor, Farndale, Foula, Haydon, Highway, Hunter, Keren, Khedive, Kintyre, Larne, Lauderdale, Liddesdale, Lookout, Mewstone, Nebb, Oakley, Octavia, Orion, Polruan, Prince Baudouin, Prince David, Prince Henry, Prins Albert, Prinses Beatrix, Product, Pursuer, Ramillies, Rhyl, Rinaldo, Rosario, Rothesay, Royalist, Satsa, Scarab, Searcher, Sirius, Skokolm, Spanker, Stalker, Stormcloud, Stornoway, Stuart Prince, Teazer, Tenacious, Termagant, Terpsichore, Thruster, Troubridge, Tumult, Tuscan, Tyrian, Ulster Queen, Welfare, Whaddon, Zetland.

FAA Sqn : 800, 807, 809, 879, 881, 882, 899
MLs: 121, 273, 299, 336, 337, 338, 451, 456, 458, 461, 462, 463, 469, 471, 555, 556, 557, 559, 560, 562, 563, 564, 567, 576, 581.
BYMS: 2009, 2022, 2026, 2027, 2171, 2172.

BURMA 1944-45
                    October 1944 - April 1945
                    May - August 1945

1944 - FAA Sqn: 815.

1944-45 - Ameer, Barpeta*, Barracuda, Cauvery, Eskimo, Flamingo, Haitan, Jumna, Kathiawar, Kedah, Kenya, Kistna, Konkan, Llanstephen Castle*, Napier, Narbada, Nepal, Newcastle, Nguva, Nigeria, Norman, Nubian, Paladin, Pathfinder, Phoebe, Queen Elizabeth, Raider, Rapid, Redpole, Rocket, Roebuck, Shoreham, Spey, Teviot, White Bear.

1945 - Agra, Bann, Bengal, Bihar, Bombay, Ceylon, Chameleon, Cumberland, Cyclone, Deveron, Emperor, Empress, Glenroy, Godavari, Halladale, Hunter, Jed, Khedive, Khyber, Kumaon, Lahore, Largs, Lulworth,

Nith, Orissa, Pamela, Patna, Penn, Persimmon, Pickle, Pincher, Plucky, Poona, Prins Albert, Punjab, Racehorse, Rajputana (m/s), Recruit, Redoubt, Rifleman, Rohilkhand, Rotherham, Royalist, Sandray, Saumarez, Scaravay, Shah, Shiel, Silvio, Stalker, Suffolk, Sussex, Sutlej, Taff, Tartar,Test, Trent, Una (not s/m), Venus, Verulam, Vestal, Vigilant, Virago, Virginia, Waveney.
FAA Sqn: 800, 804, 807, 808, 809, 845, 851, 896, 1700.

*Red Ensign

LEYTE GULF 1944   20 - 27 October 1944

Ariadne, Arunta, Australia, Gascoyne, Shropshire, Warramunga.

WALCHEREN 1944   1 November 1944

Erebus, Kingsmill, Roberts, Warspite.
ML: 146, 902 together with about 180 landing craft of various classes.

LINGAYEN GULF 1945   5- 9 January 1945

Arunta, Australia, Gascoyne, Shropshire, Warramunga, Warrego.

PALEMBANG 1945
                    24 and 29 January 1945

In this action carrier borne aircraft carried out strikes on Japanese held oil installations in Sumatra, including a strike at the Royal Dutch Oil Refinery at Pladjoe, the largest and most important in the Far East.

Illustrious, Indefatigable, Indomitable, Victorious.
FAA Sqn: 820, 849, 854, 857, 887, 888, 894, 1770, 1830, 1833, 1834, 1836, 1839, 1844.

OKINAWA 1945   26 March - 25 May 1945

Achilles, Argonaut, Avon, Ballarat, Bendigo, Black Prince, Burnie, Cairns, Chaser, Crane, Euryalus, Findhorn, Formidable, Gambia, Grenville, Howe, Illustrious, Indefatigable, Indomitable, Kalgoorlie, Kempenfelt, King George V, Launceston, Lismore, Napier, Nepal, Nizam, Norman, Parret, Pheasant,

Pirie, Quadrant, Quality, Queenborough, Quiberon, Quickmatch, Quilliam, Ruler, Slinger, Speaker, Striker, Swiftsure, Tenacious, Termagant, Troubridge, Uganda, Ulster, Undaunted, Undine, Unicorn, Urania, Urchin, Ursa, Victorious, Wager, Wessex, Whelp, Whimbrel, Whirlwind, Whyalla, Woodcock. FAA Sqn: 820, 848, 849, 854, 857, 885, 887, 894, 1770, 1830, 1833, 1834, 1836, 1839, 1840, 1841, 1842, 1844, 1845.

JAPAN 1945   16 July - 11 August 1945

Formidable, Gambia, Implacable, Indefatigable, King George V, Newfoundland, Quality, Quiberon, Tenacious, Termagant, Terpsichore, Ulysses, Undine, Urania, Victorious.
FAA Sqn: 801, 820, 848, 849, 880, 887, 894, 1771, 1772, 1834, 1836, 1841, 1842.

KOREA 1950-53   2 July 1950 - 27 July 1953

Alacrity 50-52, Alert 51, Amethyst 51-52, Anzac 51-53, Athabaskan 50-53, Bataan 52, Belfast 50-52, Birmingham 52-53, Black Swan 50-51, Cardigan Bay 50-53, Cayuga 50-52, Ceylon 50-52, Charity 50-53, Cockade 50-53, Comus 50-53, Concord 50-53, Condamine 52-53, Consort 50-53, Constance 50-52, Cossack 50-53, Crane 52-53, Crusader 52-53, Culgoa 53, Glory 51-53, Haida 52-53, Hart 50-51, Hawea 51-53, Huron 51-53, Iroquois 52-53, Jamaica 50, Kaniere 53, Kenya 50-51, Modeste 53, Morecambe Bay 50-53, Mounts Bay 50-53, Murchison 51-52, Newcastle 52-53, Nootka 51-52, Ocean 52-53, Opossum 52-53, Pukaki 50, Rotoiti 50-53, St. Brides Bay 50-53, Shoalhaven 50, Sioux 50-52, Sparrow 53, Sydney 51-52, Taupo 51-52, Telemachus 53, Theseus 50-51, Tobruk 51-53, Triumph 50, Tutira 50-51, Tyne 53, Unicorn 50-53, Warramunga 50-52, Whitesand Bay 50-53,

RFAs: Brown Ranger 50-52, Green Ranger 51-52, Wave Baron 52, Wave Chief 51-53, Wave Knight 51-53, Wave Laird 50-51, Wave Premier 50-52, Wave Prince 50-53, Wave Sovereign 52-53.

Hospital Ship: Maine 50.

FAA Sqn: 800(50), 801 (52-53), 802 (52), 804 (51-52), 805 (51-52), 807 (50-53), 808 (51-52), 810 (50-53), 812 (51-52), 817 (51-52), 821 (52-53), 825 (52), 827 (50), 898 (52-53).

VIETNAM 1967-71

Awarded to eligible units of the Royal Australian Navy by the Australian Commonwealth Navy Board:

Brisbane 1969-71, Hobart 1967-70, Perth 1967-71, Vendetta 1969-70, 723 Squadron 1967-71.

FALKLAND ISLANDS 1982
2 April – 14 June 1982

A Task Force was hastily assembled, sent thousands of miles South, and successfully recaptured the Islands from Argentinian invaders.

Active, Alacrity, Ambuscade, Andromeda, Antelope, Antrim, Ardent, Argonaut, Arrow, Avenger, Brilliant, Bristol, Broadsword, Cardiff, Conqueror, Cordella, Courageous, Coventry, Dumbarton Castle, Endurance, Exeter, Farnella, Fearless, Glamorgan, Glasgow, Hecla, Herald, Hermes, Hydra, Intrepid, Invincible, Junella, Leeds Castle, Minerva, Northella, Onyx, Penelope, Pict, Plymouth, Sheffield, Spartan, Splendid, Valiant, Yarmouth

FAA Sqn: 737, 800, 801, 809, 815, 820, 824, 825, 826, 829, 845, 846, 847, 848, 899.

RFAs:- Appleleaf, Bayleaf, Blue Rover, Brambleleaf, Engadine, Fort Austin, Fort Grange, Olmeda, Olna, Pearleaf, Plumleaf, Regent, Resource, Sir Bedivere, Sir Galahad, Sir Geraint, Sir Lancelot, Sir Percivale, Sir Tristram, Stromness, Tidepool, Tidespring,.

RMAS: Typhoon.

Merchant ships taken up from trade (STUFT): MV Anco Charger, SS Atlantic Causeway, SS Atlantic Conveyor, MV Baltic Ferry, MV British Dart, MV British Esk, MV British Tay, MV British Test, MV British Trent, MV British Wye, SS Canberra, MV Contender Bezant, MV Elk, MV Europic Ferry, MV Fort Toronto, MV Geestport, CS Iris, MT Irishman, MV Lycaon, MV Nordic Ferry, MV Norland, RMS Queen Elizabeth 2, MV Saint Edmund, MT Salvageman, MV Saxonia, MV Scottish Eagle, MV Shell Eburna, MV Stena Seaspread, MV Tor Caledonia, SS Uganda, MV Wimpey Seahorse, MT Yorkshireman.

KUWAIT 1991
17 January - 28 February 1991

Atherstone, Brave, Brazen, Brilliant, Cardiff, Cattistock, Dulverton, Exeter, Gloucester, Hecla, Herald, Hurworth, Ledbury, London, Manchester,

FAA Sqn: 815, 826, 829, 845, 846, 848,

RFAs: Argus, Bayleaf, Diligence, Fort Grange, Olna, Resource, Sir Bedivere, Sir Galahad, Sir Percivale, Sir Tristram.

PART 2
SINGLE SHIP ACTIONS

Single-ship and Boat Service Actions (*) which are normally denoted by the name of the enemy engaged, and not by a place name are as follows:

Date	Ship	Battle Honour
08.06.1940	Acasta	*'Scharnhorst'* 1940
04.02.1805	Acheron	Cape Tenez 1805
16.03.1917	Achilles	*'Leopard'* 1917
29.03.1681	Adventure	*'Golden Horse'* 1681
16.09.1681	Adventure	*'Two Lions'* 1681
19.09.1777	Alert	*'Lexington'* 1777
13.01.1797	Amazon	*'Droits de l'Homme'* 1797
13.03.1806	Amazon	*'Belle Poule'* 1806
29.07.1800 *	Amethyst	*'Cerbère'* 1800
10.11.1808	Amethyst	*'Thétis'* 1808
05.04.1809	Amethyst	*'Niémen'* 1809
13.05.1757	Antelope	*'Aquilon'* 1757
08.06.1940	Ardent	*'Scharnhorst'* 1940
04.02.1805	Arrow	Cape Tenez 1805
21.10.1794	Artois	*'Révolutionnaire'* 1794
10.04.1795	Astraea	*'Gloire'* 1795
22.07.1801*	Beaulieu	*'Chevrette'* 1801
31.03.1804	Beaver	*'Athalante'* 1804
15.08.1761	Bellona	*'Courageux'* 1761
11.11.1942	Bengal	*'Hokoku Maru'* 1942
06.01.1795	Blanche	*'Pique'* 1795
06.07.1809	Bonne Citoyenne	*'Furieuse'* 1809
21.04.1917	Broke	Dover 1917
29.03.1681	Calabash	*'Golden Horse'* 1681
14.09.1914	Carmania	*'Cap Trafalgar'* 1914
04.02.1804*	Centaur	*'Curieux'* 1804
26.08.1808	Centaur	*'Sevolod'* 1808
20.06.1743	Centurion	*'N.S. de Covadonga'* 1743
28.03.1814	Cherub	*'Essex Junior'* 1814
20.10.1849	Columbine	Kua Kam 1849
11.08.1808	Comet	*'Sylphe'* 1808
15.08.1807	Comus	*'Frederikscoarn'* 1807
03.09.1779	Countess of Scarborough	*'Pallas'* 1779
20.10.1793	Crescent	*'Réunion'* 1793
08.07.1800	Dart	*'Désirée'* 1800
11.09.1809	Diana	*'Zefier'* 1809
24.06.1795	Dido	*'Minerve'* 1795
22.07.1801*	Doris	*'Chevrette'* 1801
29.04.1758	Dorsetshire	*'Raisonnable'* 1758
13.06.1796	Dryad	*'Proserpine'* 1796
16.03.1917	Dundee	*'Leopard'* 1917
01.03.1942	Encounter	Sunda Strait 1942
15.01.1815	Endymion	*'President'* 1815
25.02.1814	Eurotas	*'Clorinde'* 1814
01.03.1942	Exeter	Sunda Strait 1942

('Sunda Strait' commemorates the final actions of the remnants of the ABDA (combined Australian, British, Dutch and Australian) Force which had been severely mauled in the Battle of the Java Sea a few days beforehand. It is an example of an award in recognition of outstanding efforts in the face of overwhelming odds.)

20.10.1798	Fisgard	*'Immortalité'* 1798
21.04.1782	Foudroyant	*'Pégase'* 1782
30.03.1800	Foudroyant	*'Guillaume Tell'* 1800
20.10.1849	Fury	Kua Kam 1849
21.01.1807*	Galatea	'Lynx' 1807
08.04.1940	Glowworm	*'Admiral Hipper'* 1940
22.05.1812	Growler	Groix Island 1812
27.03.1814	Hebrus	*'Étoile'* 1814
16.05.1795	Hussar	*'Raison'* 1795
29.07.1800*	Impetueux	*'Cerbère'* 1800
26.08.1808	Implacable	*'Sevolod'* 1808
22.04.1796	Indefatigable	*'Virginie'* 1796
13.01.1797	Indefatigable	*'Droits de l'Homme'* 1797
05.11.1940	Jervis Bay	*'Admiral Scheer'* 1940
22.05.1681	Kingfisher	Sardinia 1681
15.07.1798	Lion	*'Santa Dorotea'* 1798
30.03.1800	Lion	*'Guillaume Tell'* 1800
13.03.1795	Lively	*'Tourterelle'* 1795
29.05.1797*	Lively	*'Mutine'* 1797
13.03.1806	London	*'Marengo'* 1806
24.06.1795	Lowestoffe	*'Minerve'* 1795
21.04.1798	Mars	*'Hercule'* 1798
29.12.1669	Mary Rose	The Seven Algerines 1669
11.07.1915	Mersey	*'Konigsberg'* 1915
29.05.1797*	Minerve	*'Mutine'* 1797
28.02.1758	Monmouth	*'Foudroyant'* 1758
22.05.1812	Northumberland	Groix Island 1812
31.01.1748	Nottingham	*'Magnanime'* 1748
18.06.1793	Nymphe	*'Cléopâtre'* 1793
09.03.1797	Nymphe	*'Constance'* 1797
01.01.1809	Onyx	*'Manly'* 1809
14.09.1779	Pearl	*'Santa Monica'* 1779
1857-1858	Pearl	Amorha 1858
14.08.1813	Pelican	*'Argus'* 1813
30.03.1800	Penelope	*'Guillaume Tell'* 1800
28.02.1942	Perth	Sunda Strait 1942
21.03.1800	Peterel	*'Ligurienne'* 1800
27.10.1800*	Phaeton	*'San Josef'* 1800
20.10.1849	Phlegethon (Bengal Marine)	Kua Kam 1849
21.12.1797	Phoebe	*'Néréide'* 1797
19.02.1801	Phoebe	*'Africaine'* 1801
28.03.1814	Phoebe	*'Essex'* 1814
10.08.1805	Phoenix	*'Didon'* 1805
03-06.05.1709	Portland	*'Coventry'* 1709
31.01.1748	Portland	*'Magnanime'* 1748
09.02.1746	Portland	*'Auguste'* 1746
20.04.1667	Princess	North Sea 1667
31.08.1591	Revenge	Azores 1591
28.02.1758	Revenge	*'Orphée'* 1758
22.07.1801*	Robust	*'Chevrette'* 1801
17.06.1794	Romney	*'Sibylle'* 1794
21.10.1813	Royalist	*'Weser'* 1813
09.03.1797	St. Fiorenzo	*'Résistance'* 1797
13.02.1805	St. Fiorenzo	*'Psyché'* 1805
08.03.1808	St. Fiorenzo	*'Piédmontaise'* 1808
08.06.1796	Santa Margarita	*'Tamise'* 1796
02.03.1808	Sappho	*'Admiral Jawl'* 1808
31.03.1804	Scorpion	*'Athalante'* 1804

11.01.1810	Scorpion	*'Oreste'* 1810
21.10.1813	Scylla	*'Weser'* 1813
06.07.1808	Seahorse	*'Badere Zaffer'* 1808
25.08.1800	Seine	*'Vengeance'* 1800
23.09.1779	Serapis	*'Bonhomme Richard'* 1779
11.07.1915	Severn	*'Konigsberg'* 1915
01.06.1813	Shannon	*'Chesapeake'* 1813

(In this action between two fairly evenly matched vessels, the SHANNON (38 guns) (Captain Philip Broke) defeated the American frigate CHESAPEAKE (36 guns) (Captain Lawrence) within sight of Boston in a short but very fierce engagement)

1857-1858	Shannon	Lucknow 1857-8
12.09.1757	Southampton	*'Émeraude'* 1757
06.05.1801	Speedy	*'Gamo'* 1801
25.10.1799	Surprise	*'Hermione'* 1799
21.04.1917	Swift	Dover 1917
28.02.1799	Sybille	*'Forte'* 1799
09.11.1914	Sydney	*'Emden'* 1914
19.11.1941	Sydney	*'Kormoran'* 1941
26.04.1810	Sylvia	*'Echo'* 1810
15.03.1793*	Syren	Williamstadt 1793
18.03.1799	Telegraph	*'Hirondelle'* 1799
13.10.1796	Terpsichore	*'Mahonesa'* 1796
17.07.1761	Thetis	*'Bouffonne'* 1761
17.05.1795	Thetis	*'Prévoyante'* 1795
10.02.1810	Thistle	*'Havik'* 1810
17.07.1761	Thunderer	*'Achille'* 1761
08.01.1761	Unicorn	*'Vestale'* 1761
08.06.1796	Unicorn	*'Tribune'* 1796
22.07.1801*	Uranie	*'Chevrette'* 1801
21.02.1759	Vestal	*'Bellone'* 1759
22.02.1812	Victorious	*'Rivoli'* 1812
22.07.1801*	Ville de Paris	*'Chevrette'* 1801
30.03.1800	Vincejo	*'Guillaume Tell'* 1800
29.07.1800*	Viper	*'Cerbère'* 1800
19.05.1808	Virginie	*'Gelderland'* 1808
22.02.1812	Weazle	'Mercure' 1812
22.04.1813	Weazle	Boscaline Bay 1813
22.09.1943	X.6	*'Tirpitz'* 1943
22.09.1943	X.7	*'Tirpitz'* 1943
31.07.1945	XE.1	*'Takao'* 1945
31.07.1945	XE.3	*'Takao'* 1945

PART 3
SHIPS AND THEIR BATTLEHONOURS

The following are the Battle Honours awarded to the ships named:

* Indicates an honour awarded to a mercantile vessel
** Indicates an honour awarded to a Royal Fleet Auxiliary

Abbeydale	North Africa 1942**		
Abdiel	Jutland 1916 Biscay 1941	Crete 1941 Sicily 1943	Libya 1941
Abelia	Atlantic 1941-5	English Channel 1944	Normandy 1944
Abercrombie	Guadeloupe 1810 Salerno 1943	Dardanelles 1915-16 Mediterranean 1943	Sicily 1943
Aberdare	Libya 1941-2		
Aberdeen	Atlantic 1939-45	North Africa 1942	
Abigail	Orfordness 1666		
Aboukir	Heligoland 1914		
Acacia	English Channel 1942		
Acanthus	Norway 1941 Arctic 1943	Atlantic 1941-45 North Sea 1944	English Channel 1943
Acasta	San Domingo 1806 Atlantic 1939-40	Martinique 1809 Norway 1940	Jutland 1916 'Scharnhorst' 1940
Achates	Armada 1588 Atlantic 1940-42 Barents Sea 1942	Guadeloupe 1810 'Bismarck' 1941 Arctic 1942	Jutland 1916 North Africa 1942
Acheron	Cape Tenez 1805 Jutland 1916	Heligoland 1914 Norway 1940	Dogger Bank 1915
Achilles	Belle Isle 1761 River Plate 1939	Trafalgar 1805 Guadalcanal 1942-43	'Leopard' 1917 Okinawa 1945
Acorn	China 1856-60		
Actaeon	Belle Isle 1761	China 1856-60	
Active	Lagos 1759 Egypt 1801 Ashantee 1873-74 'Bismarck' 1941 Falkland Islands 1982	Trincomalee 1782 Lissa 1811 Jutland 1916 Diego Suarez 1942	Camperdown 1797 Pelagosa 1811 Atlantic 1939-44 Arctic 1944
Activity	Atlantic 1944	Arctic 1944	
Acute	North Sea 1942 Salerno 1943	North Africa 1942-43 Atlantic 1943	Sicily 1943

Adamant	Chesapeake 1781	Camperdown 1797	Dardanelles 1915
Adelphi	Normandy 1944		
Adonis	North Sea 1943		
Advantage	Portland 1653	Scheveningen 1653	
Adventure	Dover 1652 Lowestoft 1665 '*Golden Horse*' 1681 Belle Isle 1761	Portland 1653 Orfordness 1666 '*Two Lions*' 1681 China 1856-60	Gabbard 1653 Sole Bay 1672 Barfleur 1692 Normandy 1944
Advice	Armada 1588 Orfordness 1666 Schooneveld 1673	Portland 1653 Bugia 1671 Texel 1673	Gabbard 1653 Sole Bay 1672 Barfleur 1692
AE 2	Dardanelles 1915		
Aeolus	Bay of Biscay 1805	Martinique 1809	Baltic 1855
Aetna	Barfleur 1692 Basque Roads 1809	Louisburg 1758 *(*also see **Etna***)*	Belle Isle 1761
Affleck	Atlantic 1943-44	Normandy 1944	English Channel 1944
Africa	Trafalgar 1805		
Afridi	Belgian Coast 1916-17	Zeebrugge 1918	Norway 1940
Agamemnon	Ushant 1781 Copenhagen 1801 Crimea 1854-55	The Saints 1782 Trafalgar 1805 Dardanelles 1915-16	Genoa 1795 San Domingo 1806
Agassiz	Atlantic 1941-45		
Agincourt	Camperdown 1797	Egypt 1801	Jutland 1916
Agra	Burma 1945		
Aid	Armada 1588		
Aigle	Basque Roads 1809		
Aigon	North Sea 1941		
Ailsa Craig	Atlantic 1944	North Sea 1944	South France 1944
Aire	Atlantic 1943-45		
Airedale	Libya 1942	Arctic 1942	
Ajax	St. Vincent 1780 Egypt 1801 Baltic 1854-55 Mediterranean 1940-41 Crete 1941 Normandy 1944	St. Kitts 1782 Trafalgar 1805 Jutland 1916 Matapan 1941 Malta Convoys 1941 South France 1944	The Saints 1782 San Sebastian 1813 River Plate 1939 Greece 1941 Aegean 1944

Akbar	Java 1811		
Alacrity	China 1900	Korea 1950-52	Falkland Islands 1982
Alarm	Havana 1762 North Africa 1942-43	The Saints 1782	North Sea 1942
Alaunia	Atlantic 1939-41		
Albacore	North Africa 1942-3 Anzio 1944	Sicily 1943	Salerno 1943
Alban	Baltic 1854		
Albatross	Atlantic 1942-3	Normandy 1944	
Albemarle	Barfleur 1692		
Alberni	Atlantic 1941-44	Normandy 1944	North Sea 1944
Albion	Algiers 1816 Dardanelles 1915	Navarino 1827	Crimea 1854-55
Albrighton	Dieppe 1942 Biscay 1944	English Channel 1942-44 North Sea 1944	Normandy 1944
Albury	Dunkirk 1940	Normandy 1944	
Albyn	Belgian Coast 1915-16		
Alca	Atlantic 1942		
Alcantara	Atlantic 1940		
Alcedo	Cadiz 1596*		
Alceste	Pelagosa 1811		
Alcide	Quebec 1759 St. Vincent 1780	Martinique 1762 St. Kitts 1782	Havana 1762 The Saints 1782
Alcmene	Copenhagen 1801	Guadeloupe 1810	
Aldeborough	Belle Isle 1761		
Aldenham	Atlantic 1942 Aegean 1943	Libya 1942 Adriatic 1944	Sicily 1943 South France 1944
Alecto	The Saints 1782	Benin 1897	
Aleppine	Orfordness 1666		
Alert	'*Lexington*' 1777	The Saints 1782	Korea 1951
Alexander	Ushant 1781	Nile 1798	Egypt 1801
Alexander Scott	Normandy 1944		

Alexandra	Alexandria 1882		
Alfred	St. Vincent 1780 First of June 1794	St. Kitts 1782 St. Lucia 1796	The Saints 1782 Guadeloupe 1810
Algerian	Normandy 1944		
Algerine	China 1841-42 North Africa 1942	China 1856-60	China 1900
Algiers	Baltic 1854	Crimea 1854-55	
Algoma	Atlantic 1941-45	English Channel 1945	
Algonquin	Normandy 1944	Norway 1944	Arctic 1944-45
Alice and Francis	Sole Bay 1672		
Alisma	Atlantic 1941-45	English Channel 1945	
All Hallows	Normandy 1944		
Alliance	Acre 1799		
Alligator	Egypt 1801	Burma 1824-26	China 1841
Allington Castle	Atlantic 1944-45	Arctic 1944-45	
Alnwick Castle	Atlantic 1945	Arctic 1945	
Alresford	Dieppe 1942		
Alynbank	Atlantic 1940-43 Sicily 1943	Arctic 1942 Salerno 1943	North Africa 1942 Mediterranean 1943
Amaranthe	Martinique 1809	Guadeloupe 1810	
Amaranthus	Atlantic 1941-45		
Amarose	English Channel 1942		
Amazon	Martinique 1762 '*Belle Poule*' 1806 Norway 1940 North Africa 1942-43	'*Droits de l'Homme*' 1797 Belgian Coast 1914-16 Malta Convoys 1942	Copenhagen 1801 Atlantic 1939-43 Arctic 1942
Amberley Castle	Atlantic 1945		
Ambition	Normandy 1944		
Ambrose Pare	English Channel 1942		
Ambuscade	Finisterre 1747 Atlantic 1940-44	Lagos 1759 Arctic 1942	Jutland 1916 Falkland Islands 1982
Ameer	Burma 1944-45	East Indies 1945	
Amelia	Donegal 1798		

America	Lagos 1759 The Saints 1782	Chesapeake 1781 Cape of Good Hope 1795	St. Kitts 1782 Atlantic 1941
Amethyst	'*Cerbère*'1800 China 1856-60 Dardanelles 1915	'*Thétis*' 1808 Ashantee 1873-74 Atlantic 1945	'*Niémen*' 1809 Heligoland 1914 Korea 1951-52
Amherst	Atlantic 1941-45		
Amity	Portland 1653 Lowestoft 1665	Gabbard 1653 Four Day's Battle 1666	Porto Farina 1655 Orfordness 1666
Amphion	Lissa 1811	Baltic 1854-55	
Ampulla	North Sea 1942		
Amulo	Cadiz 1596*		
Amulree	Dunkirk 1940*		
Anchusa	Atlantic 1941-45	English Channel 1945	
Anco Charger	Falkland Islands 1982*		
Andanes	Normandy 1944		
Andrew	Dover 1652 Scheveningen 1653	Kentish Knock 1652 Porto Farina 1655	Gabbard 1653
Andomache	The Saints 1782	San Sebastian 1813	
Andromeda	St. Vincent 1780	Falkland Islands 1982	
Anemone	Dardanelles 1915-16	Atlantic 1940-43	
Angel	Portland 1653		
Angle	Norway 1940 North Sea 1943-44	Atlantic 1940-43	Arctic 1942
Anguilla	Atlantic 1944	Arctic 1945	
Ann and Joyce	Portland 1653	Gabbard 1653	
Ann and Judith	Sole Bay 1672		
Ann Melville	Normandy 1944		
Annan	Atlantic 1944	North Sea 1944	
Annapolis	Atlantic 1941-44		
Ann(e) Piercy	Portland 1653	Gabbard 1653	
Anne	Lowestoft 1665 Schooneveld 1673	Orfordness 1666 Texel 1673	Sole Bay 1672

Anne Bonaventure Armada 1588*

Anne Francis   Armada 1588*

Annet   Normandy 1944

Anson   The Saints 1782   Donegal 1798   Curaçoa 1807
                     Arctic 1942-43

Antares   Atlantic 1943-44   South France 1944

Antelope   Armada 1588   Lowestoft 1665   Four Day's Battle 1666
                     Orfordness 1666   Sole Bay 1672   Marbella 1705
                     '*Aquilon*' 1757   Atlantic 1939-44   '*Bismarck*' 1941
                     Malta Convoys 1942   North Africa 1942-43   Falkland Islands 1982

Anthony   Armada 1588*   Dunkirk 1940   Atlantic 1940-44
                     '*Bismarck*' 1941   Diego Suarez 1942   English Channel 1944-45

Antigonish   Atlantic 1945

Antigua   Martinique 1762   Atlantic 1944

Antrim   Falkland Islands 1982

Antwerp   Atlantic 1941   Libya 1942   Sicily 1943
                     Salerno 1943   South France 1944

Anzac   Korea 1951-53

Aphis   Libya 1940-42   Mediterranean 1941-43   Sicily 1943
                     Adriatic 1944   South France 1944

Apollo   St. Vincent 1780   China 1842   Crimea 1854
                     Normandy 1944

Appleleaf   Falkland Islands 1982**

Aquamarine   Atlantic 1942-43

Aquilla   North Sea 1942

Aquilon   First of June 1794   Groix Island 1795

Arab   Norway 1940   Atlantic 1940-43   Arctic 1942
                     North Sea 1943-45

Arabesque   Normandy 1944

Arabis   Atlantic 1940-42

Arachne   Burma 1824-26

Ararat   New Guinea 1943

Arawa   Atlantic 1940

Arbiter	Atlantic 1944		
Arbutus	Atlantic 1940-42		
Archangel	Cadiz 1596*	Dunkirk 1940*	
Archer	Baltic 1854-55 Biscay 1943	Heligoland 1914	Atlantic 1943-44
Arctic Explorer	Atlantic 1942		
Arctic Pioneer	Atlantic 1940		
Arctic Ranger	Atlantic 1940-42	North Africa 1942-43	
Arcturus	Atlantic 1943	South France 1944	
Ardent	Camperdown 1797 Jutland 1916 '*Scharnhorst*' 1940	Copenhagen 1801 Atlantic 1939-40 Falkland Islands 1982	Crimea 1854-55 Norway 1940
Ardrossan	North Sea 1942	Normandy 1944	
Arethusa	Ushant 1781 Crimea 1854 Norway 1940-41	St. Lucia 1796 Heligoland 1914 Malta Convoys 1941-42	Curaçoa 1807 Dogger Bank 1915 Normandy 1944
Argo	Minorca 1798		
Argonaut	Arctic 1942 Normandy 1944 Okinawa 1945	North Africa 1942 South France 1944 Falkland Islands 1982	Mediterranean 1942 Aegean 1944
Argus	Groix Island 1795 Atlantic 1941-42 Kuwait 1991**	Ashantee 1873-74 Malta Convoys 1942	Arctic 1941 North Africa 1942
Argyll	Passero 1718		
Argyllshire	Dunkirk 1940		
Ariadne	St. Lucia 1778	Leyte Gulf 1944	
Ariel	Heligoland 1914 Jutland 1916	Belgian Coast 1914	Dogger Bank 1915
Aries	South France 1944		
Ariguani	Atlantic 1941		
Aristocrat	English Channel 1942	Normandy 1944	
Ark	See **Ark Royal**		
Ark Royal	Armada 1588 Norway 1940 '*Bismarck*' 1941	Cadiz 1596 Spartivento 1940 Malta Convoys 1941	Dardanelles 1915 Mediterranean 1940-1

Arley	Dunkirk 1940		
Armana	English Channel 1942		
Armeria	Atlantic 1942-45	Normandy 1944	English Channel 1944-45
Armidale	Pacific 1942		
Arms of Holland	Portland 1653	Gabbard 1653	
Arno	Dardanelles 1915-16		
Arnprior	Atlantic 1944-45		
Arran	Atlantic 1943		
Arrogant	The Saints 1782	Baltic 1854-55	
Arrow	Copenhagen 1801 Crimea 1854-55 North Sea 1942 Sicily 1943	Cape Tenez 1805 Norway 1940 Libya 1942 Falkland Islands 1982	San Sebastian 1813 Atlantic 1940-43 Malta Convoys 1942
Arrowhead	Atlantic 1941-45		
Arsenal	Atlantic 1940		
Arthur Cavanagh	Libya 1941		
Artois	Dogger Bank 1781	'*Révolutionnaire*' 1794	
Arunta	Guadacanal 1942-43 Pacific 1942-45	Leyte Gulf 1944 New Guinea 1942-44	Lingayen Gulf 1945
Arvida	Atlantic 1941-45		
Asbestos	Atlantic 1944-45		
Ascania	Atlantic 1939-41*		
Ascension	Armada 1588*	Atlantic 1944	North Sea 1944
Ashanti	Norway 1940 Arctic 1942-43 Biscay 1944	Atlantic 1940 North Africa 1942-43 Normandy 1944	Malta Convoys 1942 English Channel 1943-44
Asia	Martinique 1794	Navarino 1827	Syria 1840
Asie	Normandy 1944		
Asp	Egypt 1801	Guadeloupe 1810	
Asphodel	Atlantic 1940-44		
Assiniboine	Atlantic 1939-45	Biscay 1944	English Channel 1944-45
Assistance	Portland 1653 Orfordness 1666	Gabbard 1653 China 1856-60	Lowestoft 1665

Association	Vigo 1702		
Assurance	Dover 1652	Portland 1653	Gabbard 1653
	Scheveningen 1653	Lowestoft 1665	Four Day's Battle 1666
	Orfordness 1666	Schooneveld 1673	Texel 1673
	Velez Malaga 1704	Martinique 1794	
Aster	Dardanelles 1915-16	Atlantic 1941	North Sea 1944
Aston Villa	Norway 1940		
Astraea	Groix Island 1795	'Gloire' 1795	St. Lucia 1796
	Egypt 1801	Tamatave 1811	Cameroons 1914
Astral	Normandy 1944		
Asturias	Atlantic 1939-40		
Atalanta	English Channel 1942	Normandy 1944	
Athabaskan	Arctic 1943-44	English Channel 1944	Korea 1950-53
Athenian	Egypt 1801		
Atherstone	English Channel 1940-2	St. Nazaire 1942	North Sea 1942-3
	Atlantic 1943	Sicily 1943	Salerno 1943
	Mediterranean 1943	South France 1944	Adriatic 1944
	Kuwait 1991		
Atholl	Atlantic 1944-45		
Atlantic Causeway	Falkland Islands 1982*		
Atlantic Conveyor	Falkland Islands 1982*		
Atlas	San Domingo 1806		
Atmah	Atlantic 1942	North Sea 1942	
Attack	Heligoland 1914	Dogger Bank 1915	Jutland 1916
Attacker	Atlantic 1943-4	Salerno 1943	South France 1944
	Aegean 1944		
Attentive	Guadeloupe 1810	Zeebrugge 1918	Belgian Coast 1914-18
Aubretia	Atlantic 1941-45	North Africa 1942-43	South France 1944
	Mediterranean 1944		
Auckland	China 1856-60 (Indian Navy)	Atlantic 1939	Norway 1940
	Greece 1941	Crete 1941	Libya 1941
Audacious	First of June 1794	Nile 1798	Gut of Gibraltar 1801
Audacity	Atlantic 1941		
Augusta	Cape François 1757		

Aurania	Atlantic 1940-41		
Auricula	Atlantic 1941-42	Diego Suarez 1942	
Aurora	St.Lucia 1778	Minorca 1798	Guadeloupe 1810
	China 1900	Dogger Bank 1915	Norway 1940
	'*Bismarck*' 1941	Mediterranean 1941-43	Malta Convoys 1941
	North Africa 1942-43	Sicily 1943	Salerno 1943
	Aegean 1943-44	South France 1944	
Aurora II	Libya 1941		
Ausonia	Atlantic 1939-41		
Australia	Atlantic 1940-1	Coral Sea 1942	Savo Island 1942
	Guadalcanal 1942-3	New Guinea 1942-4	Leyte Gulf 1944
	Lingayen Gulf 1945		
Autocarrier	Dunkirk 1940*		
Avenger	Martinique 1794	North Africa 1942	Arctic 1942
	Falkland Islands 1982		
Avon	Atlantic 1943-44	Okinawa 1945	
Avon Vale	Atlantic 1941-43	Malta Convoys 1941-42	Libya 1941-42
	Sirte 1942	North Africa 1942-43	English Channel 1943-44
	Adriatic 1944		
Avondee	Normandy 1944		
Awe	Atlantic 1944		
Aylmer	Normandy 1944	Atlantic 1944-45	
Ayrshire	Atlantic 1941-45	North Sea 1942	Arctic 1942
Azalea	Atlantic 1941-43	Normandy 1944	English Channel 1944-45
B 6	Dardanelles 1915		
B 11	Dardanelles 1915		
Babelmandeb	Egypt 1801		
Babet	Groix Island 1795		
Bacchante	Cattaro 1814	Heligoland 1914	Dardanelles 1915-16
Bacchus	Martinique 1809	Guadeloupe 1810	
Bachaquero	Diego Suarez 1942	English Channel 1942	North Africa 1942-43
	Atlantic 1943	Normandy 1944	
Baddeck	Atlantic 1941-45	English Channel 1944-45	Normandy 1944
Badger	Baltic 1855	Heligoland 1914	Jutland 1916

Badsworth	Atlantic 1941-43	Arctic 1942	Malta Convoys 1942
Baffin	Atlantic 1944		
Bagshot	Libya 1941		
Bahamas	Atlantic 1944-45	Arctic 1944	
Bahrein	Mesopotamia 1915		
Balfour	English Channel 1944	Atlantic 1944	Normandy 1944
Ballahou	Egypt 1801	Guadeloupe 1810	
Ballarat	New Guinea 1942-44	Okinawa 1945	
Ballinderry	Atlantic 1943-45		
Balsam	Atlantic 1943-45	English Channel 1944-45	Normandy 1944
Baltic Ferry	Falkland Islands 1982*		
Baltimore	Orfordness 1666	Quebec 1759	
Baluchistan	North Sea 1942		
Bamborough Castle	Atlantic 1944	Arctic 1944-45	
Banff	Atlantic 1941-43	North Africa 1942-43	Sicily 1943
Bangor	Dieppe 1942	Normandy 1944	English Channel 1944
Bann	Sicily 1943	Burma 1945	
Banshee	Crimea 1854-55		
Bantam	Sole Bay 1672		
Banterer	China 1856-60		
Barbados	Martinique 1762	St. Lucia 1778	
Barbain	Normandy 1944		
Barberry	Normandy 1944	Atlantic 1945	
Barcliff	Atlantic 1942		
Barcock	Normandy 1944		
Barcombe	Normandy 1944		
Barcoo	Pacific 1945		
Bardolf	South France 1944		

Barfleur	Vigo 1702 St. Kitts 1782 Groix Island 1795	Velez Malaga 1704 The Saints 1782 St. Vincent 1797	Passero 1718 First of June 1794 China 1900
Barford	South France 1944		
Barham	Jutland 1916 Mediterranean 1941	Matapan 1941	Crete 1941
Barholm	South France 1944		
Barle	Atlantic 1943		
Barlow	Normandy 1944		
Barmond	Anzio 1944	South France 1944	
Barndale	Anzio 1944		
Barnes Ness	Normandy 1944		
Barnwell	Normandy 1944	Atlantic 1945	
Barova	Normandy 1944		
Barpeta	Burma 1944-45*		
Barracouta	Banda Neira 1810 Ashantee 1873-74	Java 1811	China 1856-60
Barracuda	Burma 1944-45		
Barrage	Normandy 1944		
Barrie	Atlantic 1941-45	English Channel 1942	
Barrosa	Benin 1897	South Africa 1899-1900	
Bartholomew	Armada 1588*		
Barthorpe	Normandy 1944	Atlantic 1945	
Bartizan	Normandy 1944	Atlantic 1945	
Basilisk	Martinique 1762 Dardanelles 1915-16	Havana 1762 Norway 1940	Baltic 1854-55 Dunkirk 1940
Basset	North Sea 1942		
Bataan	Korea 1952		
Bath	Atlantic 1941		
Battleford	Atlantic 1941-45		
Battler	Atlantic 1942-45	Salerno 1943	East Indies 1944
Bay	English Channel 1943		

Bayfield	Atlantic 1943-44	Normandy 1944	
Bayleaf	Falkland Islands 1982**	Kuwait 1991**	
Bayntun	Atlantic 1943-44	North Sea 1945	
Bazely	Atlantic 1943-45	Arctic 1945	
Beacon	Baltic 1855	Ashantee 1873-74	Alexandria 1882
Beacon Hill	Atlantic 1944		
Beagle	Basque Roads 1809 China 1856-60 Atlantic 1940-45 English Channel 1943	San Sebastian 1813 Dardanelles 1915-16 North Africa 1942 Normandy 1944	Crimea 1854-55 Norway 1940 Arctic 1942-44
Bear	Gabbard 1653	Lowestoft 1665	
Bear Yonge	Armada 1588*		
Bearsabe	Armada 1588*		
Beaufort	Libya 1942 Sirte 1942 Aegean 1943-44	Mediterranean 1942 Sicily 1943 Anzio 1944	Malta Convoys 1942 Salerno 1943 South France 1944
Beauharnois	Atlantic 1944-45		
Beaulieu	Martinique 1794 '*Chevrette*' 1801		Camperdown 1797
Beaumaris	Normandy 1944	Atlantic 1944	
Beaver	Louisburg 1758 Atlantic 1942	'*Athalante*' 1804	Heligoland 1914
Bedford	Vigo 1702 Louisburg 1758 Chesapeake 1781 Genoa 1795	Velez Malaga 1704 Quebec 1759 St. Kitts 1782 Camperdown 1797	Marbella 1705 St. Vincent 1780 The Saints 1782
Bedouin	Narvik 1940 Arctic 1941-42	Norway 1940-41 Malta Convoys 1942	Atlantic 1940-41
Bee	Mesopotamia 1917		
Begonia	Atlantic 1941	North Sea 1941	
Begum	East Indies 1944		
Belfast	Arctic 1943 Korea 1950-52	North Cape 1943	Normandy 1944
Belle Poule	Dogger Bank 1781		

Belleisle	Havana 1762 China 1842	Trafalgar 1805 Baltic 1854-55	Martinique 1809 China 1856-60
Bellerophon	First of June 1794 Trafalgar 1805 Jutland 1916	Cornwallis' Retreat 1795 Syria 1840	Nile 1798 Crimea 1854
Bellette	Martinique 1809	Guadeloupe 1810	
Belleville	Atlantic 1945		
Belliqueux	St. Kitts 1782 Cape of Good Hope 1806	The Saints 1782	Camperdown 1797
Bellona	'*Courageux*' 1761 Jutland 1916 Norway 1944-45	Copenhagen 1801 Normandy 1944 Arctic 1944-45	Basque Roads 1809 Biscay 1944
Bellwort	Atlantic 1941-45		
Belmont	Atlantic 1941-42		
Belvoir	Arctic 1942 Aegean 1943	Sicily 1943 South France 1944	Salerno 1943 Adriatic 1944
Belzebub	Algiers 1816		
Ben Glas	Normandy 1944		
Ben-my-Chree	Dardanelles 1915-16	Dunkirk 1940*	
Ben Urie	English Channel 1942		
Benalla	New Guinea 1943-44		
Benbow	Syria 1840	Jutland 1916	
Bendigo	New Guinea 1942-44	Okinawa 1945	
Bendish	Lowestoft 1665		
Bengal	'*Hokoku Maru*' 1942	Burma 1945	
Benjamin	Gabbard 1653		
Benjamin Coleman	Normandy 1944		
Bentinck	Atlantic 1943-45	Arctic 1945	
Bentley	Atlantic 1944	Normandy 1944	
Bergamot	Atlantic 1941-45	Arctic 1942-43	Sicily 1943
Berkeley	Dieppe 1942	English Channel 1942	North Sea 1942
Berkeley Castle	Atlantic 1944		
Berkshire	Atlantic 1940	English Channel 1942	North Sea 1942-44

Bermuda	North Africa 1942	Arctic 1943	Atlantic 1943
Bern	Normandy 1944		
Berry	Biscay 1943	Atlantic 1943-44	
Bervie Braes	Normandy 1944		
Berwick	Barfleur 1692 Velez Malaga 1704 Norway 1940	Vigo 1702 Dogger Bank 1781 Spartivento 1940	Gibraltar 1704 Atlantic 1939 Arctic 1941-44
Betony	Atlantic 1943	North Sea 1943	
Bever	Libya 1942	Aegean 1944	
Beverley	Atlantic 1940-43	Malta Convoys 1941	Arctic 1942
Biarritz	Dunkirk 1940*		
Bicester	Malta Convoys 1942 South France 1944	North Africa 1942-3 Adriatic 1944	Mediterranean 1943-44 Aegean 1944
Bickerton	Normandy 1944 Arctic 1944	Atlantic 1944	English Channel 1944
Bideford	Atlantic 1939-45 Biscay 1943	Dunkirk 1940 English Channel 1945	North Africa 1942
Bienfaisant	St. Vincent 1780	Dogger Bank 1781	
Bihar	Burma 1945		
Bilsdean	English Channel 1942		
Birch	English Channel 1942-43		
Birdlip	Atlantic 1942-43		
Birkenhead	Jutland 1916		
Birmingham	Heligoland 1914 Norway 1940	Dogger Bank 1915 Korea 1952-53	Jutland 1916
Biter	Baltic 1855	North Africa 1942	Atlantic 1943-44
Bittern	Burma 1853 Alexandria 1882	China 1856-60 Norway 1940	Ashantee 1873-74
Bittersweet	Atlantic 1941-45		
Black Bull	Four Days' Battle 1666		
Black Dog	Armada 1588*		
Black Prince	Jutland 1916 English Channel 1944 Okinawa 1945	Arctic 1944 Aegean 1944	Normandy 1944 South France 1944

Black Spread Eagle	Four Days' Battle 1666		
Black Swan	Norway 1940 Korea 1950-51	North Sea 1940	Atlantic 1941-43
Blackamore Merchant	Lowestoft 1665		
Blackburn Rovers	Dunkirk 1940		
Blackfly	Mesopotamia 1917 Mediterranean 1944	Atlantic 1940-44	Arctic 1942
Blackmore	Atlantic 1943 South France 1944	Salerno 1943	Adriatic 1944
Blackpool	Dieppe 1942	English Channel 1942	Normandy 1944
Blackthorn	English Channel 1940-44		
Blackwood	Atlantic 1943-44	Normandy 1944	English Channel 1944
Blairmore	Atlantic 1943-45	Normandy 1944	
Blanche	'*Pique*' 1795	Copenhagen 1801	Jutland 1916
Blankney	Atlantic 1941-3 Sicily 1943 Mediterranean 1944	Malta Convoys 1942 Salerno 1943	Arctic 1942-43 Normandy 1944
Blast	Belle Isle 1761		
Blaze	Barfleur 1692		
Blazer	Glückstadt 1814	Baltic 1855	
Blean	North Sea 1942	North Africa 1942	
Bleasdale	Dieppe 1942 Normandy 1944	English Channel 1942-44 Atlantic 1944	North Sea 1943-45
Blencathra	North Sea 1941-45 Salerno 1943 Normandy 1944	English Channel 1942-44 Aegean 1943	Sicily 1943 Mediterranean 1944
Blenheim	St. Vincent 1797 Dardanelles 1915-16	China 1841	Baltic 1854-55
Blessing	Orfordness 1666	Texel 1673	
Bligh	Normandy 1944	Atlantic 1944-45	English Channel 1945
Blonde	Martinique 1794 China 1841-42	Egypt 1801	Guadeloupe 1810
Blossom	Gabbard 1653		

Blue Pigeon	Cadiz 1596		
Blue Rover	Falkland Islands 1982**		
Bluebell	Atlantic 1940-44 Normandy 1944	Arctic 1942-45 Mediterranean 1944	Sicily 1943
Blyth	Dieppe 1942 Normandy 1944	North Sea 1942	English Channel 1943
Boadicea	Burma 1824-26 North Africa 1942	Jutland 1916 Arctic 1942-44	Atlantic 1941-43 Normandy 1944
Boksburg	Libya 1942	Aegean 1944	
Bombardier	Atlantic 1943-45	Normandy 1944	
Bombay	Burma 1945		
Bona	Normandy 1944		
Bonaventure	Lowestoft 1665 Sole Bay 1672 Barfleur 1692	Four Days' Battle 1666 Schooneveld 1673 Malta Convoys 1941	Ordfordness 1666 Texel 1673
Bonavolia	Armada 1588		
Bond	Armada 1588*		
Bonetta	Havana 1762		
Bonito	North Sea 1942	Sicily 1943	
Bonne Citoyenne	St. Vincent 1797	Egypt 1801	'*Furieuse*' 1809
Bonner	Armada 1588*		
Bootle	Normandy 1944		
Borage	Atlantic 1942-45 Biscay 1943	Arctic 1943-44 Normandy 1944	English Channel 1943 North Sea 1944
Border Cities	Atlantic 1944-45		
Borealis	South France 1944		
Boreas	Louisburg 1758 Atlantic 1941-42	Havana 1762 North Africa 1942-43	English Channel 1940
Boscawen	Quebec 1759	Baltic 1854	
Boston	Atlantic 1942 Normandy 1944	Malta Convoys 1942 English Channel 1945	Sicily 1943
Botha	Belgian Coast 1917-18		
Bouncer	China 1860		

Bournemouth Queen	North Sea 1942		
Bowmanville	Atlantic 1944-45		
Boxer	Crimea 1855 Anzio 1944	Sicily 1943	Salerno 1943
Boy Roy	Dunkirk 1940		
Boyne	Velez Malaga 1704	St. Lucia 1778	Martinique 1794
Brackel	Camperdown 1797	Egypt 1801	
Bradford	Atlantic 1941-43	North Africa 1942	English Channel 1943
Bradman	Norway 1940		
Braes O'Mar	Normandy 1944		
Braithwaite	Normandy 1944	Atlantic 1944	North Sea 1945
Bramble	Arctic 1942		
Brambleleaf	Falkland Islands 1982**		
Bramham	Malta Convoys 1942	Arctic 1942	North Africa 1942
Brandon	Atlantic 1941-45		
Brantford	Atlantic 1942-44		
Brave	Armada 1588* Kuwait 1991	Cadiz 1596*	South France 1944
Brazen	Norway 1940	English Channel 1940	Kuwait 1991
Brazil	Portland 1653	Gabbard 1653	
Brecon	English Channel 1943 Mediterranean 1944 Atlantic 1945	Sicily 1943 South France 1944	Salerno 1943 Aegean 1944
Breconshire	Malta Convoys 1941-42	Sirte 1942	
Breda	Lowestoft 1665 Passero 1718	Four Days' Battle 1666 Atlantic 1940	Orfordness 1666
Bredon	Atlantic 1942		
Brenda	Crimea 1854		
Bressay	North Sea 1942	Normandy 1944	
Briar	Lowestoft 1665	Orfordness 1666	
Bridgewater	Atlantic 1942-43	North Sea 1942	

Bridgwater	Santa Cruz 1657	Porto Farina 1655	
Bridlington	Dieppe 1942	Normandy 1944	
Bridport	Dieppe 1942	Normandy 1944	
Brigadier	Normandy 1944		
Brigandine	Armada 1588		
Brighton Belle	Dunkirk 1940		
Brighton Queen	Belgian Coast 1915	Dunkirk 1940	
Brilliant	Belgian Coast 1914 Atlantic 1941-43 Kuwait 1991	Zeebrugge 1918 North Africa 1942-43	English Channel 1940-43 Falkland Islands 1982
Brimnes	Atlantic 1944		
Brisbane	Vietnam 1969-71		
Brisk	Navarino 1827	New Zealand 1865	
Brissenden	Atlantic 1943 English Channel 1943-5	Arctic 1943 Normandy 1944	Sicily 1943 Biscay 1944
Bristol	Santa Cruz 1657 Orfordness 1666 Finisterre 1747	Lowestoft 1665 Sole Bay 1672 Falkland Islands 1914	Four Days' Battle 1666 Texel 1673 Falkland Islands 1982
Britannia	Barfleur 1692 St. Vincent 1797	Ushant 1781 Trafalgar 1805	Genoa 1795 Crimea 1854
British Dart	Falkland Islands 1982*		
British Esk	Falkland Islands 1982*		
British Tay	Falkland Islands 1982*		
British Test	Falkland Islands 1982*		
British Trent	Falkland Islands 1982*		
British Wye	Falkland Islands 1982*		
Britomart	Algiers 1816	Arctic 1941-43	Normandy 1944
Brittany	Sicily 1943	Salerno 1943	Normandy 1944
Brixham	North Africa 1942-43 South France 1944	Sicily 1943	Salerno 1943
Broadsword	Falkland Islands 1982		
Broadwater	Atlantic 1941		
Broadway	Atlantic 1941-43	North Sea 1944	

Brock	Dunkirk 1940		
Brocklesby	Dieppe 1942 Sicily 1943	English Channel 1942-43 Salerno 1943	Atlantic 1943 Adriatic 1944
Brockville	Atlantic 1943-45		
Broke	Jutland 1916 Atlantic 1939-42 North Africa 1942	Dover 1917 North Sea 1939	Belgian Coast 1917-18 Arctic 1942
Brontes	North Sea 1944		
Broome	New Guinea 1942-44		
Brown Fish	Cadiz 1596*		
Brown Ranger	North Africa 1942**	Korea 1950-52**	
Bruiser	Sicily 1943 Atlantic 1944	Salerno 1943 South France 1944	Anzio 1944 Aegean 1944
Brunswick	First of June 1794	Cornwallis' Retreat 1795	
Bryher	Normandy 1944		
Bryony	Arctic 1942-43	Atlantic 1943	Sicily 1943
Bucephalus	Java 1811	Normandy 1944	
Buckingham	Belle Isle 1761	Atlantic 1945	
Buctouche	Atlantic 1941-45		
Bude	English Channel 1942 Salerno 1943	North Africa 1942-43 Anzio 1944	Atlantic 1943 South France 1944
Buffalo	Dogger Bank 1781		
Buggins	Armada 1588*		
Bugloss	Atlantic 1944		
Bull	Armada 1588		
Bulldog	St. Lucia 1796 English Channel 1940-45 Arctic 1942-44	Baltic 1854-55 Atlantic 1941-45	Dardanelles 1915-16 North Africa 1942
Bullen	Atlantic 1944		
Bulolo	Atlantic 1940 Anzio 1944	North Africa 1942 Normandy 1944	Sicily 1943
Bunbury	New Guinea 1943-44		
Bundaburg	New Guinea 1943-44		

Cambrian	Navarino 1827	China 1860	Arctic 1944
Cambridge	Orfordness 1666 Texel 1673 Velez Malaga 1704 Belgian Coast 1915	Sole Bay 1672 Barfleur 1692 Havana 1762	Schooneveld 1673 Vigo 1702 Syria 1840
Cambridgeshire	English Channel 1942-43	Normandy 1944	
Camel	Crimea 1855		
Cameleon	see **Chameleon**		
Camellia	Atlantic 1940-45 North Sea 1944	Arctic 1942-45 Normandy 1944	Sicily 1943
Camilla	China 1856-60		
Camito	Atlantic 1940		
Campania	Atlantic 1944	Arctic 1944-45	Norway 1944-45
Campanula	Atlantic 1940-44 English Channel 1944-45	Arctic 1942	Normandy 1944
Campbell	Norway 1940 Arctic 1942	Atlantic 1940-43 English Channel 1942-44	North Sea 1941-45 Normandy 1944
Campeltown	Atlantic 1941-42	St. Nazaire 1942	
Campeador V	Atlantic 1940		
Campion	Atlantic 1941-45		
Camrose	Atlantic 1941-45 English Channel 1945	Normandy 1944	North Sea 1944
Canada	St. Kitts 1782 Jutland 1916	The Saints 1782	Donegal 1798
Canalside	English Channel 1943		
Canberra	Savo Island 1942	Guadalcanal 1942	
Canberra	Falkland Islands 1982*		
Candytuft	Atlantic 1940-41		
Canning	Dardanelles 1915		
Canopus	San Domingo 1806	Dardanelles 1915-16	
Canso	Normandy 1944	Atlantic 1944	
Canterbury	Marbella 1705	Passero 1718	Jutland 1916
Canterbury	Dunkirk 1940*		

Canton	Atlantic 1940		
Cap-de-la Madelaine	Atlantic 1945		
Cape Argona	Dunkirk 1940	Atlantic 1940-45	Arctic 1942-43
Cape Breton	Normandy 1944	Arctic 1944	Atlantic 1944-45
Cape Chelyuskin	Norway 1940		
Cape Clear	Atlantic 1942		
Cape Comorin	North Sea 1942	English Channel 1942-43	Atlantic 1943-44
Cape Mariato	Arctic 1942-43	Atlantic 1942-45	
Cape Palliser	North Sea 1942	Arctic 1942	Atlantic 1942-44
Cape Passero	Norway 1940		
Cape Portland	North Sea 1942-43	Atlantic 1942-45	
Cape Sable	North Sea 1942		
Cape Siretoko	Norway 1940		
Cape Warwick	Atlantic 1941-42		
Capel	Normandy 1944	Atlantic 1944	English Channel 1944
Capetown	Mediterranean 1940	Normandy 1944	
Capilano	Atlantic 1944-45		
Caprice	Arctic 1944		
Capstone	English Channel 1942		
Captain	Barfleur 1692 Quebec 1759 Martinique 1809	Passero 1718 Genoa 1795	Louisburg 1758 St. Vincent 1797
Caradoc	Crimea 1854-55	Atlantic 1940	
Caraquet	Atlantic 1943-44	Normandy 1944	
Carcass	St. Lucia 1778		
Cardiff	Falkland Islands 1982	Kuwait 1991	
Cardigan Bay	Korea 1950-53		
Carisbrooke Castle	Atlantic 1944		
Carleton	Lake Champlain 1776		

Carlisle	Norway 1940 Libya 1941-42 Sicily 1943	Greece 1941 Malta Convoys 1941-42 Aegean 1943	Crete 1941 Sirte 1942
Carlplace	Atlantic 1945		
Carmania	'Cap Trafalgar' 1914		
Carnarvon	Falkland Islands 1914		
Carnarvon Castle	Atlantic 1939-42		
Carnactic	North Sea 1942		
Carnation	Atlantic 1941-42		
Carnoustie	Atlantic 1943		
Caroline	Banda Neira 1810	Java 1811	Jutland 1916
Carouse	Armada 1588*		
Carron	Baltic 1855		
Carthage	Atlantic 1942-43		
Carysfort	Syria 1840	Belgian Coast 1916	
Cassandra	Arctic 1944		
Castle	Lowestoft 1665	Orfordness 1666	
Castlenau	North Sea 1943		
Castleton	Atlantic 1940-42	North Sea 1942-44	
Castor	Guadeloupe 1810 Jutland 1916	Syria 1840	New Zealand 1845-47
Cathay	Atlantic 1940-41		
Catherine	Atlantic 1943	Normandy 1944	
Cato	Atlantic 1943	Normandy 1944	
Catterick	Salerno 1943	Aegean 1944	South France 1944
Cattistock	North Sea 1941-45 Kuwait 1991	English Channel 1942-44	Normandy 1944
Cauvery	Atlantic 1943-44	East Indies 1944	Burma 1944-45
Cava	Atlantic 1942 Anzio 1944	North Africa 1942-43	Sicily 1943
Cavalier	Arctic 1945		
Caverock	Normandy 1944		

Cavina	Atlantic 1942		
Cayman	Atlantic 1944		
Cayton Wyke	English Channel 1939	Dunkirk 1940	
Cayuga	Korea 1950-52		
Cedar	Normandy 1944		
Cedardale	Sicily 1943**		
Celandine	Atlantic 1941-45	English Channel 1944	Normandy 1944
Celia	Atlantic 1941-42	Arctic 1942	
Centaur	Havana 1762 Minorca 1798 Baltic 1855 Belgian Coast 1916-17	St. Kitts 1782 '*Curieux*' 1804 China 1860	The Saints 1782 '*Sevalod*' 1808
Centurion	Armada 1588* Portland 1653 Lowestoft 1665 Velez Malaga 1704 Louisburg 1758 St. Lucia 1778 Normandy 1944	Cadiz 1596* Gabbard 1653 Orfordness 1666 '*N.S. de Covadonga*' 1743 Quebec 1759 China 1900	Dover 1652 Santa Cruz 1657 Barfleur 1692 Finisterre 1747 Havana 1762 Jutland 1916
Cerberus	Havana 1762	Lissa 1811	
Ceres	St. Lucia 1778 Normandy 1944	Egypt 1801	Atlantic 1939
Cessnock	Sicily 1943		
Ceylon	Sabang 1944	Burma 1945	Korea 1950-52
Chakdina	Libya 1941		
Chakla	Libya 1940-41		
Challenger	San Sebastian 1813	Cameroons 1914	
Chamby	Atlantic 1941-45		
Chameleon **(Cameleon)**	Cadiz 1596*	Egypt 1801	Burma 1945
Chamois	Normandy 1944	Atlantic 1944	
Champion	St. Kitts 1782 Jutland 1916	The Saints 1782	Burma 1824-26
Chance	Armada 1588*	Normandy 1944	Atlantic 1944
Chantala	Libya 1941		

Chanticleer	Sicily 1943	Atlantic 1943	
Charity	Lowestoft 1665	Korea 1950-53	
Charles	Armada 1588 Orfordness 1666 Texel 1673	Cadiz 1596 Sole Bay 1672	Portland 1653 Schooneveld 1673
Charles Galley	Barfleur 1692	Velez Malaga 1704	
Charles Henri	English Channel 1942		
Charles Merchant	Orfordness 1666		
Charlestown	Atlantic 1941-42	North Sea 1943-44	
Charlock	Normandy 1944 Atlantic 1944-45	North Sea 1944	Arctic 1944
Charlottetown	Atlantic 1942		
Charon	First of June 1794	Groix Island 1795	Egypt 1801
Charybdis	Malta Convoys 1942 Atlantic 1943	North Africa 1942 English Channel 1943	Salerno 1943 Biscay 1943
Chase	Portland 1653		
Chaser	Atlantic 1943	Arctic 1944	Okinawa 1945
Chatham	Quiberon Bay 1759	Dardanelles 1915-16	
Chaudiere	Normandy 1944	Atlantic 1944	Biscay 1944
Chebogue	Atlantic 1944		
Chedabucto	Atlantic 1942-43		
Chelmer	Dardanelles 1915-16 English Channel 1944	Atlantic 1943-45 North Sea 1944	Normandy 1944
Chelsea	Atlantic 1940-43		
Cherub	Martinique 1809	Guadeloupe 1810	'Essex Junior' 1814
Cherubim	Cadiz 1596*		
Cherwell	Normandy 1944		
Chesapeake	China 1860		
Cheshire	Atlantic 1940-42		
Chester	Barfleur 1692	Jutland 1916	
Chesterfield	Atlantic 1941-43		
Chichester	Quiberon Bay 1759	Belle Isle 1761	Egypt 1801

Chico	Dunkirk 1940		
Chicoutimi	Atlantic 1941-44		
Chiddingfold	Norway 1941	Mediterranean 1943-44	English Channel 1945
Childers	China 1842		
Chilliwack	Atlantic 1941-45		
Chiltern	Arctic 1942		
Chitral	Atlantic 1941		
Choice	Normandy 1944		
Christopher	Jutland 1916		
Churchill	Atlantic 1941-44		
Cilicia	Atlantic 1939-42		
Circassia	Crimea 1854		
Circe	Camperdown 1797 Salerno 1943	Martinique 1809 Anzio 1944	Sicily 1943
Clacton	Dieppe 1942 Salerno 1943	North Africa 1942-43	Sicily 1943
Clare	Atlantic 1940-43	North Africa 1942-43	Sicily 1943
Clarkia	Atlantic 1940-44	English Channel 1944-45	Normandy 1944
Clayoquot	Atlantic 1942-44		
Cleopatra	Dogger Bank 1781 Belgian Coast 1916 Sicily 1943	Martinique 1809 Malta Convoys 1942	Burma 1853 Sirte 1942
Clematis	Atlantic 1940-45	English Channel 1944-45	Normandy 1944
Clevela	Atlantic 1943-44		
Cleveland	Atlantic 1942 Sicily 1943 Aegean 1944	English Channel 1942-43 Salerno 1943 Adriatic 1944	North Sea 1943 South France 1944
Clinker	Crimea 1855		
Clinton	Atlantic 1943	Aegean 1944	South France 1944
Clio	China 1842	Suez Canal 1915	Mesopotamia 1915
Cloughstone	Normandy 1944		
Clove Tree	Lowestoft 1665	Four Days' Battle 1666	

Clover	Atlantic 1941-45	North Sea 1944	Normandy 1944
Clown	China 1856-60		
Clyde	Norway 1940	Mediterranean 1941	Malta Convoys 1942
Clyne Castle	North Africa 1942	English Channel 1943	
Coast	Lowestoft 1665		
Coaticook	Atlantic 1944-45		
Cobalt	Atlantic 1941-45		
Cobourg	Atlantic 1944-45		
Cochrane	Jutland 1916		
Cockade	Korea 1950-53		
Cockatrice	Arctic 1943-44	Normandy 1944	
Cockchafer	China 1860	Sicily 1943	Mediterranean 1944
Cocker (ex **Kos 19**)	Libya 1941-42		
Codrington	Norway 1940	Dunkirk 1940	
Colac	New Guinea 1942-44	Pacific 1945	
Colchester	Santa Cruz 1657	Lowestoft 1665	
Coldstreamer	Atlantic 1943-45		
Coll	North Sea 1942	Atlantic 1943	Normandy 1944
Collingwood	Jutland 1916	Atlantic 1941-44	
Colne	Dardanelles 1915-16		
Colombo	Atlantic 1939-44 Adriatic 1944	Sicily 1943 Aegean 1944	South France 1944
Colossus	Groix Island 1795 Baltic 1855	St. Vincent 1797 Jutland 1916	Trafalgar 1805
Colsay	Normandy 1944		
Coltsfoot	Atlantic 1941-45	Malta Convoys 1942	North Africa 1942
Columbia	Belgian Coast 1914-15	Atlantic 1940-44	
Columbine	China 1841-42 South France 1944	Kua Kam 1849	Atlantic 1940-44
Combatant	Atlantic 1944		

Combustion	Sadras 1782	Providien 1782	Trincomalee 1782
Comet	First of June 1794	'*Sylphe*' 1808	Mesopotamia 1914-15
Comfort	Dunkirk 1940		
Commander Evans	English Channel 1942	Normandy 1944	
Comorin	Atlantic 1940-41		
Comus	'*Frederikscoarn*' 1807 Korea 1950-53	China 1856-60	Jutland 1916
Concord	Korea 1950-53		
Condamine	Korea 1952-53		
Condor	Alexandria 1882		
Confiance	Cayenne 1809		
Conflict	Basque Roads 1809	Baltic 1854-55	
Congre	North Sea 1942		
Conidaw	Dunkirk 1940		
Conn	Atlantic 1944-45 North Sea 1944-45	English Channel 1944	Arctic 1944
Conqueror	Lagos 1759 Jutland 1916 Biscay 1944	The Saints 1782 North Sea 1942-43 Atlantic 1944-45	Trafalgar 1805 English Channel 1943-45 Falkland Islands 1982
Consort	Korea 1950-53		
Constance	Jutland 1916	Korea 1950-52	
Constant	San Sebastian 1813		
Constant Katherine	Lowestoft 1665		
Constant Warwick	Montecristo 1652	Schooneveld 1673	
Constitution	Minorca 1798		
Contender Bezant	Falkland Islands 1982*		
Contest	Basque Roads 1809	Burma 1853	Jutland 1916
Controller	Normandy 1944		
Convert	Portland 1653	Gabbard 1653	Santa Cruz 1657
Convertine	Portland 1653 Four Days' Battle 1666	Gabbard 1653	Lowestoft 1665

Convolvulus	Atlantic 1941-44 English Channel 1945	North Africa 1942-43	Sicily 1943
Conway	China 1841		
Conway Castle	Normandy 1944		
Cooke	Normandy 1944	Atlantic 1944	English Channel 1944-45
Cootamunda	New Guinea 1944		
Coote	Aden 1839 (Indian Navy)		
Copinsay	Atlantic 1943-44		
Copper Cliff	Atlantic 1944-45	North Sea 1944	
Coquette	Ashantee 1873-4		
Corbett	Cadiz 1596*		
Cordelia	Algiers 1816	New Zealand 1860-61	Jutland 1916
Cordella	Falkland Islands 1982		
Coreopsis	Atlantic 1940-43	North Africa 1942	
Corfu	Atlantic 1940-42		
Corinthian	Atlantic 1941-43	English Channel 1942	North Sea 1942-43
Coriolanus	English Channel 1942	North Africa 1942-43	Sicily 1943
Cormorant	Quebec 1759	Minorca 1798	China 1856-59
Cornelia	Java 1811		
Cornelian	English Channel 1942-43	Normandy 1944	
Cornwall	Falkland Islands 1914	Dardanelles 1915	
Cornwallis	Amboina 1810 Dardanelles 1915	China 1842	Baltic 1855
Coromandel	China 1856-60		
Coronatia	Normandy 1944		
Coronation	Orfordness 1666		
Coronia	Normandy 1944		
Coryphene	Normandy 1944		
Cosby	English Channel 1944	North Sea 1944	Atlantic 1944-45

Cossack	Baltic 1855 Norway 1940 Malta Convoys 1941	Belgian Coast 1914-16 Atlantic 1940-41 Korea 1950-53	Narvik 1940 '*Bismarck*' 1941
Cotillion	North Sea 1941-42	Atlantic 1943-44	
Cotswold	North Sea 1941-45	English Channel 1943	Normandy 1944
Cottesmore	North Sea 1941-45	English Channel 1942-44	Normandy 1944
Cotton	Atlantic 1944	Arctic 1945	
Countess of Scarborough	'*Pallas*' 1779		
Courageous	Falkland Islands 1982		
Courageux	Ushant 1781	Genoa 1795	Bay of Biscay 1805
Courtier	Normandy 1944		
Coventry	Quiberon Bay 1759 Atlantic 1940 Crete 1941 Falkland Islands 1982	Trincomalee 1782 Spartivento 1940 Libya 1941	Norway 1940 Greece 1941 Mediterranean 1941
Coventry City	Atlantic 1941		
Coverley	North Sea 1941-43	Salerno 1943	
Cowdray	Arctic 1942 English Channel 1944	North Africa 1942 North Sea 1944-45	Atlantic 1943
Cowichan	Atlantic 1941-43	Normandy 1944	
Cowra	New Guinea 1944		
Cowslip	Atlantic 1941-45		
Cracker	Crimea 1855		
Craftsman	Normandy 1944		
Crane	Cadiz 1596 Sicily 1943 English Channel 1944	Belgian Coast 1914-17 Atlantic 1943-44 Okinawa 1945	Biscay 1943 Normandy 1944 Korea 1952-53
Cranefly	Mesopotamia 1915-17		
Cranstoun	North Sea 1944	English Channel 1944-45	Atlantic 1945
Crescent	Armada 1588* Martinique 1762	Gabbard 1653 '*Reunion*' 1793	Scheveningen 1653 Cape of Good Hope 1795
Cressy	Baltic 1854-55	Heligoland 1914	
Crested Eagle	Dunkirk 1940		

Crete	Anzio 1944		
Crevette	Normandy 1944		
Cricket	Libya 1941		
Crispin	Atlantic 1941		
Crocus	Atlantic 1940-45		
Cromarty	Diego Suarez 1942	Sicily 1943	
Cromer	Diego Suarez 1942		
Croome	Atlantic 1941-42 Aegean 1943	Libya 1942	Mediterranean 1942
Crowlin	South France 1944		
Crown	Gabbard 1653 Schooneveld 1673 Quebec 1759	Orfordness 1666 Texel 1673 Martinique 1762	Sole Bay 1672 Barfleur 1692
Cruelle	Egypt 1801		
Cruiser	China 1856-60		
Cruizer	Copenhagen 1801 Baltic 1854-55	Aden 1839	China 1841
Crusader	Belgian Coast 1914-16	Korea 1952-53	
Cubitt	Atlantic 1944-45	North Sea 1944-45	
Cuckmere	Atlantic 1943	Mediterranean 1943	
Cuckoo	Baltic 1854-55		
Culgoa	Korea 1953		
Cullen	Portland 1653		
Culloden	Lagos 1759 St. Vincent 1780 Nile 1798	Martinique 1762 First of June 1794	Havana 1762 St. Vincent 1797
Culpepper	Gabbard 1653		
Culver	North Sea 1941	Atlantic 1941-42	
Cumberland	Sadras 1758 St. Vincent 1780 Arctic 1942-43 East Indies 1944-45	Negapatam 1758 Baltic 1854 North Africa 1942 Burma 1945	Porto Novo 1759 Cameroons 1914 Sabang 1944 Malaya 1945
Cumbae	Atlantic 1943		

Curacoa	Crimea 1855 Atlantic 1940	New Zealand 1863-66 North Sea 1940-42	Norway 1940 Arctic 1942
Curlew	Crimea 1854-55	Norway 1940	
Curran	Belgian Coast 1915		
Curzon	English Channel 1944	North Sea 1944-45	
Cuttle	Martinique 1809		
Cutty Sark	Atlantic 1940		
Cyclamen	Atlantic 1940-45	Diego Suarez 1942	English Channel 1943
Cyclone	Burma 1945		
Cyclops	Egypt 1801	Syria 1840	Crimea 1854-55
Cygnet	Armada 1588 Guadeloupe 1810 Atlantic 1943-44	Portland 1653 Alexandria 1882 Arctic 1944-45	Havana 1762 Sicily 1943
Cynthia	Egypt 1801		
D 2	Heligoland 1914		
D 8	Heligoland 1914		
Dacres	Atlantic 1943	Normandy 1944	
Daffodil	Zeebrugge 1918	English Channel 1942-43	North Sea 1944
Dahlia	Atlantic 1941-44 North Sea 1944	Biscay 1943 English Channel 1944-45	Normandy 1944
Dainty	Atlantic 1940 Libya 1940-41	Mediterranean 1940-41 Malta Convoys 1941	Calabria 1940
Dakins	Normandy 1944	English Channel 1944	North Sea 1944
Dalmatia	Normandy 1944		
Damsay	North Sea 1942	Normandy 1944	
Danae	Normandy 1944		
Dandolo	Normandy 1944		
Daneman	Atlantic 1940-43	English Channel 1940	Arctic 1942-43
Dangay	Atlantic 1940		
Dangereuse	Egypt 1801		
Daniel	Armada 1588*		

Diana	Armada 1588* '*Zefier*' 1809	Louisburg 1758 Burma 1824-26	Quebec 1759 Norway 1940
Diane	Egypt 1801		
Dianella	Atlantic 1941-45 Sicily 1943	Arctic 1942-44 English Channel 1943	North Africa 1942 Normandy 1944
Dianthus	Atlantic 1941-44	English Channel 1944	Normandy 1944
Dictator	Egypt 1801		
Dido	'*Minerve*' 1795 China 1842 Mediterranean 1942-44 Salerno 1943 South France 1944	Egypt 1801 Crete 1941 Malta Convoys 1942 Aegean 1943 Arctic 1944	Syria 1840 Sirte 1942 Sicily 1943 Anzio 1944
Digby	Atlantic 1942-44		
Diligence	Kuwait 1991**		
Diligent	Camperdown 1797		
Dinard	Dunkirk 1940*		
Dingledale	North Africa 1942-43**		
Diomede	Cape of Good Hope 1806		
Director	Camperdown 1797		
Discovery	Portland 1653	Copenhagen 1801	
Disdain	Armada 1588		
Dittany	Atlantic 1943-45		
Dochet	Atlantic 1943		
Dolly	Groix Island 1795		
Dolphin	Armada 1588* Lowestoft 1665 Egypt 1801	Portland 1653 Texel 1673	Gabbard 1653 Dogger Bank 1781
Domett	Atlantic 1943-45	Normandy 1944	English Channel 1945
Dominica	Martinique 1809 Biscay 1944	Atlantic 1944-45 English Channel 1945	Normandy 1944
Donegal	San Domingo 1806	Basque Roads 1809	
Doon	English Channel 1942	North Sea 1943	Normandy 1944
Dorade II	Atlantic 1941		

Doris	*'Chevrette'* 1801 South Africa 1899-1900	Java 1811 Dardanelles 1915-16	
Dornoch	Atlantic 1943	English Channel 1943	Normandy 1944
Dorothy Gray	Atlantic 1942-43		
Dorothy Lambert	Normandy 1944		
Dorsetshire	Gibraltar 1704 Passero 1718 Atlantic 1941	Velez Malaga 1704 Quiberon Bay 1759	*'Raisonnable'* 1758 *'Bismarck'* 1941
Doterel	Basque Roads 1809		
Douglas	Atlantic 1940-44	Arctic 1942	
Douwe Aukes	Normandy 1944		
Dover	Lowestoft 1665 Martinique 1762 Amboina 1810	Orfordness 1666 Havana 1762 Ternate 1810	Sole Bay 1672 Egypt 1801
Dovey	Atlantic 1944		
Dragon	Portland 1653 Lowestoft 1665 Bugia 1671 Martinique 1762 Baltic 1854-55	Gabbard 1653 Four Days' Battle 1666 Barfleur 1692 Havana 1762 Arctic 1944	Scheveningen 1653 Orfordness 1666 Belle Isle 1761 Egypt 1801
Dragoneare	Gabbard 1653		
Dragonet	Normandy 1944		
Dragonfly	Mesopotamia 1915-17		
Drake	Lowestoft 1665	Baltic 1855	China 1856-60
Dreadnought	Armada 1588 Four Days' Battle 1666 Schooneveld 1673 Passero 1718	Cadiz 1596 Orfordness 1666 Texel 1673 Cape François 1757	Lowestoft 1665 Sole Bay 1672 Barfleur 1692 Trafalgar 1805
Driver	New Zealand 1845-47	Baltic 1854-55	
Dromedary	Martinique 1794	Ashantee 1873-74	
Druid	Belle Isle 1761 Ashantee 1873-74	Egypt 1801 Heligoland 1914	China 1841 Dogger Bank 1915
Drumheller	Atlantic 1941-45	Normandy 1944	English Channel 1944-45
Drummondville	Atlantic 1942-5		
Drury	Atlantic 1943-45	Arctic 1945	
Dryad	*'Proserpine'* 1796	Abyssinia 1868	

Dubbo	Pacific 1945		
Dublin	Louisburg 1758 Havana 1762	Quebec 1759 Dardanelles 1915	Martinique 1762 Jutland 1916
Duchess	Portland 1653 Barfleur 1692	Gabbard 1653	Scheveningen 1653
Duchess of Fife	Dunkirk 1940		
Duchess of Montrose	Belgian Coast 1915		
Duckworth	Atlantic 1943-44 Arctic 1944	Biscay 1944 English Channel 1945	Normandy 1944
Dudgeon	North Sea 1944		
Dudley	Armada 1588*		
Duff	Normandy 1944	English Channel 1944	
Dufferin	Suez Canal 1915 (RIM)		
Duke	Barfleur 1692 The Saints 1782	Quiberon Bay 1759	Ushant 1781
Duke of Edinburgh	Jutland 1916		
Duke of Wellington	Baltic 1854-55	Dieppe 1942	Normandy 1944
Duke of York	Arctic 1942-43	North Africa 1942	North Cape 1943
Dulverton	Libya 1942 Malta Convoys 1942 Aegean 1943	M S	Sirte 1942 Salerno 1943
Dumbarton Castle	Atlantic 1944-45		
Dunavon	North Sea 1942		
Dunbar	North Sea 1942	No	
Duncan	Spartivento 1940 Atlantic 1941-45	Malta Convoys 1941 Diego Suarez 1942	Mediterranean 1941
Duncton	Atlantic 1942-44	North Sea 1942	Arctic 1942
Dundalk	Dunkirk 1940		
Dundas	Atlantic 1942-45		
Dundee	'*Leopard*' 1917	Atlantic 1940	
Dunedin	Atlantic 1941		
Dunkery	North Sea 1942	Atlantic 1942-43	

Dunkirk	Lowestoft 1665 Schooneveld 1673 Quiberon Bay 1759	Orfordness 1666 Texel 1673	Sole Bay 1672 Passero 1718
Dunnottar Castle	Atlantic 1939-42		
Dunvegan	Atlantic 1941-44		
Dunvegan Castle	Atlantic 1940		
Dunver	Atlantic 1943-45		
Durban	Normandy 1944		
Dwarf	Cameroons 1914		
E 2	Dardanelles 1915		
E 4	Heligoland 1914		
E 5	Heligoland 1914		
E 6	Heligoland 1914		
E 7	Heligoland 1914	Dardanelles 1915	
E 8	Heligoland 1914		
E 9	Heligoland 1914		
E 11	Dardanelles 1915		
E 12	Dardanelles 1915		
E 14	Dardanelles 1915-16		
E 15	Dardanelles 1915		
E 20	Dardanelles 1915		
Eagle	Portland 1653 Orfordness 1666 Velez Malaga 1704 Providien 1782 Calabria 1940	Gabbard 1653 Barfleur 1692 Ushant 1747 Negapatam 1782 Mediterranean 1940	Lowestoft 1665 Gibraltar 1704 Sadras 1782 Trincomalee 1782 Malta Convoys 1942
Earl Kitchener	Atlantic 1942		
Earl of Peterborough	Dardanelles 1915-16		
East Coast	Normandy 1944		
East India London	Orfordness 1666		
East India Merchant	Orfordness 1666		

East View	Atlantic 1944-45		
Eastbourne	English Channel 1942-44 Normandy 1944	Dieppe 1942	North Africa 1942
Eastland Merchant	Gabbard 1653		
Easton	English Channel 1942 Sicily 1943	North Africa 1943 Aegean 1944	Mediterranean 1943 North Sea 1945
Eastway	South France 1944		
Ebor Wyke	Atlantic 1942-44	North Sea 1943	
Echo	Quebec 1759 Cape of Good Hope 1795 '*Bismarck*' 1941 Sicily 1943	Martinique 1762 Atlantic 1939 Arctic 1941-43 Salerno 1943	Havana 1762 Norway 1940 Malta Convoys 1942 Aegean 1943
Echuca	New Guinea 1943-44		
Eclair	Martinique 1809		
Eclipse	New Zealand 1863-66 Sicily 1943 Atlantic 1943	Norway 1940 Salerno 1943	Arctic 1941-43 Aegean 1943
Eday	Atlantic 1942	North Africa 1942-43	Sicily 1943
Edgar	Sole Bay 1672 Barfleur 1692 St. Vincent 1780 Dardanelles 1915-16	Schooneveld 1673 Lagos 1759 Ushant 1781	Texel 1673 Havana 1762 Copenhagen 1801
Edinburgh	Ushant 1747 Baltic 1854-55 Atlantic 1941	Cape François 1757 Norway 1940-41 Malta Convoys 1941	Syria 1840 '*Bismarck*' 1941 Arctic 1941-42
Edmunston	Atlantic 1942-45	Biscay 1943	
Edward	Armada 1588		
Edward Bonaventure	Armada 1588*		
Effingham	Atlantic 1939-40	Norway 1940	
Eggesford	Sicily 1943 South France 1944	Salerno 1943	Adriatic 1944
Egilsay	English Channel 1942		
Eglantine	Norway 1941	Atlantic 1941-44	Arctic 1943-45
Eglinton	Atlantic 1940 Normandy 1944	English Channel 1940-44	North Sea 1941-44
Egmont	Genoa 1795	St. Vincent 1797	

Egret	Atlantic 1939-42	North Africa 1942-43	Biscay 1943
Eileen Emma	Dunkirk 1940		
Ekins	Atlantic 1944	English Channel 1944	North Sea 1944-45
El Carmen	Egypt 1801		
Elbury	North Africa 1942-43		
Electra	Atlantic 1939-40 Arctic 1941	Norway 1940 Malaya 1942	'*Bismarck*' 1941
Elephant	Copenhagen 1801		
Elgin	English Channel 1942	Normandy 1944	
Elizabeth	Armada 1588* Orfordness 1666 Negapatam 1758	Cadiz 1596* Barfleur 1692 Porto Novo 1759	Montecristo 1652 Sadras 1758 Guadeloupe 1810
Elizabeth and Ann	Portland 1653		
Elizabeth Bonaventure	Armada 1588		
Elizabeth Drake	Armada 1588*		
Elizabeth Founes	Armada 1588*		
Elizabeth Jonas	Armada 1588	Cadiz 1596*	
Elk	China 1856-60	Falkland Islands 1982*	
Ellesmere	Norway 1940 Normandy 1944	Atlantic 1940-44	English Channel 1942-45
Elm	Atlantic 1942-44	Arctic 1944	
Elphinstone	New Zealand 1845-47 (Indian Navy)		
Else Rykens	North Sea 1941		
Emerald	Basque Roads 1809	Atlantic 1939-40	Normandy 1944
Emperor	Atlantic 1943-44 Aegean 1944 Burma 1945	Norway 1944 South France 1944 East Indies 1945	Normandy 1944 Malaya 1945
Emperor of India	Dunkirk 1940		
Employment	Gabbard 1653		
Empress	Atlantic 1944	Burma 1945	
Empyrean	North Africa 1942		
Enchantress	Atlantic 1939-45	Mediterranean 1942	North Africa 1942-43

Encounter	Cape of Good Hope 1806	Basque Roads 1809	China 1856-60
	Ashantee 1973-74	Atlantic 1939	Norway 1940
	Spartivento 1940	Mediterranean 1941	Libya 1941
	Malta Convoys 1941	Malaya 1942	Sunda Strait 1942
Endeavour	Cadiz 1596*		
Endurance	Falkland Islands 1982		
Endymion	The Saints 1782	*'President'* 1815	China 1842
	China 1900	Dardanelles 1915-16	
Engadine	Jutland 1916	Atlantic 1943	
Engadine	Falkland Islands 1982**		
Ennerdale	English Channel 1942**	North Africa 1942**	Sicily 1943**
Ensay	English Channel 1942	Salerno 1943	
Enterprise	Atlantic 1939-40	Norway 1940	Biscay 1943
	Normandy 1944		
Enterprize	Havana 1762		
Entrance	Dover 1652	Portland 1653	Gabbard 1653
Entreprenante	Egypt 1801	Trafalgar 1805	
Epervier	San Domingo 1806		
Erebus	Belgian Coast 1916-18	Zeebrugge 1918	English Channel 1940-44
	North Sea 1941	Atlantic 1943	Mediterranean 1943
	Sicily 1943	Normandy 1944	Walcheren 1944
Erica	Atlantic 1940-41	Libya 1942	
Eridanes	Normandy 1944		
Eridge	Libya 1941-42	Malta Convoys 1941-42	Sirte 1942
	Mediterranean 1942		
Erin	Jutland 1916	Atlantic 1940	
Eriksay	Atlantic 1943-45		
Erne	Atlantic 1942-45	North Africa 1942	Sicily 1943
Eroican	North Sea 1942	Normandy 1944	
Erraid	Atlantic 1945		
Escapade	Atlantic 1939-45	Norway 1940	Arctic 1941-42
	Malta Convoys 1942		
Escort	Belle Isle 1761	Atlantic 1939-40	North Sea 1940

Esk	Baltic 1855 Atlantic 1939	China 1856-60 Norway 1940	New Zealand 1863-66 Dunkirk 1940
Eskdale	Arctic 1942	English Channel 1942-43	
Eskimo	Narvik 1940 Arctic 1942 Normandy 1944 East Indies 1945	Norway 1940-41 North Africa 1942-43 English Channel 1944	Malta Convoys 1942 Sicily 1943 Burma 1944-45
Esperance Bay	Atlantic 1940-41		
Espiegle	Egypt 1801 Salerno 1943	Mesopotamia 1914-16 Anzio 1944	Sicily 1943
Espoir	Cape of Good Hope 1806		
Esquimalt	Atlantic 1943-44		
Essex	Gabbard 1653 Vigo 1702 Passero 1718	Four Days' Battle 1666 Gibraltar 1704 Quiberon Bay 1759	Barfleur 1692 Velez Malaga 1704 Belle Isle 1761
Essington	Atlantic 1943-45 Biscay 1944	Arctic 1944 English Channel 1944-45	Normandy 1944
Estrello D'Alva	North Sea 1942		
Estrella Do Orto	North Sea 1942		
Ethalion	Donegal 1798	Martinique 1809	
Etna (and **Aetna**)	Lagos 1759		
Etruscan	Normandy 1944		
Ettrick	Atlantic 1943-45		
Europa	Egypt 1801		
Europe	Chesapeake 1781		
Europic Ferry	Falkland Islands 1982*		
Eurotas	'Clorinde' 1814		
Eurus	Quebec 1759	Egypt 1801	
Euryalus	Trafalgar 1805 Dardanelles 1915 Sirte 1942 Okinawa 1945	Baltic 1854-5 Malta Convoys 1941-42 Sicily 1943	Heligoland 1914 Mediterranean 1941-43 Salerno 1943
Eurydice	St. Kitts 1782	The Saints 1782	Martinique 1809
Evadne	Atlantic 1942-45		
Evelyn Rose	North Sea 1942		

Evenlode	Atlantic 1943-44		
Excellent	St. Vincent 1797	Belgian Coast 1914-16	
Exchange	Cadiz 1596*	Portland 1653	Gabbard 1653
Exe	Atlantic 1942-45	North Africa 1942	
Exeter	Sadras 1782 Trincomalee 1782 Sunda Strait 1942	Providien 1782 River Plate 1939 Falkland Islands 1982	Negapatam 1782 Malaya 1942 Kuwait 1991
Exeter Merchant	Scheveningen 1653		
Exmoor	Atlantic 1941-42 Sicily 1943 Mediterranean 1944	North Sea 1941 Salerno 1943	Libya 1942 Aegean 1943-44
Exmouth	Baltic 1855 Atlantic 1939	Belgian Coast 1914	Dardanelles 1915
Expedition	Cadiz 1596* Scheveningen 1653 Barfleur 1692 Egypt 1801	Portland 1653 Four Days' Battle 1666 Marbella 1705	Gabbard 1653 Orfordness 1666 St. Kitts 1782
Experience	Cadiz 1596*		
Experiment	Martinique 1794	Egypt 1801	
Explosion	Copenhagen 1801		
Express	Martinique 1809	Dunkirk 1940	
Extravagant	Barfleur 1692		
Eyebright	Atlantic 1941-45		
Fair Sisters	Gabbard 1653		
Fairfax	Dover 1652 Orfordness 1666 Atlantic 1944	Portland 1653 Sole Bay 1672	Santa Cruz 1657 Texel 1673
Fairway	Normandy 1944		
Fal	Atlantic 1943-45		
Falcon	Gabbard 1653 Barfleur 1692 New Zealand 1863-66	Schooneveld 1673 Finisterre 1747 Belgian Coast 1914-17	Texel 1673 Baltic 1855
Falk	Libya 1941-42		
Falkland	Finisterre 1747	Quiberon Bay 1759	Martinique 1762
Falmouth	Portland 1653 Jutland 1916	Gabbard 1653 East Indies 1940	Heligoland 1914

Fame	Lowestoft 1665 Norway 1940	The Saints 1782 Atlantic 1942-44	China 1900 Normandy 1944
Fancy	Armada 1588	Crimea 1855	Normandy 1944
Fandango	Atlantic 1940-43		
Fanfan	Orfordness 1666		
Fantome	Atlantic 1943		
Fareham	Libya 1941		
Farndale	Atlantic 1941 Libya 1941-42 Sicily 1943 Aegean 1944	Malta Convoys 1941 Arctic 1942 Salerno 1943 North Sea 1945	Mediterranean 1941 North Africa 1942-43 South France 1944
Farne	Normandy 1944		
Farnella	Falkland Islands 1982		
Farnham	Libya 1942		
Farnham Castle	Arctic 1945		
Faulknor	Jutland 1916 Ostend 1918 Spartivento 1940 Mediterranean 1943-44 Aegean 1943	Belgian Coast 1917-18 Atlantic 1939-43 Malta Convoys 1941 Sicily 1943 Anzio 1944	Zeebrugge 1918 Norway 1940 Arctic 1942-43 Salerno 1943 Normandy 1944
Favourite	Lagos 1759		
Fawn	Martinique 1809	Guadeloupe 1810	Belgian Coast 1914-18
Fearless	Heligoland 1914 Atlantic 1941 Falkland Islands 1982	Jutland 1916 Mediterranean 1941	Norway 1940 Malta Convoys 1941
Felixstowe	Dieppe 1942 Sicily 1943	English Channel 1942 Salerno 1943	North Africa 1942-43
Fencer	Atlantic 1943-44 Arctic 1944	Norway 1944	North Sea 1944
Fenella	Dunkirk 1940*		
Fennel	Atlantic 1941-45		
Fergus	Atlantic 1945		
Fernie	English Channel 1940-44 Normandy 1944	North Sea 1941-45	Dieppe 1942
Fernmoor	Normandy 1944		

Ferret	Havana 1762 Belgian Coast 1917	Heligoland 1914	Dogger Bank 1915
Fervent	Basque Roads 1809		
Fetlar	Atlantic 1943-44		
Fiaray	Normandy 1944		
Fidelity	Atlantic 1942	English Channel 1942	
Fidget	Dunkirk 1940		
Fiji	Crete 1941		
Filey Bay	North Africa 1942-43		
Filla	North Sea 1942		
Findhorn	Atlantic 1943-44	East Indies 1944	Okinawa 1945
Fiona	Libya 1940-41		
Fir	English Channel 1942-45		
Firebrand	Velez Malaga 1704	Crimea 1854-55	
Firedrake	Belle Isle 1761 Norway 1940 Malta Convoys 1941	Heligoland 1914 Spartivento 1940	Atlantic 1939-42 Mediterranean 1940-41
Firefly	Baltic 1855	Mesopotamia 1915-17	
Firm	Crimea 1855	China 1856-60	
Firmament	Libya 1942		
Firme	Velez Malaga 1704		
Fisgard	'*Immortalite*' 1798	Curaçoa 1807	
Fisher Boy	Dunkirk 1940		
Fishguard	Atlantic 1941-43	Sicily 1943	
Fitzroy	Dunkirk 1940 Atlantic 1944-45	English Channel 1944 North Sea 1944-45	Arctic 1944
Flamborough	Belle Isle 1761		
Flame	Barfleur 1692		
Flamer	Crimea 1855	China 1860	
Flamingo	North Sea 1939-40 Crete 1941	Norway 1940 Libya 1941	Greece 1941 Burma 1944-45

Flatholm	Atlantic 1944		
Fleetwood	Norway 1940 Mediterranean 1944	Atlantic 1940-44 English Channel 1945	North Africa 1942-43
Fleur de Lys	Atlantic 1940-41	Malta Convoys 1941	
Flint	Atlantic 1943	Normandy 1944	
Flint Castle	Atlantic 1944-45		
Flirt	Belgian Coast 1914-15		
Flora	The Saints 1782	Egypt 1801	
Florentina	Egypt 1801		
Flores	North Sea 1942-43		
Fluellen	English Channel 1942	North Africa 1942	
Fly	Belle Isle 1761 Anzio 1944	Sicily 1943	Salerno 1943
Flyboat	Armada 1588*		
Flycatcher	Mesopotamia 1915-17		
Foley	Atlantic 1943-44		
Folkestone	Atlantic 1940-44		
Forecast	Dunkirk 1940		
Foresight	Armada 1588 Scheveningen 1653 Orfordness 1666 Belgian Coast 1914 Mediterranean 1941	Portland 1653 Porto Farina 1655 Schooneveld 1673 Dardanelles 1915-16 Malta Convoys 1941-42	Gabbard 1653 Santa Cruz 1657 Texel 1673 Atlantic 1941 Arctic 1942
Forest Hill	Atlantic 1944		
Forester	Lowestoft 1665 Guadeloupe 1810 Dogger Bank 1915 Norway 1940 Arctic 1942-43	Sole Bay 1672 China 1856-60 Atlantic 1939-44 Spartivento 1940 Normandy 1944	Martinique 1809 Heligoland 1914 Narvik 1940 Malta Convoys 1941 English Channel 1944
Formidable	The Saints 1782 Mediterranean 1941 Sicily 1943 Okinawa 1945	Matapan 1941 East Indies 1941 Salerno 1943 Japan 1945	Crete 1941 North Africa 1942-43 Norway 1944
Fort Austin	Falkland Islands 1982**		
Fort Frances	Atlantic 1945		
Fort Grange	Falkland Islands 1982**	Kuwait 1991**	

Fort Toronto	Falkland Islands 1982*		
Fort William	Atlantic 1943	Normandy 1944	
Fort York	Atlantic 1943	Normandy 1944	
Forte	Benin 1897	South Africa 1899-1900	
Fortitude	Dogger Bank 1781	Genoa 1795	
Fortune	Armada 1588* Orfordness 1666 North Sea 1940	Portland 1653 Jutland 1916 Malta Convoys 1941-42	Gabbard 1653 Atlantic 1939
Fossbeck	Normandy 1944		
Foudroyant	Martinique 1762 '*Guillaume Tell*' 1800	'*Pégase*' 1782 Egypt 1801	Donegal 1798
Foula	North Africa 1942-43	South France 1944	
Foulness	Normandy 1944		
Fountain	Lowestoft 1665	Sole Bay 1672	
Fowey	Quebec 1759	Atlantic 1939-45	
Fox	Gabbard 1653 Genoa 1795 Burma 1852-53	Orfordness 1666 St. Vincent 1797	Barfleur 1692 Egypt 1801
Foxhound	Basque Roads 1809 Narvik 1940 Malta Convoys 1941	Dardanelles 1915 Norway 1940	Atlantic 1939-41 Mediterranean 1941
Foxtrot	Atlantic 1940-43	North Sea 1941-42	Sicily 1943
Frances	Armada 1588*		
Franklin	Normandy 1944		
Fraser	Atlantic 1939		
Fraserburgh	Normandy 1944		
Fratton	Normandy 1944		
Fredericton	Atlantic 1942-45		
Freesia	Atlantic 1941-42	Diego Suarez 1942	
Freija	Guadeloupe 1810	San Sebastian 1813	
French Ruby **Friendship**	Sole Bay 1672 Texel 1673	Schooneveld 1673 Atlantic 1943-45	Texel 1673 Normandy 1944
Fritillary	Atlantic 1941-45	Diego Suarez 1942	

Frobisher	Normandy 1944		
Frolic	Martinique 1809	Guadeloupe 1810	
Frontenac	Atlantic 1944-45		
Fuday	Normandy 1944		
Fulminate	Egypt 1801		
Furious	Crimea 1854-55	China 1856-60	Narvik 1940
	Norway 1940-44	Malta Convoys 1942	North Africa 1942-43
Furnace	Belle Isle 1761		
Fury	St. Lucia 1796	Egypt 1801	Algiers 1816
	Kua Kam 1849	Crimea 1854	China 1856-60
	Dardanelles 1915-16	Spartivento 1940	Mediterranean 1941
	Malta Convoys 1941-42	Atlantic 1941-43	Arctic 1942-43
	Sicily 1943	Salerno 1943	Aegean 1943
	Normandy 1944		
Fusilier	Atlantic 1943-45	Normandy 1944	
Fyldea	Dunkirk 1940		
Gadfly	Mesopotamia 1915-17		
Gairsay	Normandy 1944		
Galatea	Groix Island 1795	*'Lynx'* 1807	Tamatave 1811
	Jutland 1916	Norway 1940	*'Bismarck'* 1941
	Mediterranean 1941		
Gallant	Atlantic 1939	Dunkirk 1940	Spartivento 1940
	Mediterranean 1940-41	Malta Convoys 1941	
Gallego	Armada 1588*		
Galt	Atlantic 1941-45		
Gambia	Sabang 1944	Okinawa 1945	Japan 1945
Gananoque	Atlantic 1942-45		
Ganges	St. Lucia 1796	Copenhagen 1801	Syria 1840
Ganilly	English Channel 1943	Normandy 1944	
Gardenia	Atlantic 1940-42	North Africa 1942	
Gardiner	Atlantic 1943-45		
Garland	Dover 1652	Kentish Knock 1652	Lowestoft 1665
	Bugia 1671	Velez Malaga 1704	Passero 1718
	Jutland 1961	Atlantic 1940-43	Arctic 1942
	Mediterranean 1944		

Plate 1 - **Warspite**: The battleship **Warspite** won one Honour for the name in World War I and 14 in World War II, giving her a massive total of 25. Completed in March 1915, she underwent several major modernisations during her long career, altering her appearance, but retaining her main armament of eight 15-inch guns. She was sold for breaking up in 1946, and ran aground on her way to the breakers in 1947. The name has been used subsequently by a nuclear submarine.

SWIFTSURE

Submitted

Arthur Cochrane
Clarenceux King of Arms
A.A.H.

25 February 19**44**

Passed as
SEALED PATTERN

E.B.C. Dicken
Assistant Controller
for the Board

Admiralty 28 - 2 - 19**44**

Plate 2 - **Swiftsure**: The cruiser **Swiftsure** was completed early enough in the Second World War to add one more honour to the 19 already held by the name, which goes back to 'Armada 1588'. She was badly damaged in a collision in 1953. Never repaired, she was broken up in 1962. More recently the name has been borne by a nuclear submarine.

8

UNICORN

Submitted

Passed as
SEALED PATTERN

haisich for Deputy Controller

A.A.H.

for the Board

19

Admiralty *29 January* 19 41

Plate 3 - **Unicorn**: The aircraft carrier **Unicorn** was built for maintenance duties but was employed operationally in the Second World War. She gained three of the fifteen Honours of the name, the last in the Korean War. The name of the previous **Unicorn**, a 'wooden wall' of 1824, was changed to **Cressy** in 1941 to release the name for the carrier, and when the carrier was broken up in 1959, **Cressy** reverted to **Unicorn**, and in 1968 was handed over for preservation. The name has since been borne by a submarine - now the Canadian **Windsor**.

Courageous

800

Submitted

A.A.H.

Passed as
SEALED PATTERN

for the Board

Plate 4 - *800 Squadron*: First formed in April 1933 using Nimrod and Osprey aircraft, *800 Squadron* was re-equipped with Skuas in 1938 and joined the newly completed aircraft carrier *Ark Royal* in 1939. The Squadron was in the thick of the action during the Norwegian campaign, and, as its 13 World War II Honours gained indicate, served widely in a variety of zones. In July 1943 it became the first FAA Squadron equipped with Hellcats. When in Korea in 1950 it operated with Seafires from the carrier *Triumph*. The Squadron was disbanded in 1972. It was reformed with Sea Harriers in 1980 and served in the Falklands War in 1982 in the carrier *Hermes*.

Plate 5- **Invincible**: The Battle Honours Board of the present aircraft carrier shows her eight Battle Honours including those for the Falkland Islands in 1914 and the 1982 Falkland Islands, showing the continuity that exits in naval history. Two other ships, **Bristol** and **Glasgow**, also have both these honours, despite there being only eight ships with the 1914 award.

Plate 6 - **Antelope**: A destroyer which gained 4 Battle Honours for her name in World War II. She survived the war and was broken up in 1946. Seven other Honours had been gained by previous ships of the name, including 'Armada 1588', and a later ship won an Honour in the Falklands War.

Plate 7 - *Arrow*: The frigate *Arrow* is seen returning form the Falklands War in 1982 where she gained the 11th Honour awarded to the name. She was sold to Pakistan in 1994, being renamed *Khaibur*.

Plate 8 - *SS Atlantic Conveyor*: This Roll-on Roll-off Cargo Vessel was requisitioned on 16 April 1982, and was modified at Devonport to carry aircraft. She sailed for the South Atlantic with Naval Part 1840 embarked, but still under her mercantile colours. She was lost to Exocet attack off the Falkland Islands, being hit on 25 May and sinking on 29 May.

Plate 9 - **Bamborough Castle**: The corvette gained both Honours awarded to the name. These sturdy ships intro-duced the Squid anti-submarine mortar to counter the U-boat threat to good effect. She sank **U-387** in the Arctic in December 1944.

Plate 10 - **Betony**: This Modified Flower class corvette won both Honours attached to the name in World War II. She transferred to the Royal Indian Navy in 1945, and then to Thailand in 1947, being lost in 1951 during the Korean War.

Plate 11 - **Calder**: Built in America, **Calder** was one of many Captain Class frigates that helped win the Battle of the Atlantic, where she won the one Honour attached to the name. She was named after Admiral Sir Robert Calder, who was Captain of the Fleet to Jervis at St. Vincent. She helped sink **U-1172** and **U-774** in 1945.

Plate 12 - **Centurion**: This remarkable ship served in two World Wars, gaining one battle honour in each, the first at Jutland as a battleship with a main armament of 13.5-inch guns, the second at Normandy as a blockship. Between the wars she served as a target ship, and in the Second World War she also served as a dummy battleship, a measure of the British desperate shortage of ships.

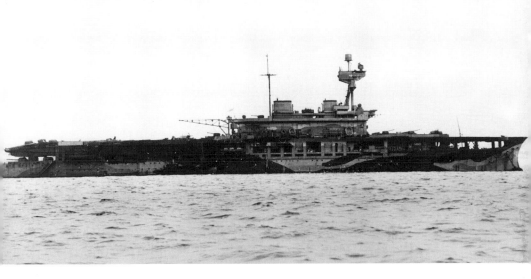

Plate 13 - *Eagle*: A long-standing name in the Royal Navy, going back to the 16th Century, *Eagle* won 3 of the 15 Honours of the name before she was lost on a Malta Convoy in August 1942. She had been laid down as a Chilean battleship and was completed as an aircraft carrier in 1924.

Plate 14 - *Euryalus*: Carrying the Honour 'Trafalgar 1805', the cruiser *Euryalus* won a further 6 Honours for her name to make a total of 10 for the name. She took part in fierce fighting the Mediterranean and later served at Okinawa. She was broken up in 1959.

Plate 15 - **Faulknor**: The 'F' Class destroyers took part in many actions in World War II. **Faulknor**, the Leader of the Flotilla, was typical, adding 11 Honours to the 4 already held by the name. She was named after Robert Faulknor (1763-1795) who was killed whilst commanding the **Blanche** in an action with the French **Pique**, which in itself became a Single Ship Action Battle Honour.

Plate 16 - **Grey Goose**: Originally known as **Steam Gun Boat 9**, she was later named. She saw much action in the Channel, gaining three Battle Honours for the name whilst serving with both number and later, the name. Used for engine trials after the war, she was sold in 1957.

Plate 17 - *Jervis*: *Jervis* won all 13 Honours of the name in World War II, a number only surpassed by Warspite, and equalled by *Orion*, *Nubian* and *Tartar*. Named after Admiral of the Fleet Sir John Jervis, Earl St. Vincent (1735-1832).

Plate 18 - *Nubian*: The Tribal class destroyers, completed just before World War II, had a very active war. *Nubian* (and her sister ship *Tartar*) won 13 Honours. Her predecessor was damaged in World War I, and part of her was joined to part of her (also damaged) sister, *Zulu*, becoming a new ship named *Zubian*, which won one Battle Honour in World War I.

Plate 19 - *Orion*: The light cruiser *Orion* had a very active war, gaining 13 Battle Honours for the name, bringing the total to 20, which include 'Trafalgar 1805' and 'Jutland 1916'. She was very badly damaged during the evacuation from Crete in 1941, but was repaired and returned to the Mediterranean by 1943 to continue gaining Honours for her name.

Plate 20 - *Prince of Wales*: This ill fated battleship won two Honours for her name before she was lost off Malaya in 1941. During her service she did win Honours for her part in the sinking of the German battleship *Bismarck*, and also for guarding convoys to sustain the fortress island of Malta. She was armed with ten 14-inch guns mounted in two quadruple and one twin turret.

Plate 21 - **Repulse**: The battle cruiser **Repulse** gained three Honours for her name before she was lost to Japanese aircraft off Malaya in December 1941. Her career had spanned two World Wars and she had been worked very hard in the two and a half years of war prior to her loss, allowing no time for modernisation to meet the threat from air attack.

Plate 22 - **HMCS Sackville**: This Canadian corvette was commissioned in December 1941 and won one Honour in the Atlantic. She has been preserved at Halifax, Nova Scotia, as a tribute to the many Canadians who took part in that great campaign.

Plate 23 - **Shropshire**: The cruiser **Shropshire** won all seven of the name's Honours, four of them whilst serving with the Royal Australian Navy, to which she was transferred in 1943 to replace her sister **Canberra**, which had been lost in action.

Plate 24 - **Sir Tristram**: There are three Honours for this name, two won by the Landing Ship Logistic of the Royal Fleet Auxiliary, which was damaged by bombing off San Carlos in the Falkland Islands and was brought back to the U.K. for major repair work.

Plate 25 - **HMAS Sydney**: The Royal Australian Navy cruiser **Sydney** gained four Battle Honours for her name, including a Single Ship Action. Her predecessor had also gained a Single Ship Action Battle Honour. The name has been re-used several times since, and a later **Sydney** gained the Battle Honour 'Korea 1951-52'.

Plate 26 - **Triton**: **Triton** gained two Honours. She was the first of her class, completing in November 1938. She was lost in the Adriatic in December 1940. Production of this successful design of submarine continued throughout the war, and some served until the late 1960's in modernised and streamlined forms.

Plate 27 - *Ursula*: A pre-war design, *Ursula* carried six torpedo tubes, though later vessels of the class only carried four. These small submarines carried out much work in home and Mediterranean waters. *Ursula* won six Honours for her name. She was lent to Russia from 1944 to 1949, and was broken up in 1950. The name has recently been used for another submarine (1992-2003) which has now been transferred to Canada under the name *Corner Brook*.

Plate 28 - *Victorious*: The carrier *Victorious* won 11 of the 12 Honours of the name. The earlier Honour was a Single-Ship action. She was commissioned in March 1941, and, after very active war service, underwent a major modernisation to extend her life. She was not broken up until 1969.

Garlies	Atlantic 1943-44	Normandy 1944	
Garth	North Sea 1941-45 Normandy 1944	English Channel 1942-44	Dieppe 1942
Gascoyne	Leyte Gulf 1944 Pacific 1945	New Guinea 1944	Lingayen Gulf 1945
Gaston Riviere	English Channel 1942		
Gateshead	Atlantic 1943	Normandy 1944	
Gatineau	Atlantic 1943-44	Normandy 1944	
Gaul	Norway 1940		
Gavotte	North Sea 1941 Salerno 1943	Atlantic 1942-43	Sicily 1943
Gawler	Sicily 1943		
Gazelle	Dardanelles 1915-16	Atlantic 1943-44	Normandy 1944
Geelong	New Guinea 1944		
Geestport	Falkland Islands 1982*		
General Birdwood	Normandy 1944		
General Craufurd	Belgian Coast 1915-18	Zeebrugge 1918	
General Wolfe	Belgian Coast 1916-18		
Genista	Atlantic 1942	Diego Suarez 1942	
Genoa	Navarino 1827		
Gentian	Atlantic 1940-44	English Channel 1944-45	Normandy 1944
George	Armada 1588 Porto Farina 1655 Orfordness 1666	Cadiz 1596* Santa Cruz 1657	Gabbard 1653 Lowestoft 1665
George Bonaventure	Armada 1588*		
George Noble	Armada 1588*		
Georgetown	Atlantic 1940-43		
Georgette	Normandy 1944		
Georgian	Atlantic 1941-44	Normandy 1944	
Geraldton	Sicily 1943		
Geranium	Atlantic 1940-45 English Channel 1944	Malta Convoys 1942 Normandy 1944	North Africa 1942

Gervais Rentoul	Dunkirk 1940		
Geyser	Baltic 1855		
Gibraltar	Lagos 1759	First of June 1794	Egypt 1801
	Basque Roads 1809		
Giffard	Atlantic 1944		
Gift	Armada 1588*	Portland 1653	Gabbard 1653
	Scheveningen 1653		
Gift of God	Armada 1588*	Cadiz 1596*	
Gilliflower	Portland 1653		
Gilly Flower	Gabbard 1653		
Gilsay	Normandy 1944		
Gipsy	Belgian Coast 1914-17	Atlantic 1939	
Girl Gladys	Dunkirk 1940		
Girl Pamela	Dunkirk 1940		
Glace Bay	Atlantic 1944-45		
Gladiator	Baltic 1854	Crimea 1854-55	
Gladiolus	Atlantic 1940-41		
Gladstone	New Guinea 1943-44		
Glaisdale	English Channel 1942-44		
Glamorgan	Falkland Islands 1982		
Glasgow	Lagos 1759	Havana 1762	Algiers 1816
	Navarino 1827	Falkland Islands 1914	Norway 1940
	Arctic 1943	Biscay 1943	Normandy 1944
	Falkland Islands 1982		
Glatton	Copenhagen 1801	Crimea 1855	
Gleaner	Baltic 1855	Atlantic 1940-41	North Sea 1941-42
	Arctic 1942-44	Normandy 1944	
Glen Avon	Belgian Coast 1915	Dunkirk 1940	
Glen Gower	Dunkirk 1940		
Glenarm	Atlantic 1943-44		
Glenearn	Greece 1941	Libya 1941	Mediterranean 1941
	Normandy 1944		
Glenelg	New Guinea 1943-44		

Glengyle	Greece 1941 Mediterranean 1941 Sicily 1943	Crete 1941 Dieppe 1942 Salerno 1943	Libya 1941 North Africa 1942 Anzio 1944
Glenroy	Crete 1941 Burma 1945	Libya 1941	Normandy 1944
Globe	Gabbard 1653		
Gloire	Martinique 1809	Guadeloupe 1810	
Glorious	Norway 1940		
Glory	First of June 1794	Dardanelles 1915	Korea 1951-53
Gloucester	Lowestoft 1665 Sole Bay 1672 Ushant 1747 Matapan 1941 Mediterranean 1941	Four Days' Battle 1666 Schooneveld 1673 Jutland 1916 Crete 1941 Kuwait 1991	Orfordness 1666 Texel 1673 Calabria 1940 Malta Convoys 1941
Glowworm	Atlantic 1939	Norway 1940	*'Admiral Hipper'* 1940
Gloxinia	Atlantic 1940-44 Libya 1941-42	Spartivento 1940 Mediterranean 1943	Malta Convoys 1941 English Channel 1945
Gnat	Mesopotamia 1916-17	Mediterranean 1941	Libya 1941
Goatfell	North Sea 1942	Normandy 1944	
Goathland	Atlantic 1943 North Sea 1944	English Channel 1943	Normandy 1944
Godavari	Atlantic 1943	East Indies 1944	Burma 1945
Goderich	Atlantic 1942-45		
Godetia	Atlantic 1940-43 Normandy 1944	Biscay 1943 English Channel 1945	North Sea 1944
Goldcock	North Sea 1943		
Golden Cock	Scheveningen 1653		
Golden Dragon	Cadiz 1596*		
Golden Eagle	Dunkirk 1940	Normandy 1944	
Golden Fleece	Gabbard 1653		
Golden Gift	Dunkirk 1940		
Golden Hind	Armada 1588*		
Golden Lion	Armada 1588*	Lowestoft 1665	
(Golden) Lion	Armada 1588		

Golden Noble	Armada 1588*		
Golden Phoenix	Orfordness 1666		
Golden Ryall	Armada 1588*		
Golden Sunbeam	Dunkirk 1940		
Goliath	St. Vincent 1797	Nile 1798	Dardanelles 1915
Good Design	Egypt 1801		
Good Hope	English Channel 1945		
Goodall	Atlantic 1944	Arctic 1945	
Goodson	Normandy 1944	Atlantic 1944	English Channel 1944
Goodwin	North Sea 1942		
Gore	Atlantic 1943-44	Normandy 1944	
Gorée	Martinique 1809		
Gorgon	Egypt 1801 Belgian Coast 1918	Syria 1840 Atlantic 1943	Baltic 1854-55 Normandy 1944
Gorleston	Atlantic 1941-43		
Goshawk	Heligoland 1914	Dogger Bank 1915	Jutland 1916
Gossamer	Dunkirk 1940 North Sea 1942	Atlantic 1940-41	Arctic 1941-42
Goth	North Africa 1942-43		
Goulburn	New Guinea 1944		
Gould	Atlantic 1943-44		
Gozo	Egypt 1801 East Indies 1945	Atlantic 1943	Normandy 1944
Grace	Armada 1588*		
Grace of God	Armada 1588*	Cadiz 1596*	
Gracie Fields	Dunkirk 1940		
Grafton	Barfleur 1692 Velez Malaga 1704 Dardanelles 1915-16	Vigo 1702 Passero 1718 Atlantic 1939	Gibraltar 1704 Porto Novo 1759 Dunkirk 1940
Gramont	Louisburg 1758	Lagos 1759	
Grampian	Normandy 1944		
Grampus	Dardanelles 1915		

Granado	Martinique 1762	Havana 1762	
Granby	Atlantic 1942-44		
Grandmere	Atlantic 1943-45		
Granicus	Algiers 1816		
Gransha	Belgian Coast 1915		
Graph	Biscay 1942	Arctic 1942-43	North Sea 1943
Grappler	Baltic 1855		
Grassholm	Normandy 1944		
Grasshopper	China 1860	Dardanelles 1915-16	
Grayfly	Mesopotamia 1916-17		
Grayling	North Sea 1942	Sicily 1943	
Great Admiral	Atlantic 1943		
Great Charity	Lowestoft 1665		
Great Gift	Orfordness 1666		
Great Katherine	Cadiz 1596*		
Great President	Portland 1653	Gabbard 1653	Scheveningen 1653
Grecian	Atlantic 1943-44	Normandy 1944	
Green Dragon	Cadiz 1596*		
Green Howard	Normandy 1944		
Green Ranger	Korea 1951-52**		
Greenfly	Mesopotamia 1916-17	North Sea 1944	
Greenwich	Orfordness 1666 Texel 1673	Sole Bay 1672 Barfleur 1692	Schooneveld 1673 Marbella 1705
Grenada	Guadeloupe 1810		
Grenade	Atlantic 1939	Norway 1940	Dunkirk 1940
Grenadier	Atlantic 1943-45	North Sea 1943	Normandy 1944
Grenville	Atlantic 1939 Anzio 1944 Okinawa 1945	English Channel 1943 Normandy 1944	Mediterranean 1943-44 Adriatic 1944
Grey Fox **(SGB 4)**	English Channel 1943	Normandy 1944	

Grey Goose (SGB 9)	Dieppe 1942	English Channel 1942-43	Normandy 1944
Grey Owl (SGB 5)	Dieppe 1942	English Channel 1943-44	Normandy 1944
Grey Seal (SGB 3)	English Channel 1943	Normandy 1944	
Grey Shark (SGB 6)	English Channel 1943	Normandy 1944	
Grey Wolf (SGB 8)	Dieppe 1942	English Channel 1943	Normandy 1944
Greyhound	Armada 1588 Four Days' Battle 1666 Egypt 1801 Norway 1940 Matapan 1941 Mediterranean 1941	Dover 1652 Barfleur 1692 Belgian Coast 1915-18 Dunkirk 1940 Crete 1941 Malta Convoys 1941	Kentish Knock 1652 Martinique 1762 Atlantic 1939 Spartivento 1940 Libya 1941
Gribb	Libya 1942	Aegean 1944	
Griffin	Armada 1588* Velez Malaga 1704 Mediterranean 1940-41 Crete 1941 Atlantic 1942	Barfleur 1692 Passero 1718 Matapan 1941 Malta Convoys 1941-42 English Channel 1943	Vigo 1702 Norway 1940 Greece 1941 Libya 1941-42
Grimsby	Greece 1941	Crete 1941	Libya 1941
Grimsby Town	Dunkirk 1940	English Channel 1942-43	Normandy 1944
Grimstead	English Channel 1942		
Grindall	Atlantic 1943-45		
Grinder	Crimea 1855		
Grive	Dunkirk 1940*		
Gros Inlet	St. Kitts 1782		
Grou	Normandy 1944	Atlantic 1944	Arctic 1944
Grove	Libya 1942	Atlantic 1942	Arctic 1942
Growler	Basque Roads 1809	Groix Island 1812	Baltic 1855
Gruinard	Atlantic 1943		
Guadeloupe	Chesapeake 1781	Guadeloupe 1810	
Guardian	Norway 1940	Sicily 1943	
Guardsman	Atlantic 1944-45		
Guelph	Atlantic 1944-45		

Guernsey	Lowestoft 1665	Texel 1673	Lagos 1759
Guilder de Ruyter	Orfordness 1666		
Guillemot	Dunkirk 1940	North Sea 1942-45	
Guinea	Kentish Knock 1652 Lowestoft 1665	Portland 1653 Orfordness 1666	Gabbard 1653
Gulnare	Normandy 1944		
Gulzar	Dunkirk 1940		
Gunner	North Sea 1942	Normandy 1944	
Gurkha	Belgian Coast 1914-16 Atlantic 1941	Norway 1940 Mediterranean 1941	North Sea 1940 Malta Convoys 1941-42
Guysborough	Atlantic 1943-44	Normandy 1944	
Gweal	English Channel 1943-44	Normandy 1944	
Gympie	New Guinea 1944		
H.49	North Sea 1940		
Haarlem	Atlantic 1940-44	Mediterranean 1943	East Indies 1943
Hadleigh Castle	Atlantic 1943-44		
Haerlem	Egypt 1801		
Haida	Arctic 1943-45 Biscay 1944	English Channel 1944 Korea 1952-53	Normandy 1944
Hailstorm	Libya 1941		
Haitan	Burma 1944-45		
Halcyon	Dunkirk 1940	Arctic 1941-44	Normandy 1944
Half-moon	Barfleur 1692		
Halifax	Louisburg 1758	Quebec 1759	Atlantic 1942-45
Halladale	Burma 1945		
Hallowell	Atlantic 1944-45		
Halse	Armada 1588*		
Halsted	Normandy 1944	English Channel 1944	North Sea 1944
Hambledon	North Sea 1941-44 Salerno 1943 Normandy 1944	English Channel 1943 Aegean 1943	Sicily 1943 Mediterranean 1944

Hambro' Merchant	Lowestoft 1665		
Hamburg Merchant	Gabbard 1653		
Hamilton	Atlantic 1942-43		
Hamlet	Arctic 1941	Atlantic 1941-44	
Hammond	Norway 1940		
Hampshire	Gabbard 1653 Orfordness 1666 Jutland 1916	Santa Cruz 1657 Schooneveld 1673	Lowestoft 1665 Texel 1673
Hampton Court	Barfleur 1692 Belle Isle 1761	Marbella 1705 Havana 1762	Puerto Bello 1739
Handmaid	Armada 1588*		
Hanna Ray	Normandy 1944		
Hannibal	Portland 1653 Baltic 1854	Gabbard 1653 Crimea 1855	Scheveningen 1653
Happy Entrance	Dover 1652 Four Days' Battle 1666	Portland 1653	Gabbard 1653
Happy Return	Lowestoft 1665 Texel 1673	Orfordness 1666	Schooneveld 1673
Hard Bargain	Texel 1673		
Hardinge	Suez Canal 1915 (RIM)		
Hardy	Crimea 1855 Atlantic 1940	China 1860 Narvik 1940	Jutland 1916 Arctic 1943-44
Hare	Velez Malaga 1704		
Hargood	Atlantic 1944	Normandy 1944	
Harlequin	China 1842		
Harpy	Copenhagen 1801 Dardanelles 1915	Java 1811	Crimea 1854-55
Harrier	Baltic 1855 Normandy 1944	New Zealand 1863-66	Arctic 1941-43
Hart	Armada 1588 Atlantic 1944-45	Normandy 1944 Korea 1950-51	English Channel 1944
Hartland	Atlantic 1941-42	English Channel 1942	North Africa 1942
Harvester	Dunkirk 1940	Atlantic 1940-43	

Hascosay	Atlantic 1944		
Haslemere	Normandy 1944		
Hastings	Syria 1840 Atlantic 1940-43	Burma 1852 Biscay 1943	Baltic 1855
Hasty	Atlantic 1939 Spada 1940 Greece 1941 Malta Convoys 1941-42	Norway 1940 Mediterranean 1940-41 Crete 1941 Sirte 1942	Calabria 1940 Matapan 1941 Libya 1941-42
Hatsuse	English Channel 1942		
Haughty	Martinique 1809	China 1856-60	
Havant	Dunkirk 1940	Atlantic 1940	
Havelock	Dardanelles 1915-16 Biscay 1943	Norway 1940 English Channel 1944	Atlantic 1940-45 Normandy 1944
Havock	Baltic 1855 Narvik 1940 Mediterranean 1940-41 Crete 1941 Sirte 1942	China 1860 Norway 1940 Matapan 1941 Libya 1941-42	Atlantic 1939 Spada 1940 Greece 1941 Malta Convoys 1941-42
Hawea	Korea 1951-53		
Hawk	Barfleur 1692	Vigo 1702	
Hawke	Louisburg 1758	Baltic 1855	
Hawkesbury	Atlantic 1944-45 (RCN)	New Guinea 1944 (RAN)	Pacific 1945 (RAN)
Hawkins	Normandy 1944		
Hawkyns	Armada 1588*		
Haydon	Sicily 1943 South France 1944	Salerno 1943 North Sea 1945	Aegean 1943
Hazard	Armada 1588* Syria 1840 Belgian Coast 1914 Atlantic 1943-44	Martinique 1809 China 1842 Arctic 1941-42	Guadeloupe 1810 New Zealand 1845-47 Sicily 1943
Hazel	Atlantic 1942-44		
Heartsease	Armada 1588*	Gabbard 1653	Atlantic 1940-41
Hearty	Glückstadt 1814		
Hearty Anne	Armada 1588*		
Heathen	Armada 1588*		

Heather	Atlantic 1940-45 English Channel 1944-45	Arctic 1943	Normandy 1944
Hebe	St. Lucia 1796 Arctic 1941-42	Egypt 1801 Malta Convoys 1942	Dunkirk 1940 Sicily 1943
Hebrus	'*Étoile*' 1814	Algiers 1816	
Hecate	Java 1811		
Hecla	Copenhagen 1801 Alexandria 1882	Algiers 1816 Falkland Islands 1982	Baltic 1854 Kuwait 1991
Hector	Egypt 1801	Dardanelles 1915-16	
Hedgehog	Aegean 1943		
Helicon	Alexandria 1882		
Heliotrope	Dardanelles 1915-16	Atlantic 1940-42	
Helmsdale	Atlantic 1943-44		
Helverson	Orfordness 1666		
Hengist	North Africa 1942-43	Salerno 1943	
Henrietta	Lowestoft 1665 Schooneveld 1673	Four Days' Battle 1666 Texel 1673	Orfordness 1666
Henry	Lowestoft 1665 Sole Bay 1672	Four Days' Battle 1666 Schooneveld 1673	Orfordness 1666 Texel 1673
Hepatica	Atlantic 1940-45		
Herald	China 1841	Falkland Islands 1982	Kuwait 1991
Hercules	Armada 1588* The Saints 1782	Cadiz 1596* Jutland 1916	Quiberon Bay 1759
Hereward	Atlantic 1940 Libya 1940 Greece 1941	Calabria 1940 Mediterranean 1940-41 Crete 1941	Spartivento 1940 Matapan 1941 Malta Convoys 1941
Hermes	Burma 1852	Atlantic 1940	Falkland Islands 1982
Hermione	'*Bismarck*' 1941 Diego Suarez 1942	Mediterranean 1941	Malta Convoys 1941-42
Hero	Quiberon Bay 1759 Providien 1782 Bay of Biscay 1805 Norway 1940 Greece 1941 Libya 1941-42	Belle Isle 1761 Negapatam 1782 Basque Roads 1809 Calabria 1940 Crete 1941 Malta Convoys 1941-42	Sadras 1782 Trincomalee 1782 Narvik 1940 Spada 1940 Mediterranean 1941 Sirte 1942
Heroine	Egypt 1801	Normandy 1944	

Heron	Algiers 1816	Atlantic 1940	
Herschell	Atlantic 1943	English Channel 1943	Normandy 1944
Hertfordshire	Atlantic 1943		
Hespeler	Atlantic 1944-45		
Hesper	Java 1811	China 1856-60	
Hesperus	Norway 1940	Atlantic 1940-45	English Channel 1945
Heythrop	Atlantic 1941	Malta Convoys 1941-42	Libya 1941-42
Hibernia	Dardanelles 1915-16		
Hibiscus	Atlantic 1940-42		
Highflyer	Crimea 1854-55	China 1856-60	
Highlander	Norway 1940	Atlantic 1940-45	
Highway	South France 1944		
Hilary	Atlantic 1941-42 Normandy 1944	Sicily 1943	Salerno 1943
Himalaya	New Zealand 1863-66	Ashantee 1873-74	Suez Canal 1915
Hind	Quebec 1759 Heligoland 1914	Navarino 1827 Normandy 1944	Baltic 1855
Hobart	Mediterranean 1941 Guadalcanal 1942-43	Coral Sea 1942 Pacific 1945	Savo Island 1942 Vietnam 1967-70
Hogue	Baltic 1854-55	Heligoland 1914	
Holcombe	Sicily 1943	Salerno 1943	Mediterranean 1943
Holderness	North Sea 1942-45		
Holdfast	Normandy 1944		
Holly	San Sebastian 1813		
Hollyhock	Atlantic 1940-41		
Holmes	Normandy 1944 English Channel 1944-45	North Sea 1944	Atlantic 1944-45
Homeguard	Atlantic 1944-45		
Honesty	Atlantic 1943		
Honeysuckle	Dardanelles 1915-16 Sicily 1943	Atlantic 1940-45 English Channel 1944	Arctic 1942-45 Normandy 1944
Hong Kong	China 1856-60		

Hood	*'Bismarck'* 1941		
Hope	Armada 1588	Barfleur 1692	Cape of Good Hope 1795
Hope Hawkyns	Armada 1588*		
Hopeful Luke	Gabbard 1653		
Hopewell	Armada 1588*	Texel 1673	Barfleur 1692
Horatio	English Channel 1942	North Africa 1942	
Hornbeam	English Channel 1942	North Sea 1943	Normandy 1944
Hornet	China 1856-60	Dogger Bank 1915	
Hornpipe	Atlantic 1940	North Sea 1941-43	Anzio 1944
Horseman	Lowestoft 1665		
Hoste	Atlantic 1944		
Hostile	Atlantic 1939-40 Calabria 1940	Narvik 1940	Norway 1940
Hotham	Normandy 1944		
Hotspur	Narvik 1940 Atlantic 1940-44 Crete 1941	Spartivento 1940 Matapan 1941 Libya 1941-42	Mediterranean 1940-41 Greece 1941 Normandy 1944
Hound	Gabbard 1653 Four Days' Battle 1666 Normandy 1944	Scheveningen 1653 Barfleur 1692	Lowestoft 1665 Arctic 1943-44
House of Sweeds	Four Days' Battle 1666(de Swyte)		Orfordness 1666
Hoverfly	Mesopotamia 1917		
Howard	Cadiz 1596*		
Howe	Arctic 1942-43	Sicily 1943	Okinawa 1945
Hoy	North Africa 1942		
Hoy of Sandwich	Cadiz 1596*		
Huddersfield Town	Atlantic 1940		
Hugh Walpole	Atlantic 1941-43	Arctic 1941-42	Normandy 1944
Humber	Belgian Coast 1914	Dardanelles 1915	
Humberstone	Atlantic 1944-45		
Hunda	North Africa 1942-43		

Hunter	Gabbard 1653	Scheveningen 1653	Barfleur 1692
	Vigo 1702	Velez Malaga 1704	Louisburg 1758
	Quebec 1759	Atlantic 1939-40	Narvik 1940
	Salerno 1943	Atlantic 1943-44	South France 1944
	Aegean 1944	Burma 1945	
Huntley	Libya 1941		
Huntsville	Atlantic 1944-45		
Huron	Arctic 1943-45	English Channel 1944	Normandy 1944
	Korea 1951-53		
Hurricane	Atlantic 1940-44	Biscay 1943	
Hursley	Mediterranean 1942-43	Sicily 1943	Aegean 1943
Hurst Castle	Atlantic 1944		
Hurworth	Atlantic 1941	Sirte 1942	Mediterranean 1942
	Malta Convoys 1942	Libya 1942	Sicily 1943
	Aegean 1943	Kuwait 1991	
Husky	Atlantic 1940		
Hussar	'Raison' 1795	Java 1811	Dardanelles 1915-16
	Arctic 1941-44	North Africa 1942-43	Atlantic 1943
	Normandy 1944		
Hutchins	Armada 1588*		
Hyacinth	China 1841-42	Spartivento 1940	Greece 1941
	Malta Convoys 1941	Libya 1941-42	Mediterranean 1941-43
	Sicily 1943	East Indies 1943	
Hyderabad	Atlantic 1942-45	Arctic 1942-43	Barents Sea 1942
	North Sea 1942	Sicily 1943	English Channel 1943
Hydra	Syria 1840	Dogger Bank 1915	Jutland 1916
	North Sea 1943	Arctic 1943-44	Normandy 1944
	Falkland Islands 1982		
Hydrangea	Atlantic 1941-44	English Channel 1945	
Hyena	St. Vincent 1780		
Hyperion	Atlantic 1939	Calabria 1940	Spada 1940
	Libya 1940	Mediterranean 1940	
Hythe	Malta Convoys 1942	Sicily 1943	
Ibis	Atlantic 1941-42	North Africa 1942	
Ibis II	Normandy 1944		

Icarus Atlantic 1939-44 North Sea 1939 Narvik 1940
Norway 1940-41 Dunkirk 1940 *'Bismarck'* 1941
Arctic 1941-43 Malta Convoys 1942 Normandy 1944
English Channel 1945

Ideshire English Channel 1942

Ijuin English Channel 1942 Normandy 1944

Ilex Atlantic 1939 Calabria 1940 Spada 1940
Mediterranean 1940-43 Matapan 1941 Crete 1941
Malta Convoys 1941 Sicily 1943 Salerno 1943

Ilfracombe Dieppe 1942 English Channel 1942 North Africa 1942
Atlantic 1943-45 Normandy 1944

Illustrious Genoa 1795 Basque Roads 1809 Java 1811
Taranto 1940 Mediterranean 1940-41 Malta Convoys 1941
Diego Suarez 1942 Salerno 1943 Sabang 1944
East Indies 1944 Palembang 1945 Okinawa 1945

Imersay East Indies 1945

Imhoff Libya 1942

Imogen Atlantic 1939 North Sea 1940

Imperial Atlantic 1939 Norway 1940 Crete 1941
Mediterranean 1941

Imperialist Atlantic 1941-43 North Africa 1942

Imperieuse Basque Roads 1809 Baltic 1854-55 China 1860

Impetueux *'Cerbère'* 1800

Implacable *'Sevolod'* 1808 Syria 1840 Dardanelles 1915
Norway 1944 Japan 1945

Impregnable First of June 1794 Algiers 1816

Impulsive Norway 1940 Dunkirk 1940 Arctic 1941-44
Atlantic 1942-43 English Channel 1944 Normandy 1944

Incendiary First of June 1794 Groix Island 1795

Inchcolm North Africa 1942-43

Inchgower English Channel 1942

Inchkeith Atlantic 1942

Inchmarnock Atlantic 1942 North Africa 1942-43 Sicily 1943

Inconstant Genoa 1795 Egypt 1801 Jutland 1916
Diego Suarez 1942 Arctic 1942-44 Atlantic 1943-44
Sicily 1943 English Channel 1944 Normandy 1944

Indefatigable	*'Virginie'* 1796 Jutland 1916 Okinawa 1945	*'Droits de l'Homme'* 1797 East Indies 1945 Japan 1945	Basque Roads 1809 Palembang 1945
Indian Star	Atlantic 1940-42	North Sea 1941-42	Arctic 1942
Indomitable	Dogger Bank 1915 Diego Suarez 1942 Palembang 1945	Jutland 1916 Sicily 1943 Okinawa 1945	Malta Convoys 1942 East Indies 1944-45
Industry	Gabbard 1653	Crimea 1854-55	
Infernal	Belle Isle 1761	Algiers 1816	
Inflexible	Lake Champlain 1776 Crimea 1854-55 Falkland Islands 1914	Egypt 1801 China 1856-60 Dardanelles 1915	New Zealand 1845-47 Alexandria 1882 Jutland 1916
Inglefield	Atlantic 1939-43 *'Bismarck'* 1941 Sicily 1943 Mediterranean 1944	North Sea 1940 Malta Convoys 1942 Salerno 1943	Norway 1940-42 Arctic 1942-43 Anzio 1944
Inglis	Normandy 1944	Atlantic 1944-45	
Ingonish	Atlantic 1944		
Inkpen	Atlantic 1942		
Inman	Atlantic 1944-45		
Insolent	Basque Roads 1809	China 1856-60	
Intrepid	Lagos 1759 St. Kitts 1782 Atlantic 1939-41 Norway 1941-42 Sicily 1943 Falkland Islands 1982	Quiberon Bay 1759 Martinique 1809 Dunkirk 1940 Arctic 1941-43 Salerno 1943	Havana 1762 Zeebrugge 1918 *'Bismarck'* 1941 Malta Convoys 1942 Aegean 1943
Inver	Atlantic 1943-45		
Invercauld	North Sea 1942		
Inverforth	Dunkirk 1940		
Invicta	Dieppe 1942	Normandy 1944	
Invincible	St. Vincent 1780 Alexandria 1882 Jutland 1916	St. Kitts 1782 Heligoland 1914 Falkland Islands 1982	First of June 1794 Falkland Islands 1914
Iphigenia	Egypt 1801	Zeebrugge 1918	
Ipswich	Sicily 1943	East Indies 1944	
Iris	Chesapeake 1781 English Channel 1942	New Zealand 1860-61 Falkland Islands 1982*	Belgian Coast 1918

Iris II	Zeebrugge 1918		
Irishman	Falkland Islands 1982*		
Iron Duke	Jutland 1916		
Iroquois	Atlantic 1943 Norway 1945	Arctic 1943-45 Korea 1952-53	Biscay 1943-44
Irresistible	Martinique 1794 Belgian Coast 1941	Groix Island 1795 Dardanelles 1915	St. Vincent 1797
Isis	St. Lucia 1778 Negapatam 1782 Copenhagen 1801 Greece 1941 Sicily 1943	Sadras 1782 Trincomalee 1782 Atlantic 1939-43 Crete 1941 Normandy 1944	Providien 1782 Camperdown 1797 Norway 1940 Mediterranean 1941-43
Islay	Mediterranean 1942	Sicily 1943	
Isle of Guernsey	Dunkirk 1940*		
Isle of Thanet	Dunkirk 1940*		
Isobel	Normandy 1944		
Istria	English Channel 1945		
Itchen	Atlantic 1943		
Ithuriel	Atlantic 1942	Malta Convoys 1942	North Africa 1942
Ivanhoe	Atlantic 1939	Norway 1940	Dunkirk 1940
Jacinth	Atlantic 1940		
Jackal	Heligoland 1914 Norway 1940 Mediterranean 1941	Dogger Bank 1915 English Channel 1940 Libya 1941-42	Atlantic 1939-41 Crete 1941
Jackdaw	Baltic 1855		
Jacketa	Dunkirk 1940		
Jacob	Armada 1588*	Cadiz 1596*	
Jacqueline Clasine	Normandy 1944		
Jade	Mediterranean 1941		
Jaguar	Dunkirk 1940 Matapan 1941 Libya 1941-42	Atlantic 1940 Crete 1941 Malta Convoys 1941-42	Spartivento 1940 Mediterranean 1941
Jamaica	Copenhagen 1801 Barents Sea 1942	Arctic 1942-44 North Cape 1943	North Africa 1942 Korea 1950

James	Dover 1652	Kentish Knock 1652	Gabbard 1653
	Scheveningen 1653		
James Lay	Normandy 1944		
James Watt	Baltic 1854-55		
Jane Bonaventure	Armada 1588*		
Janissary	Egypt 1801		
Janus	Baltic 1854	China 1856-60	Atlantic 1939
	Norway 1940	Libya 1940	Calabria 1940
	Mediterranean 1940-44	Matapan 1941	Sfax 1941
	Crete 1941	Malta Convoys 1941	Anzio 1944
	Adriatic 1944		
Jardine	Norway 1940		
Jaseur	Atlantic 1945		
Jasmine	Atlantic 1941-42	Diego Suarez 1942	
Jason	Atlantic 1940	North Sea 1941-42	Arctic 1943
	Normandy 1944		
Jasper	Crimea 1855	Atlantic 1940	English Channel 1942
	North Sea 1945		
Jaunty	North Africa 1942-43		
Javelin	Atlantic 1940	Norway 1940	Dunkirk 1940
	Diego Suarez 1942	Mediterranean 1942-43	Arctic 1942
	English Channel 1944	Normandy 1944	
Jed	Dardanelles 1915-16	Atlantic 1943-44	Burma 1945
Jefferies	Velez Malaga 1704		
Jersey	Santa Cruz 1657	Lowestoft 1665	Orfordness 1666
	Lagos 1759	Mediterranean 1941	
Jervis	Libya 1940-42	Mediterranean 1940-44	Matapan 1941
	Sfax 1941	Crete 1941	Malta Convoys 1941-42
	Sirte 1942	Sicily 1943	Salerno 1943
	Aegean 1943	Anzio 1944	Adriatic 1944
	Normandy 1944		
Jervis Bay	Atlantic 1940	'*Admiral Scheer*' 1940	
Jewel	Armada 1588*		
John	Armada 1588*		
John and Abigail	Gabbard 1653	Lowestoft 1665	
John and Francis	Cadiz 1596*		

John and Katherine	Scheveningen 1653	Lowestoft 1665	
John and Thomas	Lowestoft 1665	Orfordness 1666	
John Cattling	Dunkirk 1940		
John Trelawney	Armada 1588*		
John Young	Armada 1588*		
Joliette	Atlantic 1944		
Jonas	Armada 1588*	Cadiz 1596*	
Jonathan	Cadiz 1596*	Gabbard 1653	
Jonquiere	Atlantic 1944		
Jonquil	Dardanelles 1915 North Africa 1942	Atlantic 1941-45	Malta Convoys 1942
Joshua	Cadiz 1596*		
Jude	Normandy 1944		
Juliet	Atlantic 1942 Sicily 1943	English Channel 1942	North Africa 1942-43
Julnar	Mesopotamia 1916		
Jumna	Atlantic 1941 Burma 1944-45	Sicily 1943	East Indies 1944
Junella	Falkland Islands 1982		
Juniper	San Sebastian 1813	Norway 1940	
Juno	Louisburg 1758 Libya 1940 Crete 1941	Atlantic 1939 Mediterranean 1940-41 Malta Convoys 1941	Calabria 1940 Matapan 1941
Jupiter	Cape of Good Hope 1795 Malaya 1942	China 1841-42	Mediterranean 1941
Jupiter II	Belgian Coast 1915-16		
Jura	North Sea 1942	North Africa 1942-43	
Kai	Libya 1941		
Kalan	English Channel 1942		
Kale	Atlantic 1943		
Kalgoorlie	Pacific 1942	Okinawa 1945	

Kamloops	Atlantic 1941-45		
Kamsack	Atlantic 1942-45		
Kandahar	East Indies 1940 Libya 1941	Greece 1941 Mediterranean 1941	Crete 1941 Malta Convoys 1941
Kangaroo	Egypt 1801	Belgian Coast 1914-16	
Kaniere	Korea 1953		
Kapunda	New Guinea 1943-44		
Kapuskasing	Atlantic 1944-45		
Karanja	Diego Suarez 1942	North Africa 1942	
Kashmir	North Sea 1939	Crete 1941	Mediterranean 1941
Katharine	Armada 1588*		
Katherine	Portland 1653 Sole Bay 1672	Lowestoft 1665 Texel 1673	Orfordness 1666
Kathiawar	Burma 1944-45		
Katoomba	New Guinea 1942-44		
Keats	Normandy 1944	Atlantic 1944-45	
Kedah	Burma 1944-45		
Keith	Atlantic 1939-40	Dunkirk 1940	
Kellett	Dunkirk 1940	North Sea 1943	Normandy 1944
Kelly	Atlantic 1939 Crete 1941	Norway 1940	Mediterranean 1941
Kelvin	Atlantic 1940 Mediterranean 1941-43 Aegean 1944	Spartivento 1940 Malta Convoys 1942 Normandy 1944	Crete 1941 Sirte 1942
Kempenfelt	Jutland 1916 Normandy 1944	Atlantic 1939 Okinawa 1945	Anzio 1944
Kempthorne	Atlantic 1944-45		
Kempton	Belgian Coast 1917		
Kenilworth Castle	Atlantic 1944	North Sea 1945	
Kennet	Dardanelles 1915-16	North Sea 1941	
Kennington	Louisburg 1758		
Kenogomi	Atlantic 1941-45		

Kenora	Atlantic 1942-45	Normandy 1944	
Kent	Porto Farina 1655	Lowestoft 1665	Orfordness 1666
	Barfleur 1692	Vigo 1702	Velez Malaga 1704
	Passero 1718	Ushant 1747	Egypt 1801
	Falkland Islands 1914	Atlantic 1940	Mediterranean 1940
	Arctic 1942-43	Norway 1944	
Kentish	Portland 1653	Gabbard 1653	
Kentville	Atlantic 1944-45		
Kenya	Atlantic 1941	'*Bismarck*' 1941	Malta Convoys 1941-42
	Arctic 1941-42	Norway 1941	Sabang 1944
	Burma 1944-45	Korea 1950-51	
Keppel	Atlantic 1940-43	Malta Convoys 1942	Arctic 1942-45
	Normandy 1944	English Channel 1944	
Keren	Diego Suarez 1942	North Africa 1942	Sicily 1943
	South France 1944		
Kerneval	Normandy 1944		
Kerrera	Atlantic 1942	North Africa 1942	Sicily 1943
Kestrel	China 1856-60		
Khartoum	East Indies 1940		
Khedive	Aegean 1944	South France 1944	East Indies 1945
	Burma 1945		
Khyber	Atlantic 1942	Burma 1945	
Kiama	New Guinea 1944	Pacific 1945	
Kilbirnie	Atlantic 1944-45		
Kilbride	Atlantic 1944		
Killarney	Dunkirk 1940*		
Killegray	North Sea 1942	Atlantic 1942	
Kilmarnock	Mediterranean 1944	Atlantic 1944-45	
Kilmartin	Atlantic 1944-45		
Kimelford	Atlantic 1944-45		
Kilmington	Atlantic 1945		
Kilmore	Atlantic 1945		
Kimberley	Narvik 1940	Norway 1940	East Indies 1940
	Greece 1941	Crete 1941	Libya 1941-42
	Malta Convoys 1941	Aegean 1944	Adriatic 1944

Kincardine	Atlantic 1944-45		
King Ferdinando	Gabbard 1653	Lowestoft 1665	
King George	Camperdown 1797	Basque Roads 1809	
King George V	Jutland 1916	Dunkirk 1940*	Atlantic 1941
	'*Bismarck*' 1941	Arctic 1942-43	Sicily 1943
	Okinawa 1945	Japan 1945	
King Orry	Dunkirk 1940		
King Sol	Atlantic 1940-43	Arctic 1942	Sicily 1943
Kingcup	Atlantic 1941-45	Normandy 1944	North Sea 1944
	English Channel 1944-45		
Kingfisher	Sardinia 1681	San Domingo 1806	Dunkirk 1940
Kings Grey	North Sea 1942	Normandy 1944	
Kingsmill	Normandy 1944	Walcheren 1944	English Channel 1944
Kingston	Gibraltar 1704	Velez Malaga 1704	Louisburg 1758
	Quiberon Bay 1759	Atlantic 1939	North Sea 1939
	East Indies 1940	Greece 1941	Crete 1941
	Malta Convoys 1941-42	Libya 1941	Sirte 1942
Kingston Agate	North Sea 1942	Atlantic 1944	
Kingston Alalite	Dunkirk 1940		
Kingston Amber	North Sea 1942	Atlantic 1943-44	
Kingston Andalusite	Dunkirk 1940	English Channel 1942	Normandy 1944
Kingston Beryl	Atlantic 1942		
Kingston Chrysoberyl	English Channel 1940-43	Normandy 1944	
Kingston Chrysolite	Atlantic 1940-43	North Africa 1942	
Kingston Coral	Libya 1942		
Kingston Crsytal	Libya 1942		
Kingston Olivina	North Sea 1942		
Kingston Olivine	Dunkirk 1940		
Kintyre	North Sea 1942	North Africa 1942-43	South France 1944
Kipling	Norway 1940	Atlantic 1940	Crete 1941
	Mediterranean 1941	Malta Convoys 1941-42	Libya 1941-42
	Sirte 1942		

133

Kirkella	Atlantic 1942-44		
Kistna	Atlantic 1943	Burma 1944-45	
Kitchener	Atlantic 1942-43	Normandy 1944	English Channel 1944-45
Kite	Atlantic 1943-44 Arctic 1944	Biscay 1943	Normandy 1944
Kittiwake	North Sea 1941-44	English Channel 1942	
Kiwi	Atlantic 1942	Guadalcanal 1942-43	
Klo	Libya 1941-42		
Knaresborough Castle	Atlantic 1944-45		
Kokanee	Atlantic 1944-45		
Konkan	Atlantic 1942	Burma 1944-45	
Kootenay	Atlantic 1943-45 Normandy 1944	English Channel 1944	Biscay 1944
Kos 19	see **Cocker**		
Kos 21	see **Whippet**		
Kos 22	Crete 1941		
Kos 23	Crete 1941		
Kumaon	Burma 1945		
La Hulloise	Atlantic 1945		
La Malbaie	Atlantic 1942-45		
La Malouine	Atlantic 1940-43	Arctic 1942	
La Nantaise	Normandy 1944		
Labuan	English Channel 1945		
Lacennia	Atlantic 1941-45		
Lacerta	North Sea 1942		
Lachine	Atlantic 1942-45		
Lachlan	Pacific 1945		
Lachute	Atlantic 1945		
Laconia	Atlantic 1940-41		

Lady Beryl	Atlantic 1943-44		
Lady Elsa	Atlantic 1940-42		
Lady Estelle	North Sea 1942		
Lady Hogarth	Atlantic 1941-45		
Lady Ismay	Belgian Coast 1915		
Lady Lillian	Atlantic 1940		
Lady Madeleine	Atlantic 1940-45	North Sea 1942	Arctic 1942-3
Lady of Mann	Dunkirk 1940*		
Lady Philomena	Dunkirk 1940		
Lady Shirley	Atlantic 1941		
Ladybird	Libya 1940-41	Mediterranean 1940-41	
Laertes	Heligoland 1914	Dogger Bank 1915	
Laforey	Heligoland 1914 Malta Convoys 1941-42 Sicily 1943 Anzio 1944	Dogger Bank 1915 Diego Suarez 1942 Salerno 1943	Dardanelles 1915-16 Atlantic 1942 Mediterranean 1943-44
Lagan	Atlantic 1943		
Lahore	Burma 1945		
Lamb	Armada 1588*		
Lamerton	Atlantic 1941-42 Sicily 1943 Mediterranean 1943	Arctic 1942 Salerno 1943 Adriatic 1944	North Africa 1942-43 Aegean 1943
Lanark	Atlantic 1944-45		
Lancaster	Louisburg 1758 Arctic 1942	Camperdown 1797 North Sea 1943-45	Atlantic 1941
Lancaster Castle	Arctic 1945		
Lance	Heligoland 1914 Malta Convoys 1941-42	Belgian Coast 1917	Mediterranean 1941
Lancer	Atlantic 1943-45	Normandy 1944	
Land of Promise	Orfordness 1666		
Landguard	Atlantic 1941-43	North Africa 1942	Biscay 1943
Landrail	Heligoland 1914	Dogger Bank 1915	Jutland 1916
Langlaate	Libya 1942	Aegean 1944	

Langport	Santa Cruz 1657		
Lanner	Crete 1941		
Lapwing	Heligoland 1914 Jutland 1916 Arctic 1944-45	Belgian Coast 1914 Normandy 1944	Dogger Bank 1915 North Sea 1944
Largs	Atlantic 1942 Mediterranean 1943	North Africa 1942 Normandy 1944	Sicily 1943 Burma 1945
Lark	Armada 1588* Baltic 1855 Normandy 1944 Arctic 1944-45	Velez Malaga 1704 Heligoland 1914 English Channel 1944	Marbella 1705 Dogger Bank 1915 North Sea 1944
Larkspur	Atlantic 1941		
Larne	Burma 1824-26 Normandy 1944	China 1841 South France 1944	Aegean 1944
Larwood	Norway 1940		
Lasalle	Atlantic 1945		
Latimer	Normandy 1944		
Latona	Dogger Bank 1781 Libya 1941	First of June 1794	Curaçoa 1807
Latrobe	New Guinea 1943-44	Pacific 1945	
Lauderdale	North Sea 1942 Mediterranean 1943	Atlantic 1942 South France 1944	Sicily 1943 Adriatic 1944
Launceston	Belle Isle 1761	East Indies 1944	Okinawa 1945
Launceston Castle	Atlantic 1944		
Laura	Guadeloupe 1810		
Laurel	Portland 1653 Heligoland 1914 Jutland 1916	Gabbard 1653 Belgian Coast 1914-16 North Africa 1942	Scheveningen 1653 Dogger Bank 1915
Lauzon	Atlantic 1944-45		
Lavender	Atlantic 1941-45	English Channel 1944	Normandy 1944
Laverock	Normandy 1944		
Lawford	Heligoland 1914 Normandy 1944	Dogger Bank 1915	Dardanelles 1915-16
Lawrence	Mesopotamia 1914-15		
Lawson	Atlantic 1944	Normandy 1944	

Leamington	Atlantic 1941-43	Arctic 1942	
Leander	Nile 1798 Kula Gulf 1943	Algiers 1816	Crimea 1854-55
Leaside	Atlantic 1944-45		
Leda	Egypt 1801 Atlantic 1939-41	Cape of Good Hope 1806 Dunkirk 1940	Java 1811 Arctic 1941-42
Ledbury	Malta Convoys 1942 Salerno 1943 Kuwait 1991	Arctic 1942-43 Adriatic 1944	Sicily 1943 Aegean 1944
Lee	China 1856-59		
Leeds	North Sea 1941-45		
Leeds Castle	Atlantic 1945	Falkland Islands 1982	
Leeds United	Atlantic 1940	English Channel 1942	
Legion	Heligoland 1914 Atlantic 1941 Mediterranean 1941	Dogger Bank 1915 Cape Bon 1941 Malta Convoys 1941-42	Norway 1941 Libya 1941-42 Sirte 1942
Leicester	Armada 1588*		
Leicester City	North Sea 1943-44		
Leith	Atlantic 1939-44	North Africa 1942	English Channel 1945
Lennox(*Lenox)**	***Barfleur 1692 ***Passero 1718 East Indies 1945	***Gibraltar 1704 Heligoland 1914	***Velez Malaga 1704 Normandy 1944
Leonian	Normandy 1944		
Leonidas	Heligoland 1914		
Leopard	Lowestoft 1665 Sole Bay 1672 Egypt 1801	Four Days' Battle 1666 Texel 1673 Baltic 1854	Orfordness 1666 Marbella 1705 Crimea 1855
Lephreto	Normandy 1944		
Lerwick	English Channel 1942		
Lethbridge	Atlantic 1941-45		
Letitia	Atlantic 1939-40		
Levant	Martinique 1762		
Leven	China 1856-60	Belgian Coast 1915-16	
Leviathan	First of June 1794	Minorca 1798	Trafalgar 1805
Levis	Atlantic 1941-45		

Lewes	North Sea 1942		
Lewis Pelly	Mesopotamia 1914-15		
Leyland	Atlantic 1942	North Africa 1942	
Liberty	Martinique 1809 Jutland 1916	Heligoland 1914	Dogger Bank 1915
Liddesdale	North Sea 1941-43 Salerno 1943 Mediterranean 1944	Atlantic 1943 Aegean 1944	Sicily 1943 South France 1944
Liffey	Burma 1824-26		
Lightfoot	Belgian Coast 1916 Normandy 1944	Zeebrugge 1918 East Indies 1945	Atlantic 1943
Lightning	Barfleur 1692 Louisburg 1758 Diego Suarez 1942	Vigo 1702 Baltic 1854-55	Velez Malaga 1704 Malta Convoys 1941-42
Lilac	Normandy 1944		
Lilly	Four Days' Battle 1666		
Limbourne	English Channel 1942-43	North Sea 1943	
Linaria	Atlantic 1943		
Lincoln	Atlantic 1941-43	North Sea 1942-44	
Lincoln City	Atlantic 1940		
Lincolnshire	English Channel 1942-43	Normandy 1944	
Lindisfarne	Normandy 1944		
Lindsay	Normandy 1944	English Channel 1944	Atlantic 1944-45
Lingay	East Indies 1945		
Lingfield	Zeebrugge 1918		
Linnet	Heligoland 1914	North Africa 1942-43	
Lion	Armada 1588 Gabbard 1653 Schooneveld 1673 Ushant 1747 Java 1811 Jutland 1916	Cadiz 1596 Lowestoft 1665 Texel 1673 '*Santa Dorotea*' 1798 Heligoland 1914	Portland 1653 Orfordness 1666 Barfleur 1692 '*Guillaume Tell*' 1800 Dogger Bank 1915
Lioness	Cadiz 1596*	English Channel 1945	
Lion's Whelp	Cadiz 1596		
Lisbon Merchant	Portland 1653	Gabbard 1653	

Lismore	Sicily 1943	Okinawa 1945	
Lithgow	New Guinea 1942-44	Pacific 1945	
Little Hare	Armada 1588*		
Little John	Armada 1588*		
Little Katherine	Four Days' Battle 1666		
Little Unicorn	Four Days' Battle 1666		
Little Victory	Bugia 1671		
Lively	*'Tourterelle'* 1795 Atlantic 1941 Libya 1942	St. Vincent 1797 Mediterranean 1941 Sirte 1942	*'Mutine'* 1797 Malta Convoys 1941-42
Liverpool	Heligoland 1914 Arctic 1942	Mediterranean 1940 Malta Convoys 1942	Calabria 1940
Lizard	Orfordness 1666 Martinique 1762 Belgian Coast 1914	Texel 1673 Havana 1762 Jutland 1916	Quebec 1759 Heligoland 1914
Llandudno	Normandy 1944		
Llanstephan Castle	Burma 1944-45*		
Llanthony	Dunkirk 1940		
Llewellyn	Heligoland 1914		
Lobelia	Atlantic 1941-44		
Loch Achanalt	English Channel 1945		
Loch Achray	Atlantic 1945		
Loch Alvie	Arctic 1944-45	English Channel 1945	
Loch Craggie	Atlantic 1945		
Loch Dunvegan	Arctic 1944	North Sea 1945	
Loch Eck	Atlantic 1945	North Sea 1945	
Loch Fada	Normandy 1944	English Channel 1945	Atlantic 1945
Loch Fyne	Atlantic 1945	English Channel 1945	
Loch Gary	Dunkirk 1940*		
Loch Glendhu	Atlantic 1945		
Loch Insh	Atlantic 1944	Arctic 1945	

Loch Killin	Normandy 1944 English Channel 1945	Atlantic 1944	Biscay 1944
Loch More	Atlantic 1945		
Loch Oskaig	North Africa 1942-43	Atlantic 1943	
Loch Quoich	Atlantic 1945		
Loch Ruthven	English Channel 1945	Atlantic 1945	
Loch Scavaig	Atlantic 1945		
Loch Shin	Norway 1940	Atlantic 1945	Arctic 1945
Loch Tulla	Atlantic 1944		
Lochinvar	Belgian Coast 1916-17		
Lochy	Normandy 1944		
Lockeport	Atlantic 1943		
Locust	Baltic 1854-55 English Channel 1942-44	Dunkirk 1940 Normandy 1944	Dieppe 1942
Loire	Guadeloupe 1810		
London	Kentish Knock 1652 Lowestoft 1665 Texel 1673 Groix Island 1795 Crimea 1854-55 Arctic 1941-43	Gabbard 1653 Sole Bay 1672 Barfleur 1692 Copenhagen 1801 Dardanelles 1915 East Indies 1944-45	Scheveningen 1653 Schooneveld 1673 Chesapeake 1781 '*Marengo*' 1806 Atlantic 1941 Kuwait 1991
London Merchant	Orfordness 1666		
Londonderry	Atlantic 1939-45 Normandy 1944	North Sea 1940 English Channel 1944-45	North Africa 1942-43
Long Branch	Atlantic 1944-45		
Longa	English Channel 1945		
Longueuil	Atlantic 1944-45		
Loo	Passero 1718		
Lookout	Heligoland 1914 Malta Convoys 1942 Sicily 1943 South France 1944	Dogger Bank 1915 Arctic 1942 Salerno 1943	Diego Suarez 1942 North Africa 1942-43 Mediterranean 1943-45
Loosestrife	Atlantic 1942-45 English Channel 1944-45	North Sea 1944	Normandy 1944
Lord Ashfield	Normandy 1944		

Lord Austin	North Sea 1942	Arctic 1942-43	Normandy 1944
Lord Caven	Dunkirk 1940		
Lord Clive	Belgian Coast 1915-18	Zeebrugge 1918	
Lord Essenden	English Channel 1942-43	Normandy 1944	
Lord Hailsham	English Channel 1942-43		
Lord Hotham	Atlantic 1940-42	North Africa 1942	
Lord Howard	Dunkirk 1940		
Lord Howe	Dunkirk 1940	English Channel 1942	North Sea 1942
Lord Inchcape	Dunkirk 1940		
Lord Melchett	Normandy 1944		
Lord Middleton	Arctic 1942	Atlantic 1942-44	Normandy 1944
Lord Nelson	Dardanelles 1915-1916		
Lord Nuffield	Atlantic 1942-44	North Africa 1942-43	
Lord Plender	North Sea 1944	English Channel 1945	
Lord Snowden	English Channel 1942		
Lord Stanhope	English Channel 1942-44	Atlantic 1943	Normandy 1944
Lord Stonehaven	English Channel 1942		
Lord Wakefield	English Channel 1943-44	Normandy 1944	
Lorina	Dunkirk 1940*		
Loring	Atlantic 1945		
Lossie	Atlantic 1943-44		
Lotus	North Africa 1942-43 Sicily 1943	Arctic 1942-45 Atlantic 1944-45	Mediterranean 1942
Louis	Heligoland 1914 Atlantic 1944	Dogger Bank 1915 Biscay 1944	Dardanelles 1915 Arctic 1944
Louisa	Gut of Gibraltar 1801		
Louisburg	Atlantic 1941-45	Normandy 1944	English Channel 1944-45
Lowestoffe	Quebec 1759	Genoa 1795	*'Minerve'* 1795
Lowestoft	Heligoland 1914 North Sea 1940-45	Dogger Bank 1915	Atlantic 1940-45

Loyal	Sicily 1943 Anzio 1944	Salerno 1943 Adriatic 1944	Mediterranean 1943
Loyal Convert	Lake Champlain 1776		
Loyal George	Lowestoft 1665	Four Days' Battle 1666	
Loyal London	Orfordness 1666		
Loyal Merchant	Lowestoft 1665	Orfordness 1666	
Loyalty	Gabbard 1653	Normandy 1944	Arctic 1944
Lucifer	Heligoland 1914	Dogger Bank 1915	Belgian Coast 1916
Ludlow	Atlantic 1941-42	North Sea 1942-45	
Lulworth	Atlantic 1941-43	North Africa 1942	Burma 1945
Lundy	English Channel 1943		
Lunenburg	Atlantic 1942-45 English Channel 1944	North Africa 1942-43	Normandy 1944
Lurcher	Havana 1762	Heligoland 1914	
Lycaon	Falkland Islands 1982*		
Lydd	Dunkirk 1940	North Sea 1942	Normandy 1944
Lydiard	Heligoland 1914 Jutland 1916	Dogger Bank 1915	Dardanelles 1915-16
Lyme	Santa Cruz 1657	Lagos 1759	
Lyme Regis	Normandy 1944		
Lynn	Belle Isle 1761		
Lynton	North Sea 1942		
Lynx	Crimea 1854-55		
Lyre	Basque Roads 1809	San Sebastian 1813	
Lysander	Heligoland 1914	Dogger Bank 1915	Belgian Coast 1915-16
Macbeth	Atlantic 1941-44	North Sea 1944	Arctic 1944
Macedonia	Falkland Islands 1914		
Mackay	Atlantic 1939-40 North Sea 1942-45	Dunkirk 1940 English Channel 1942-44	Arctic 1942 Normandy 1944
Maderas	Lowestoft 1665		
Madras	St. Lucia 1796	Egypt 1801	

Maenad	Jutland 1916		
Magic	Jutland 1916		
Magicienne	San Domingo 1806 Baltic 1854-55	San Sebastian 1813 China 1860	Syria 1840
Magnanime	Quiberon Bay 1759 Trincomalee 1782	Providien 1782 Donegal 1798	Negapatam 1782
Magnet	Crimea 1855		
Magnificent	The Saints 1782	Dardanelles 1915	
Magnolia	Atlantic 1942	North Sea 1942	
Magpie	Baltic 1855 Normandy 1944	Benin 1897 Arctic 1944	Atlantic 1943-44
Mahé	Aden 1839 (Indian Navy)		
Mahone	Atlantic 1942-45		
Mahratta	Arctic 1943-44		
Maid of Orleans	Dunkirk 1940*		
Maidstone	Santa Cruz 1657	Quiberon Bay 1759	North Africa 1942-43
Maine	Korea 1950** (Hospital Ship)		
Majestic	First of June 1794 Dardanelles 1915	Nile 1798	Baltic 1854-55
Majesty	Arctic 1942		
Makeshift	Armada 1588*		
Malaga Merchant	Gabbard 1653	Scheveningen 1653	
Malaya	Jutland 1916 Mediterranean 1940-41	Calabria 1940 Malta Convoys 1941-42	Atlantic 1940-41 English Channel 1944
Malcolm	North Sea 1940 Arctic 1942 English Channel 1943	Dunkirk 1940 Malta Convoys 1942	Atlantic 1940-45 North Africa 1942
Malines	Dunkirk 1940*	Atlantic 1941	Libya 1942
Mallard	North Sea 1941-43		
Mallow	Atlantic 1940-43	North Sea 1942	
Maloja	Atlantic 1940-41		
Malpeque	Atlantic 1941-42	Normandy 1944	
Malta	Egypt 1801		

Man-o-war	Atlantic 1940-45	North Sea 1941	Sicily 1943
Manchester	Norway 1940 Arctic 1942	Spartivento 1940 Kuwait 1991	Malta Convoys 1941-42
Mandate	Jutland 1916		
Mangrove	English Channel 1942		
Manica	Dardanelles 1915		
Manington	Armada 1588*		
Manly	Baltic 1855	Belgian Coast 1916-18	Zeebrugge 1918
Manners	Jutland 1916	Atlantic 1944-45	
Manor	English Channel 1942		
Mansfield	Belgian Coast 1916-18 Atlantic 1941-44	Zeebrugge 1918	Norway 1941
Mantis	Mesopotamia 1916-17		
Manxman	Dunkirk 1940*	Malta Convoys 1941-2	
Maori	Belgian Coast 1914-15 Cape Bon 1941	Norway 1940 Atlantic 1941	'*Bismarck*' 1941 Malta Convoys 1941-42
Maplin	Atlantic 1941-42		
Marauder	Normandy 1944		
Margaree	Atlantic 1940		
Margaret	Armada 1588*	Norway 1940	
Margaret and John	Armada 1588*		
Marguerite	Atlantic 1941		
Maria	Lake Champlain 1776		
Marie Jose Rosette	Normandy 1944		
Marigold	Armada 1588* North Africa 1942	Atlantic 1941-42	Mediterranean 1941
Marksman	Jutland 1916		
Marlborough	Martinique 1762 The Saints 1782	Havana 1762 First of June 1794	St. Vincent 1780 Jutland 1916
Marmaduke	Gabbard 1653	Lowestoft 1665	Orfordness 1666
Marmion	Dunkirk 1940		

Marmion II	Belgian Coast 1915		
Marne	Jutland 1916 Aegean 1944	Arctic 1942-44	Malta Convoys 1942
Maron	Atlantic 1941-42	North Sea 1942	
Mars	Quiberon Bay 1759 Trafalgar 1805	Cornwallis' Retreat 1795 Dardanelles 1915-16	*'Hercule'* 1798
Marsdale	Atlantic 1941-42		
Marshal Ney	Belgian Coast 1915		
Marshal Soult	Belgian Coast 1915-18	Zeebrugge 1918	
Martial	Basque Roads 1809	Jutland 1916	
Martin	Dover 1652 Lowestoft 1665 North Africa 1942	Portland 1653 Camperdown 1797 Atlantic 1942	Gabbard 1653 Arctic 1942
Martinet	Normandy 1944		
Marvel	Jutland 1916		
Mary	Gabbard 1653 Bugia 1671 Texel 1673	Lowestoft 1665 Sole Bay 1672 Vigo 1702	Orfordness 1666 Schooneveld 1673
Mary Ann	Cadiz 1596*		
Mary ketch	Portland 1653		
Mary Galley	Barfleur 1692		
Mary Margaret	Cadiz 1596*		
Mary Prize	Scheveningen 1653		
Mary Rose	Armada 1588 Four Days' Battle 1666 Sole Bay 1672 Jutland 1916	Cadiz 1596 Orfordness 1666 Schooneveld 1673 Scandanavian Convoys 1917	Lowestoft 1665 The Seven Algerines 1669 Texel 1673
Maryborough	Sicily 1943		
Marygold	Cadiz 1596*		
Maryland Merchant	Lowestoft 1665		
Mashona	Norway 1940	*'Bismarck'* 1941	
Massoudieh	Mesopotamia 1915		
Mastiff	Baltic 1855 Zeebrugge 1918	Dogger Bank 1915	Belgian Coast 1916-18

Matabele	Norway 1940	Arctic 1941-42	
Matane	Normandy 1944	Atlantic 1944	Arctic 1945
Matapedia	Atlantic 1941-45		
Matchless	Belgian Coast 1916-18 Malta Convoys 1942	Zeebrugge 1918 North Cape 1943	Arctic 1942-44
Mathias	Orfordness 1666		
Matthew	Armada 1588*		
Mauritius	Atlantic 1941 Mediterranean 1943-44 Biscay 1944	Sicily 1943 Anzio 1944 Norway 1945	Salerno 1943 Normandy 1944
May	Libya 1941		
Mayflower	Armada 1588* Normandy 1944	Scheveningen 1653 English Channel 1945	Atlantic 1941-43
Mayfly	Mesopotamia 1916-17		
Mazurka	North Sea 1941-42	Atlantic 1942-44	
Meadowsweet	Atlantic 1942-44		
Medea	Trincomalee 1782	Syria 1840	Belgian Coast 1916
Mediator	Basque Roads 1809		
Medicine Hat	Atlantic 1943		
Medina	Crimea 1854-55		
Medway	Quebec 1759	Ushant 1781	
Medway Queen	Dunkirk 1940		
Megaera	Groix Island 1795	Crimea 1854-55	
Melampe	Belle Isle 1761		
Melampus	Donegal 1798	Guadeloupe 1810	
Melbourne	Norway 1940		
Melbreak	English Channel 1943-44 North Sea 1945	Normandy 1944	Atlantic 1944-45
Meleager	Genoa 1795		
Melita	Normandy 1944	Atlantic 1945	East Indies 1945
Melpomene	Belgian Coast 1916-18	Zeebrugge 1918	
Melville	China 1841	Atlantic 1942-45	

146

Menace	Jutland 1916		
Mendip	. North Sea 1941-45 Salerno 1943	English Channel 1942-43 Mediterranean 1943	Sicily 1943 Normandy 1944
Menalaus	Belgian Coast 1915		
Menestheus	Atlantic 1941		
Mentor	Dogger Bank 1915	Belgian Coast 1917-18	Zeebrugge 1918
Meon	Normandy 1944	English Channel 1944	Atlantic 1944-45
Merceditta	Atlantic 1940		
Merchant Royal	Armada 1588*		
Mercury	Havana 1762		
Mere Honour	Cadiz 1596		
Merlin	Armada 1588 Scheveningen 1653 Ashantee 1873-74	Portland 1653 Port Farina 1655	Gabbard 1653 Baltic 1855
Mermaid	Cadiz 1596* Porto Farina 1655	Dover 1652 Belgian Coast 1914-17	Gabbard 1653 Arctic 1944
Merrittonia	Atlantic 1945		
Mersey	Belgian Coast 1914-15	*'Konigsberg'* 1915	
Meteor	Crimea 1855 Atlantic 1942-43 Mediterranean 1945	Dogger Bank 1915 North Africa 1942	Arctic 1942-44 Aegean 1944
Mewstone	South France 1944		
Meynell	English Channel 1941-43 Normandy 1944	North Sea 1941-45	Arctic 1943
Michael	Jutland 1916		
Midas	Dunkirk 1940		
Middleboro'	Gabbard 1653		
Middlesex	Atlantic 1944-45		
Middleton	Arctic 1942-43 Normandy 1944	Malta Convoys 1942 English Channel 1944	Atlantic 1944 North Sea 1944-45
Midge	Jutland 1916		
Midland	Atlantic 1942-45		
Mignonette	Atlantic 1941-45 English Channel 1945	Normandy 1944	North Sea 1944

Mikasa	Normandy 1944		
Milbrook	Jutland 1916		
Mildenhall	Atlantic 1939		
Mildura	New Guinea 1944		
Milford	Lowestoft 1665	Atlantic 1940-44	
Milford Countess	Libya 1941		
Milford Duchess	English Channel 1942		
Millet	North Sea 1942		
Milltown	Atlantic 1942-44	Normandy 1944	
Milne	Dogger Bank 1915 North Africa 1942	Belgian Coast 1916 Atlantic 1942-43	Arctic 1942-44
Mimico	Normandy 1944	English Channel 1945	Atlantic 1945
Mimosa	Atlantic 1941-42		
Minas	Atlantic 1941-44	Normandy 1944	
Minden	Java 1811	Algiers 1816	
Mindful	Jutland 1916		
Miner	Mesopotamia 1914-16		
Minerva	Quiberon Bay 1759 Falkland Islands 1982	Suez Canal 1915	Dardanelles 1915
Minerve	St. Vincent 1797	*'Mutine'* 1797	Egypt 1801
Minion	Armada 1588*	Cadiz 1596*	Jutland 1916
Minna	Crimea 1854	Atlantic 1943	
Minorca	Egypt 1801		
Minos	Dogger Bank 1915		
Minotaur	Nile 1798 Jutland 1916	Egypt 1801	Trafalgar 1805
Minster	North Sea 1942	Normandy 1944	
Minuet	North Sea 1941-43	Salerno 1943	
Mirabelle	Normandy 1944		
Miranda	Baltic 1854 Dogger Bank 1915	Crimea 1854-55 Belgian Coast 1916-18	New Zealand 1863-66

Mischief	Jutland 1916		
Miscou	Atlantic 1944		
Misoa	North Africa 1942	Mediterranean 1943	Normandy 1944
Moa	Atlantic 1941	Guadalcanal 1942-43	
Modeste	Martinique 1762 China 1841-42	Egypt 1801 Crimea 1854	Java 1811 Korea 1953
Mohawk	Belgian Coast 1915-16 Libya 1940 Sfax 1941	Norway 1940 Mediterranean 1940-41 Malta Convoys 1941	Calabria 1940 Matapan 1941
Monarca	Sadras 1782 Trincomalee 1782	Providien 1782	Negapatam 1782
Monarch	St. Vincent 1780 Cape of Good Hope 1795 Baltic 1854 Jutland 1916	St. Kitts 1782 Camperdown 1797 Alexandria 1882	The Saints 1782 Copenhagen 1801 South Africa 1899-1900
Mona's Isle	Dunkirk 1940	North Sea 1942-43	
Mona's Queen	Dunkirk 1940*		
Monck	Lowestoft 1665 Schooneveld 1673 Gibraltar 1704	Orfordness 1666 Texel 1673 Velez Malaga 1704	Sole Bay 1672 Barfleur 1692
Moncton	Atlantic 1942-43		
Mondovi	Egypt 1801		
Monkshood	Atlantic 1941-44	Biscay 1943	
Monmouth	Sole Bay 1672 Vigo 1702 Finisterre 1747 Belle Isle 1761 Negapatam 1782 Egypt 1801	Texel 1673 Gibraltar 1704 Ushant 1747 Sadras 1782 Trincomalee 1782	Barfleur 1692 Velez Malaga 1704 '*Foudroyant*' 1758 Providien 1782 Camperdown 1797
Monnow	Atlantic 1944-45	Arctic 1944-45	North Sea 1945
Mons	Jutland 1916		
Monsieur	Ushant 1781		
Montagu	St. Vincent 1780 First of June 1794	St. Kitts 1782 Camperdown 1797	The Saints 1782
Montbretia	Atlantic 1941-42		
Montclare	Atlantic 1939-41		
Montgomery	Atlantic 1941-43		

Montreal	Atlantic 1944-45		
Montrose	Atlantic 1939-40 North Sea 1942-44	Dunkirk 1940 English Channel 1943-44	Arctic 1942-43 Normandy 1944
Mooltan	Atlantic 1940		
Moon	Armada 1588	Cadiz 1596	Jutland 1916
Moonshine	Armada 1588*		
Moonstone	East Indies 1940		
Moorsman	Atlantic 1945		
Moorsom	Jutland 1916 Normandy 1944	Belgian Coast 1917-18 Atlantic 1944	Zeebrugge 1918 North Sea 1944
Moosejaw	Atlantic 1941-43	Normandy 1944	English Channel 1944-45
Morden	Atlantic 1941-45		
Morecambe Bay	Korea 1950-53		
Moresby	Jutland 1916		
Moreton Bay	Atlantic 1940		
Morne Fortunée	Curaçoa 1807	Guadeloupe 1810	
Morning Star	Jutland 1916		
Morpeth Castle	Atlantic 1944-45		
Morris	Dogger Bank 1915 Zeebrugge 1918	Jutland 1916	Belgian Coast 1917-18
Morris Dance	English Channel 1942	Atlantic 1943	
Mosambique	Martinique 1809		
Moselle	Genoa 1795	Cape of Good Hope 1795	
Moslem	Crimea 1855		
Mosquito	Navarino 1827	Dardanelles 1915	Dunkirk 1940
Moth	Mesopotamia 1916-17		
Mounsey	Jutland 1916 Arctic 1944	Normandy 1944	Atlantic 1944
Mountague	Lowestoft 1665 Barfleur 1692 Passero 1718	Orfordness 1666 Gibraltar 1704 Quiberon Bay 1759	Sole Bay 1672 Velez Malaga 1704
Mounts Bay	Korea 1950-53		

Mourne	Atlantic 1943-44	Normandy 1944	English Channel 1944
Mousa	English Channel 1942	Salerno 1943	
Moy	Libya 1941-42		
Moyola	Atlantic 1943-44		
Mulgrave	Atlantic 1943-44	Normandy 1944	
Mull	North Africa 1942-43	Mediterranean 1944	
Mullett	Sicily 1943		
Munster	Jutland 1916		
Murchison	Korea 1951-52		
Muroto	Greece 1941	Libya 1941	Normandy 1944
Murray	Belgian Coast 1916		
Musketeer	Arctic 1942-44 Aegean 1944	Atlantic 1943	North Cape 1943
Mutine	Nile 1798 Salerno 1943	Algiers 1816	Sicily 1943
Muzaffri	Mesopotamia 1915-16		
Myngs	Zeebrugge 1918	Norway 1944	Arctic 1944-45
Myosotis	Atlantic 1941-43	English Channel 1945	
Myrmidon	Belgian Coast 1914-16		
Mystic	Jutland 1916		
Nab Wyke	Atlantic 1941-44		
Nadder	East Indies 1944		
Naiad	Trafalgar 1805 Malta Convoys 1941-42	Crete 1941	Mediterranean 1941
Nairana	Atlantic 1944	Arctic 1944-45	Norway 1945
Namur	Velez Malaga 1704 Lagos 1759 The Saints 1782	Finisterre 1747 Quiberon Bay 1759 St. Vincent 1797	Louisburg 1758 Havana 1762 Bay of Biscay 1805
Nanaimo	Atlantic 1941-44		
Nankin	China 1856-60		
Nantwich	Santa Cruz 1657		

Napanee	Atlantic 1941-45		
Napier	Crete 1941 Okinawa 1945	Libya 1941	Burma 1944-45
Narbada	English Channel 1943	Burma 1944-45	
Narbrough	Jutland 1916 Atlantic 1945	Normandy 1944	English Channel 1944
Narcissus	Atlantic 1941-45	Normandy 1944	
Narwhal	Jutland 1916 Norway 1940	Atlantic 1939	North Sea 1940
Nasprite	North Africa 1942**		
Nassau	Gibraltar 1704	Velez Malaga 1704	
Nasturtium	Atlantic 1940-45	Normandy 1944	English Channel 1944-45
Natal	North Sea 1945		
Nautilus	Martinique 1794	Dunkirk 1940	
Neave	Normandy 1944		
Nebb	Libya 1941	South France 1944	
Negresse	Egypt 1801		
Negro	North Africa 1942-43		
Neil Mackay	North Sea 1941		
Neil Smith	Normandy 1944		
Nelson	Malta Convoys 1941-42 Salerno 1943	North Africa 1942-43 Mediterranean 1943	Sicily 1943 Normandy 1944
Nene	Biscay 1943 North Sea 1945	Atlantic 1943-44	Arctic 1944-45
Nepal	Burma 1944-45	Okinawa 1945	
Neptune	Barfleur 1692 Martinique 1809 Atlantic 1939 '*Bismarck*' 1941	Quebec 1759 Baltic 1854 Calabria 1940 Malta Convoys 1941	Trafalgar 1805 Jutland 1916 Mediterranean 1940
Nerissa	Jutland 1916		
Ness	Atlantic 1943-44	English Channel 1945	
Nessus	Jutland 1916		
Nestor	Jutland 1916 Malta Convoys 1941-42	'*Bismarck*' 1941	Atlantic 1941

152

Netley	Guadeloupe 1810		
Netsukis	Dunkirk 1940		
New Glasgow	Atlantic 1944-45		
New Waterford	Atlantic 1944		
New Westminster	Atlantic 1942-45		
New York City	Atlantic 1944		
New Zealand	Heligoland 1914	Dogger Bank 1915	Jutland 1916
Newark	Velez Malaga 1704 North Sea 1943-44	Lagos 1759	Atlantic 1941-42
Newbury	Santa Cruz 1657		
Newcastle	Porto Farina 1655 Orfordness 1666 Marbella 1705 Porto Novo 1759 Korea 1952-53	Santa Cruz 1657 Schooneveld 1673 Sadras 1758 Spartivento 1940	Lowestoft 1665 Texel 1673 Negapatam 1758 Burma 1944-45
Newfoundland	Mediterranean 1943	Sicily 1943	Japan 1945
Newmarket	Atlantic 1941-42	Arctic 1942	
Newport	Velez Malaga 1704 Arctic 1942	Atlantic 1941	English Channel 1942
Nguva	Burma 1944-45		
Niagara	Atlantic 1940-44		
Niblick	Normandy 1944		
Nicator	Jutland 1916		
Nicodemus	Portland 1653	Gabbard 1653	
Nigella	Atlantic 1941-42	Diego Suarez 1942	
Niger	First of June 1794 Crimea 1854-55 Dunkirk 1940	St. Vincent 1797 China 1856-60 Atlantic 1941	Egypt 1801 New Zealand 1860-61 Arctic 1941-42
Nigeria	Atlantic 1941 Malta Convoys 1942 East Indies 1945	Norway 1941 Sabang 1944	Arctic 1942 Burma 1944-45
Night Hawk	English Channel 1942		
Nightingale	Armada 1588* Lowestoft 1665 Martinique 1762	Kentish Knock 1652 Louisburg 1758	Portland 1653 Quebec 1759

Nile	Baltic 1854-55		
Nimrod	Basque Roads 1809 Belgian Coast 1917	China 1841	China 1856-60
Nipigon	Atlantic 1941-45		
Nisus	Java 1811		
Nith	Normandy 1944	Burma 1945	
Nizam	Malta Convoys 1941 Okinawa 1945	Crete 1941	Libya 1941
Noble	Jutland 1916		
Nomad	Jutland 1916		
Nonpareil	Armada 1588	Cadiz 1596	
Nonsuch	Kentish Knock 1652 Texel 1673 Jutland 1916	Portland 1653 St.Lucia 1778	Gabbard 1653 The Saints 1782
Nootka	Korea 1951-52		
Noranda	Atlantic 1943-45		
Nordic Ferry	Falkland Islands 1982*		
Norfolk	Velez Malaga 1704 Atlantic 1941 North Cape 1943	Norway 1940 Arctic 1941-43	'*Bismarck*' 1941 North Africa 1942
Norland	Falkland Islands 1982*		
Norman	Burma 1944-45	East Indies 1944	Okinawa 1945
Normania	Dunkirk 1940*		
Norsyd	Atlantic 1944-45		
North Bay	Atlantic 1944-45		
North Lynn	Normandy 1944		
North Star	China 1842	New Zealand 1845-47	Zeebrugge 1918
Northcoates	Normandy 1944		
Northella	Falkland Islands 1982		
Northern Dawn	Atlantic 1940-42		
Northern Foam	North Sea 1942	Atlantic 1943-45	Normandy 1944
Northern Gem	Norway 1940 Arctic 1942-43	Atlantic 1940-45 Normandy 1944	Barents Sea 1942

Northern Gift	Atlantic 1943-45	Normandy 1944	
Northern Pride	Atlantic 1940-45	Arctic 1942-43	Normandy 1944
Northern Reward	Atlantic 1943-45	Normandy 1944	
Northern Sky	Atlantic 1943-45	Normandy 1944	
Northern Spray	Atlantic 1940-45	Arctic 1942	Normandy 1944
Northern Sun	Atlantic 1942-45	North Sea 1942	Normandy 1944
Northern Wave	Atlantic 1939-45	Arctic 1942-43	Normandy 1944
Northumberland	Barfleur 1692	Vigo 1702	Louisburg 1758
	Quebec 1759	Egypt 1801	San Domingo 1806
	Groix Island 1812		
Northward Ho	English Channel 1942		
Northway	Normandy 1944		
Norwich	Scheveningen 1653	Puerto Bello 1739	Martinique 1762
Norwich City	Atlantic 1940-42		
Notre Dame de France	English Channel 1942-43	Normandy 1944	
Nottingham	Gibraltar 1704	Velez Malaga 1704	Marbella 1705
	Finisterre 1747	Ushant 1747	'*Magnanime*' 1748
	Louisburg 1758	Martinique 1762	Havana 1762
	Heligoland 1914	Dogger Bank 1915	Jutland 1916
Notts County	Atlantic 1940-42	Arctic 1942	
Nubian	Belgian Coast 1914-15	Norway 1940	Calabria 1940
	Libya 1940	Mediterranean 1940-43	Matapan 1941
	Sfax 1941	Greece 1941	Crete 1941
	Malta Convoys 1941	Sicily 1943	Salerno 1943
	Arctic 1944	Burma 1944-45	
Nugent	Belgian Coast 1917		
Nyasaland	Atlantic 1944-45		
Nymphe	St. Kitts 1782	'*Cléopâtre*' 1793	Groix Island 1795
	'*Constance*' 1797		
Oak	Portland 1653	Gabbard 1653	Scheveningen 1653
	Jutland 1916		
Oakham Castle	Atlantic 1945		
Oakley	Arctic 1942	Sicily 1943	South France 1944
	North Sea 1945		

Oakville	Atlantic 1942-45		
Oasis	Atlantic 1943		
Obdurate	Jutland 1916 Atlantic 1943	Arctic 1942-45	Barents Sea 1942
Obedient	Jutland 1916 Atlantic 1943	Arctic 1942-44 Normandy 1944	Barents Sea 1942
Oberon	Crimea 1855		
Observateur	Guadeloupe 1810		
Ocean	Ushant 1781 Dardanelles 1915	Mesopotamia 1914 Korea 1952-53	Suez Canal 1915
Ocean Brine	North Sea 1942		
Ocean View	English Channel 1942		
Octavia	Abyssinia 1868	South France 1944	
Odin	Baltic 1854 Mesopotamia 1914-17	Crimea 1855	China 1860
Odzani	Atlantic 1943-45		
Offa	Norway 1941 Sicily 1943 Atlantic 1943	Arctic 1941-45 Salerno 1943 English Channel 1944	North Africa 1942-43 Mediterranean 1943 Normandy 1944
Ogano	North Sea 1942		
Old James	Lowestoft 1665 Schooneveld 1673	Orfordness 1666 Texel 1673	Sole Bay 1672
Old Warwick	Portland 1653		
Olive	North Sea 1942	English Channel 1942-44	
Olivina	Normandy 1944		
Olmeda	Falkland Islands 1982**		
Olna	Falkland Islands 1982**	Kuwait 1991**	
Olvina	Dunkirk 1940	English Channel 1942-44	
Olympus	Malta Convoys 1941-42		
Ommering	English Channel 1942		
Oneida	Crimea 1855		
Onslaught	Jutland 1916 Normandy 1944	Arctic 1942-45 Norway 1945	Atlantic 1943

Onslow	Jutland 1916	Norway 1941-45	Arctic 1941-45
	Atlantic 1942	Malta Convoys 1942	North Africa 1942
	Barents Sea 1942	Biscay 1944	Normandy 1944
Onyx	'*Manly*' 1809	North Sea 1943	Arctic 1944
	Normandy 1944	Falkland Islands 1982	
Opal	Jutland 1916		
Ophelia	Jutland 1916	Arctic 1941-42	Atlantic 1942
	North Sea 1942		
Opossum	China 1856-60	Korea 1952-53	
Opportune	Arctic 1942-45	North Africa 1942	Atlantic 1943
	North Cape 1943	Normandy 1944	
Orangeville	Atlantic 1944-45		
Orchis	Atlantic 1941-44	North Sea 1942	Normandy 1944
	English Channel 1944		
Orduna	Atlantic 1942		
Oresay	North Sea 1942		
Orestes	Arctic 1944	Normandy 1944	
Orfasy	Atlantic 1942-43		
Orford	Vigo 1702	Velez Malaga 1704	Passero 1718
	Louisburg 1758	Quebec 1759	Havana 1762
Oribi	Norway 1941	Malta Convoys 1941	Arctic 1942-44
	North Africa 1942	Atlantic 1942-43	Normandy 1944
Orient Star	Atlantic 1939		
Orillia	Atlantic 1941-45		
Oriole	Dunkirk 1940		
Orion	First of June 1794	Groix Island 1795	St. Vincent 1797
	Nile 1798	Trafalgar 1805	Baltic 1855
	Jutland 1916	Atlantic 1939	Calabria 1940
	Mediterranean 1940-44	Matapan 1941	Greece 1941
	Crete 1941	Malta Convoys 1941	Sicily 1943
	Salerno 1943	Anzio 1944	Aegean 1944
	Normandy 1944	South France 1944	
Orissa	Atlantic 1942	Burma 1945	
Orkney	North Sea 1945		
Orlando	China 1900		
Orpheus	Guadeloupe 1810		

Orwell	Arctic 1942-45 Normandy 1944	Barents Sea 1942 Norway 1945	Atlantic 1943
Oshawa	Atlantic 1944-45		
Osiris	Mediterranean 1940	Malta Convoys 1941	Sicily 1943
Osiris II	Dardanelles 1915-16		
Osprey	New Zealand 1845-47		
Ossory	Barfleur 1692	Jutland 1916	
Othello	North Sea 1942	North Africa 1942	
Ottawa	Atlantic 1939-45 English Channel 1944	Biscay 1944	Normandy 1944
Otter	Copenhagen 1801	Baltic 1854-55	
Otus	Malta Convoys 1941		
Otway	Atlantic 1940		
Our Bairns	Dunkirk 1940		
Ouse	Libya 1941		
Outremont	Atlantic 1944	Arctic 1944	Normandy 1944
Owen Sound	Atlantic 1944-45		
Owl	Jutland 1916		
Owner's Love	Barfleur 1692		
Oxford	Lowestoft 1665	Barfleur 1692	
Oxford Castle	Atlantic 1944-45		
Oxlip	Arctic 1942-45 Normandy 1944	Atlantic 1942-45	Sicily 1943
Oxna	Atlantic 1943		
P.31	(see **Uproar**)		
P.32	Malta Convoys 1941		
P.33	Mediterranean 1941		
P.34	(see **Ultimatum**)		
P.35	(see **Umbra**)		
P.36	Malta Convoys 1941		

P.37	(see **Unbending**)		
P.42	(see **Unbroken**)		
P.43	(see **Unison**)		
P.44	(see **United**)		
P.45	(see **Unrivalled**)		
P.46	(see **Unruffled**)		
P.48	North Africa 1942		
P.51	(see **Unseen**)		
P.54	(see **Unshaken**)		
P.211	(see **Safari**)		
P.212	(see **Sahib**)		
P.217	(see **Sibyl**)		
P.219	(see **Seraph**)		
P.221	(see **Shakespeare**)		
P.222	North Africa 1942	Malta Convoys 1942	
P.228	(see **Splendid**)		
P.247	(see **Saracen**)		
P.511	English Channel 1943		
P.614	Arctic 1942		
P.615	Arctic 1942		
Pakenham	Diego Suarez 1942	Mediterranean 1942-43	
Paladin	Diego Suarez 1942 East Indies 1944	Mediterranean 1943 Burma 1944-45	Sicily 1943
Pallas	Cornwallis' Retreat 1795	Egypt 1801	Basque Roads 1809
Palomares	Arctic 1942 Salerno 1943	Atlantic 1942 Anzio 1944	North Africa 1942
Pamela	Burma 1945		
Pandora	Mediterranean 1940-41	Malta Convoys 1941-42	
Pangbourne	Dunkirk 1940	English Channel 1944	Normandy 1944
Pansy	Armada 1588*		

Panther	Velez Malaga 1704 North Africa 1942-43 Mediterranean 1943	Diego Suarez 1942 Sicily 1943 Aegean 1943	Atlantic 1942-43 Salerno 1943
Papua	Atlantic 1944-45		
Paradox	Portland 1653		
Paragon	Montecristo 1652		
Paris	Dunkirk 1940*		
Parkes	New Guinea 1944		
Parktown	Libya 1942		
Parramatta	Libya 1941		
Parrett	Atlantic 1943	East Indies 1944	Okinawa 1945
Parrsboro	English Channel 1942	Atlantic 1943	Normandy 1944
Parry Sound	Atlantic 1944-45		
Parthian	Mediterranean 1940-43	Malta Convoys 1942	Sicily 1943
Partridge	Scandanavian Convoys 1917	North Africa 1942	Malta Convoys 1942
Pasley	Atlantic 1944	Arctic 1945	
Passport	Armada 1588*		
Pathfinder	Malta Convoys 1942 Sicily 1943 Burma 1944-45	North Africa 1942-43 Salerno 1943	Atlantic 1942-43 Aegean 1943
Patna	Burma 1945		
Patroller	Atlantic 1944-45		
Patti	English Channel 1942		
Paul	Portland 1653	Gabbard 1653	Orfordness 1666
Paxton	Dunkirk 1940		
Paynter	Arctic 1942	Atlantic 1942-44	
Peacock	Arctic 1944	Atlantic 1945	
Pearl	Armada 1588* Porto Farina 1655 'Santa Monica' 1779 Amorha 1858 Normandy 1944	Portland 1653 Texel 1673 Egypt 1801 English Channel 1942-44	Gabbard 1653 Chesapeake 1781 China 1860 North Sea 1942
Pearleaf	Sicily 1943**	Falkland Islands 1982**	

Peary	Belgian Coast 1915		
Pegasus	St. Vincent 1780 Atlantic 1940-41	First of June 1794	Egypt 1801
Peggy Hutton	Normandy 1944		
Pelican	Armada 1588* Gabbard 1653 St. Lucia 1778 Jutland 1916 North Africa 1942	Kentish Knock 1652 Scheveningen 1653 St. Lucia 1796 Norway 1940 Normandy 1944	Portland 1653 Quebec 1759 '*Argus*' 1813 Atlantic 1942-44 English Channel 1944
Pellew	Scandanavian Convoys 1917		
Pelorus	Martinique 1809 Normandy 1944	Guadeloupe 1810 Atlantic 1945	New Zealand 1860-61 East Indies 1945
Pelter	Baltic 1855		
Pembroke	Lowestoft 1665 Finisterre 1747 Havana 1762	Vigo 1702 Louisburg 1758 Baltic 1855	Marbella 1705 Quebec 1759
Penelope	'*Guillaume Tell*' 1800 Baltic 1854 Mediterranean 1941-43 Sicily 1943 Anzio 1944	Egypt 1801 Alexandria 1882 Malta Convoys 1941-42 Salerno 1943 Falkland Islands 1982	Martinique 1809 Norway 1940 Sirte 1942 Aegean 1943
Penetang	Atlantic 1945		
Penn	Malta Convoys 1942 Mediterranean 1943 Aegean 1943	North Africa 1942-43 Sicily 1943 Burma 1945	Atlantic 1942-43 Salerno 1943
Pennywort	Atlantic 1942-45	North Sea 1943-44	Normandy 1944
Pentland Firth	Atlantic 1940	North Sea 1942	
Pentstemon	Atlantic 1941-42	North Africa 1942-43	Sicily 1943
Penylan	English Channel 1942		
Penzance	Martinique 1762	Atlantic 1940	
Peony	Dardanelles 1915-16 Malta Convoys 1941	Atlantic 1940 Libya 1941-42	Spartivento 1940
Perdrant	Normandy 1944		
Perim	Atlantic 1944-45	English Channel 1945	
Periwinkle	Atlantic 1940-41		
Perlen	Guadeloupe 1810		
Persephone	Normandy 1944		

Persian	Normandy 1944	East Indies 1945	
Persimmon	Burma 1945		
Perth	Atlantic 1939 Crete 1941 Vietnam 1967-71	Matapan 1941 Malta Convoys 1941	Greece 1941 Sunda Strait 1942
Petard	Jutland 1916 Salerno 1943	Mediterranean 1942-43 Aegean 1943	Sicily 1943 East Indies 1944
Peter	Cadiz 1596*	Gabbard 1653	
Peterborough	Atlantic 1944-45		
Peterel	Minorca 1798	*'Ligurienne'* 1800	Egypt 1801
Peterhead	English Channel 1942 Normandy 1944	Atlantic 1943	North Sea 1943
Petrolia	Atlantic 1944-45		
Petunia	Atlantic 1941-45	English Channel 1944-45	Normandy 1944
Pevensey Castle	Atlantic 1944		
Phaeton	Barfleur 1692 *'San Josef'* 1800	First of June 1794 Java 1811	Cornwallis' Retreat 1795 Jutland 1916
Pheasant	Sicily 1943	Atlantic 1943-44	Okinawa 1945
Philante	Atlantic 1940-42	North Africa 1942	
Philomel	Navarino 1827	Benin 1897	South Africa 1899-1900
Phlegethon	(Bengal Marine)	Kua Kam 1849	
Phoebe	*'Néréide'* 1797 Tamatave 1811 Benin 1897 Greece 1941 Aegean 1943 East Indies 1944	*'Africaine'* 1801 Java 1811 Belgian Coast 1917-18 Crete 1941 Mediterranean 1944 Burma 1944-45	Trafalgar 1805 *'Essex'* 1814 Zeebrugge 1918 Malta Convoys 1942 Sabang 1944
Phoenix	Montecristo 1652 Sole Bay 1672 Egypt 1801 Syria 1840 Dogger Bank 1915	Gabbard 1653 Vigo 1702 *'Didon'* 1805 China 1900	Scheveningen 1653 Velez Malaga 1704 Bay of Biscay 1805 Heligoland 1914
Phrontis	North Sea 1942		
Pickle	Trafalgar 1805 Burma 1945	Baltic 1855	Normandy 1944
Picotee	Atlantic 1940-41		
Pict	Atlantic 1942-43	Falkland Islands 1982	

Pictou	Atlantic 1941-45		
Piedmontaise	Banda Neira 1810		
Piercer	Glückstadt 1814		
Pigmy	Egypt 1801	Baltic 1854	Crimea 1854
Pimpernel	Atlantic 1941-45	Biscay 1943	
Pincher	Baltic 1855 Burma 1945	Normandy 1944	Atlantic 1945
Pine	English Channel 1942-44		
Pink	North Sea 1942 Normandy 1944	Atlantic 1942-44	English Channel 1944
Pintail	North Sea 1940-41		
Pioneer	China 1856-60		
Pippin	Armada 1588*		
Pique	Egypt 1801 Normandy 1944	Syria 1840	China 1856-60
Pirie	New Guinea 1943-44	Okinawa 1945	
Pirouette	North Sea 1941-42 Salerno 1943	Atlantic 1942	Sicily 1943
Pitstruan	North Sea 1942	Normandy 1944	
Plantagenet	Normandy 1944		
Pleasure	Cadiz 1596*		
Plinlimmon	Dunkirk 1940		
Plover	Portland 1653 Normandy 1944	China 1842	China 1856-59
Plucky	Normandy 1944	Burma 1945	
Plumleaf	Falkland Islands 1982**		
Plumper	Guadeloupe 1810		
Plym	Atlantic 1943	Sicily 1943	
Plymouth	Porto Farina 1655 Four Days' Battle 1666 Texel 1673	Santa Cruz 1657 Orfordness 1666 Falkland Islands 1982	Lowestoft 1665 Sole Bay 1672
Pointer	English Channel 1942		
Polka	North Sea 1941-45		

Polly Johnson Dunkirk 1940

Polo Norte North Sea 1942

Polruan

Dieppe 1942	North Africa 1942-43	Atlantic 1943
Sicily 1943	Salerno 1943	South France 1944

Polyanthus Atlantic 1941-43

Polythemus Copenhagen 1801 Trafalgar 1805

Pompée Martinique 1809 Guadeloupe 1810

Poole Diego Suarez 1942 Sicily 1943 Normandy 1944

Poona Burma 1945

Popinjay Cadiz 1596*

Poppy

North Sea 1942-44	Mediterranean 1942-44	Arctic 1942-44
North Africa 1942	Sicily 1943	Atlantic 1943-45
Normandy 1944	English Channel 1944	

Porcher Atlantic 1943

Porcupine

Quebec 1759	Havana 1762	Baltic 1854-55
North Africa 1942		

Porpoise

Baltic 1855	Jutland 1916	Norway 1940
Atlantic 1940-41	Malta Convoys 1942	Mediterranean 1942
Malaya 1944		

Port Arthur

Atlantic 1942-44	Mediterranean 1943	Normandy 1944
English Channel 1945		

Port Colborne

Atlantic 1944-45	English Channel 1944	Normandy 1944
Arctic 1944	North Sea 1945	

Port d'Espagne Martinique 1809

Port Hope Atlantic 1943-45

Port Mahon Louisburg 1758 Egypt 1801

Portage Atlantic 1944-45

Portchester Castle Atlantic 1944

Portland

Scheveningen 1653	Lowestoft 1665	Four Days' Battle 1666
Orfordness 1666	'*Coventry*' 1709	'*Auguste*' 1746
Ushant 1747	'*Magnanime*' 1748	Lagos 1759
Quiberon Bay 1759		

Portsdown North Sea 1942 Atlantic 1942-44

Portsmouth

Dover 1652	Gabbard 1653	Scheveningen 1653
Lowestoft 1665	Four Days' Battle 1666	Orfordness 1666
Bugia 1671	Texel 1673	Barfleur 1692

Posthorse	Cadiz 1596*		
Postillion	Atlantic 1944-45	Normandy 1944	East Indies 1945
Potentilla	Atlantic 1942-43	North Sea 1944	Normandy 1944
Potts	Armada 1588*		
Poulette	Genoa 1795		
Poundmaker	Atlantic 1944-45		
Powerful	Camperdown 1797	Syria 1840	South Africa 1899-1900
Pozarica	Atlantic 1942	Arctic 1942	North Africa 1942-43
Prague	Dunkirk 1940*		
Premier	Atlantic 1944	Arctic 1945	Norway 1945
Prescott	Atlantic 1941-45 English Channel 1944-45	North Africa 1942-43	Normandy 1944
President	Portland 1653 Java 1811	Gabbard 1653 San Sebastian 1813	Scheveningen 1653
Preston	St. Lucia 1778	Dogger Bank 1781	
Preston North End	North Sea 1943-44		
Pretoria Castle	Atlantic 1940-42		
Primrose	Armada 1588* North Sea 1942	Cadiz 1596* English Channel 1944	Atlantic 1940-45 Normandy 1944
Primula	Atlantic 1940-44	Libya 1942	Sicily 1943
Prince	Sole Bay 1672 Lagos 1759	Schooneveld 1673 Groix Island 1795	Texel 1673 Trafalgar 1805
Prince Baudouin	Normandy 1944	South France 1944	
Prince Charles	Norway 1941 Dieppe 1942 Normandy 1944	North Sea 1942 Sicily 1943	English Channel 1942 Salerno 1943
Prince David	Atlantic 1941 Aegean 1944	Aleutians 1942 (RCN) South France 1944	Normandy 1944
Prince Edward	Dardanelles 1915-16		
Prince Eugene	Belgian Coast 1915-18	Zeebrugge 1918	Ostend 1918
Prince Frederick	Finisterre 1747	Louisburg 1758	Quebec 1759
Prince George	Velez Malaga 1704 St. Kitts 1782 St. Vincent 1795	Finisterre 1747 The Saints 1782 Dardanelles 1915-16	St. Vincent 1780 Groix Island 1795

Prince Henry	Aleutians 1942 (RCN)	Aegean 1944	South France 1944
Prince Leopold	Norway 1941 Salerno 1943	Dieppe 1942 Normandy 1944	Sicily1943 English Channel 1944
Prince of Orange	Louisburg 1758	Quebec 1759	Belle Isle 1761
Prince of Wales	St. Lucia 1778 '*Bismarck*' 1941	Groix Island 1795 Malta Convoys 1941	Dardanelles 1915
Prince Regent	Baltic 1854		
Prince Robert	Aleutians 1942 (RCN)	Atlantic 1943-44	English Channel 1944
Prince Rupert	Belgian Coast 1915-16	Atlantic 1944	
Prince Victor	Normandy 1944		
Prince William	St. Kitts 1782	The Saints 1782	
Princess	Lowestoft 1665 North Sea 1667 Texel 1673	Four Days' Battle 1666 Sole Bay 1672	Orfordness 1666 Schooneveld 1673
Princess Alice	Baltic 1855		
Princess Amelia	Louisburg 1758	Quebec 1759	Dogger Bank 1781
Princess Anne	Velez Malaga 1704		
Princess Charlotte	Syria 1840		
Princess Elizabeth	Dunkirk 1940		
Princess Iris	English Channel 1942-44		
Princess Louisa	Puerto Bello 1739	Finisterre 1747	Ushant 1747
Princess Maria	Portland 1653	Gabbard 1653	Porto Farina 1655
Princess Maud	Dunkirk 1940*		
Princess Royal	Genoa 1795 Heligoland 1914	Baltic 1854 Dogger Bank 1915	Crimea 1855 Jutland 1916
Princessa	St. Kitts 1782	The Saints 1782	
Prins Albert	Norway 1941 Sicily 1943 South France 1944	Dieppe 1942 Salerno 1943 Burma 1945	English Channel 1942 Normandy 1944
Prinses Astrid	Dieppe 1942 Normandy 1944	Sicily 1943	Salerno 1943
Prinses Beatrix	Norway 1941 Sicily 1943 Anzio 1944	Dieppe 1942 Salerno 1943 South France 1944	North Africa 1942-43 Mediterranean 1943

Prinses Josephine Charlotte	Sicily 1943	Salerno 1943	Normandy 1944
Probe	Normandy 1944		
Procris	Java 1811		
Proctor	Normandy 1944		
Prodigal	Atlantic 1943		
Product	South France 1944		
Prometheus	Algiers 1816		
Prompt	Baltic 1855	Atlantic 1945	
Proof	Normandy 1944		
Proserpine	Suez Canal 1915		
Prospect	Atlantic 1943	English Channel 1945	
Prosperous	Portland 1653	Gabbard 1653	Scheveningen 1653
Protea	Libya 1941-42 Atlantic 1943-44	Mediterranean 1942-44 Aegean 1944	Sicily 1943
Protector	Sadras 1758 Norway 1940	Negapatam 1758 Libya 1940-41	Cape of Good Hope 1806
Proteus	Mediterranean 1941-42	Malta Convoys 1942	
Prothée	The Saints 1782		
Providence	Portland 1653 Orfordness 1666	Gabbard 1653 Schooneveld 1673	Lowestoft 1665
Prowess	Normandy 1944		
Prudence	Armada 1588*	Cadiz 1596*	
Prudent	Chesapeake 1781	St. Kitts 1782	
Prudent Mary	Gabbard 1653	Lowestoft 1665	Texel 1673
Prudente	Ushant 1781		
Psyche	Java 1811		
Puckeridge	English Channel 1942	North Africa 1942-43	Sicily 1943
Puffin	English Channel 1939	Atlantic 1940	North Sea 1941-45
Pukaki	Korea 1950		
Pultusk	Martinique 1809	Guadeloupe 1810	

Puncher	Atlantic 1944		
Punjab	Burma 1945		
Punjabi	Narvik 1940 Arctic 1941-42	Atlantic 1940-42 *'Bismarck'* 1941	Norway 1941
Pursuer	Atlantic 1943-45 South France 1944	Norway 1944 Aegean 1944	Normandy 1944
Pylades	China 1841	Baltic 1855	Atlantic 1944
Pytchley	North Sea 1942-45 Normandy 1944	English Channel 1942-44	Arctic 1943
Quadrant	Arctic 1942-43	Okinawa 1945	
Quadrille	North Sea 1941-42 Normandy 1944	Atlantic 1942-44	English Channel 1943
Quail	Sicily 1943	Salerno 1943	Mediterranean 1943
Qualicum	North Sea 1942 Normandy 1944	Atlantic 1943	English Channel 1944
Quality	North Africa 1942-43 Japan 1945	Sabang 1944	Okinawa 1945
Quantock	North Sea 1941-45 Salerno 1943	Atlantic 1943 Adriatic 1944	Sicily 1943
Qu'Appelle	Atlantic 1944	Normandy 1944	Biscay 1944
Quebec	Martinique 1794		
Queen	Ushant 1781 Crimea 1854-55 Norway 1945	First of June 1794 Dardanelles 1915 Arctic 1945	Groix Island 1795 Atlantic 1944
Queen Charlotte	First of June 1794	Groix Island 1795	Algiers 1816
Queen Elizabeth	Dardanelles 1915 Burma 1944-45	Crete 1941 East Indies 1945	Sabang 1944
Queen Elizabeth 2	Falkland Islands 1982*		
Queen Emma	Norway 1941 Sicily1943 Normandy 1944	Dieppe 1942 Atlantic 1943	North Africa 1942-43 Mediterranean 1943
Queen Mary	Heligoland 1914	Jutland 1916	
Queen of the Channel	Dunkirk 1940*		
Queen of Kent	Normandy 1944		

Queen of Thanet	Dunkirk 1940	Normandy 1944	
Queen Victoria	Belgian Coat 1915	Dardanelles 1915-16	
Queenborough	Sadras 1758 Arctic 1942-43 Mediterranean 1943	Negapatam 1758 Sicily 1943 East Indies 1944	Porto Novo 1759 Salerno 1943 Okinawa 1945
Quentin	Malta Convoys 1942 Mediterranean 1942	North Africa 1942	Atlantic 1942
Quesnel	Atlantic 1942-45		
Quiberon	Mediterranean 1942 East Indies 1944	North Africa 1942-43 Okinawa 1945	Atlantic 1943 Japan 1945
Quickmatch	English Channel 1942 Okinawa 1945	Atlantic 1943	Sabang 1944
Quilliam	Sicily1943 Sabang 1944	Salerno 1943 East Indies 1944	Mediterranean 1943 Okinawa 1945
Quinte	Atlantic 1942		
Quittance	Cadiz 1596		
Quorn	North Sea 1941-44	English Channel 1942-44	Normandy 1944
Racehorse	Quebec 1759 China 1856-60 Sabang 1944	Tamatave 1811 Belgian Coast 1915-16 East Indies 1945	New Zealand 1845-47 Atlantic 1943 Burma 1945
Rachel	Sole Bay 1672	Schooneveld 1673	
Racoon	Dardanelles 1915-16		
Radiant	Belgian Coast 1917		
Radnor Castle	English Channel 1942		
Raglan	Dardanelles 1915-16		
Raider	Arctic 1942-43 Mediterranean 1943 Burma 1944-45	Sicily 1943 Sabang 1944	Salerno 1943 East Indies 1944
Rainbow	Armada 1588 Gabbard 1653 Four Days' Battle 1666 Schooneveld 1673	Cadiz 1596 Scheveningen 1653 Orfordness 1666 Texel 1673	Portland 1653 Lowestoft 1665 Sole Bay 1672 Lagos 1759
Raisonnable	Martinique 1762	Copenhagen 1801	Cape of Good Hope 1806
Rajah	Atlantic 1944		
Rajputana	Atlantic 1940-41 (AMC)	Atlantic 1942 (m/s)	Burma 1945(m/s)

Ramillies	First of June 1794 Mediterranean 1940 Normandy 1944	Copenhagen 1801 Atlantic 1941 South France 1944	Spartivento 1940 Diego Suarez 1942
Ramsey	Atlantic 1941-42		
Ranee	Atlantic 1945		
Ranelagh	Vigo 1702	Gibraltar 1704	Velez Malaga 1704
Ranen	Norway 1940		
Ranger	First of June 1794		
Ranpura	Atlantic 1940-43		
Raphael	Armada 1588*		
Rapid	Atlantic 1943 East Indies 1945	Sabang 1944	Burma 1944-45
Rat of Wight	Armada 1588*		
Rattler	First of June 1794	Burma 1852	
Rattlesnake	Martinique 1794 Ashantee 1873 Arctic 1944	Cape of Good Hope 1795 Dardanelles 1915-16 Normandy 1944	China 1841-42 North Sea 1942
Ravager	Atlantic 1943		
Raven	Portland 1653 St. Vincent 1797	Gabbard 1653 Crimea 1855	Scheveningen 1653
Ravenswood	Belgian Coast 1915		
Rayon	North Sea 1942		
Reading	Atlantic 1941-42		
Ready	Normandy 1944	Arctic 1944	
Reaper	Atlantic 1944		
Reboundo	English Channel 1942		
Recovery	Scheveningen 1653		
Recruit	Martinique 1809 Normandy 1944	Crimea 1855 Atlantic 1945	Belgian Coast 1917 Burma 1945
Reculver	Atlantic 1942		
Red Deer	Atlantic 1942-45		
Red Lion	Armada 1588*		
Redbreast	Glückstadt 1814	Baltic 1855	

Redmill	English Channel 1944 Atlantic 1945	Arctic 1944	North Sea 1944-45
Redoubt	Atlantic 1943	East Indies 1945	Burma 1945
Redoubtable	Belgian Coast 1915		
Redpole	Basque Roads 1809 Burma 1944-45	Atlantic 1943-44	Normandy 1944
Redshank	Atlantic 1943		
Redwing	Baltic 1855		
Redwood	English Channel 1944		
Reformation	Portland 1653	Gabbard 1653	
Regardo	North Sea 1942		
Regent	Mediterranean 1940-41	Falkland Islands 1982**	
Regina	Atlantic 1942-44 Normandy 1944	Mediterranean 1943	English Channel 1944
Registan	Atlantic 1941		
Regulus	Egypt 1801		
Reighton Wyke	North Sea 1942 Salerno 1943	Atlantic 1942-43	Sicily 1943
Reindeer	Atlantic 1940		
Release	Armada 1588*		
Relentless	Sabang 1944	East Indies 1944-45	
Renard	Dardanelles 1915		
Renominée	Egypt 1801		
Renown	Gabbard 1653 Egypt 1801 Atlantic 1940 Malta Convoys 1941-42 Sabang 1944	Scheveningen 1653 Norway 1940 '*Bismarck*' 1941 Arctic 1942 East Indies 1944	Ushant 1781 Spartivento 1940 Mediterranean 1941 North Africa 1942
Repulse	Cadiz 1596 Atlantic 1939-40	Martinique 1762 Norway 1940	The Saints 1782 '*Bismarck*' 1941
Reserve	Lowestoft 1665	Four Days' Battle 1666	New Guinea 1943-44
Resistance	Baltic 1854		

Resolution	Kentish Knock 1652	Gabbard 1653	Scheveningen 1653
	Lowestoft 1665	Orfordness 1666	Sole Bay 1672
	Schooneveldt 1673	Texel 1673	Barfleur 1692
	Quiberon Bay 1759	St. Vincent 1780	St. Kitts 1782
	The Saints 1782	Basque Roads 1809	Atlantic 1939-40
	Norway 1940		
Resource	Egypt 1801	Falkland Islands 1982**	Kuwait 1991**
Restigouche	Atlantic 1939-45	North Sea 1940	Mediterranean 1943
	Biscay 1944	Normandy 1944	
Restive	North Africa 1942-43		
Restoration	Barfleur 1692		
Retako	North Sea 1942		
Retalick	Normandy 1944	English Channel 1944	Atlantic 1944
	North Sea 1945		
Retribution	Crimea 1854	Baltic 1855	China 1860
Retriever	Belgian Coast 1917	Atlantic 1942	Arctic 1942
	North Sea 1942		
Return	Lowestoft 1665		
Returno	North Africa 1942		
Reuben	Dover 1652		
Revenge	Armada 1588	Azores 1591	Lowestoft 1665
	Four Days' Battle 1666	Orfordness 1666	Bugia 1671
	Schooneveldt 1673	Marbella 1705	'*Orphée*' 1758
	Quiberon Bay 1759	Trafalgar 1805	Basque Roads 1809
	Syria 1840	Belgian Coast 1914-15	Jutland 1916
	Atlantic 1939-41	English Channel 1940	
Revolutionnaire	Groix Island 1795	Bay of Biscay 1805	San Sebastian 1813
Reynard	China 1860		
Rhadamanthus	Baltic 1854		
Rhine	Norway 1940		
Rhododendron	Atlantic 1940-45	English Channel 1942	North Africa 1942
	Barents Sea 1942	Arctic 1942-45	Sicily 1943
	Normandy 1944		
Rhyl	Dieppe 1942	English Channel 1942	North Africa 1942-43
	Sicily 1943	Salerno 1943	South France 1944
Riano	Normandy 1944		
Ribble	Dardanelles 1915-16		

Richard	Four Days' Battle 1666	Orfordness 1666	
Richard Duffield	Armada 1588*		
Richard and Martha	Portland 1653	Gabbard 1653	Orfordness 1666
Richmond	Quebec 1759 Arctic 1942	Havana 1762	Atlantic 1941-43
Rifleman	Normandy 1944	Burma 1945	
Righto	English Channel 1942	Normandy 1944	
Rigoletto	Normandy 1944		
Rimouski	Atlantic 1942-45	English Channel 1944-45	Normandy 1944
Rinaldo	Belgian Coast 1914 South France 1944	North Sea 1942 Aegean 1944	Anzio 1944
Ringdove	Martinique 1809 Atlantic 1943	Guadeloupe 1810	China 1860
Ringwood	North Sea 1942	Normandy 1944	
Riou	Normandy 1944	North Sea 1945	
Ripley	Atlantic 1941-42		
Ripon	Passero 1718	Havana 1762	
River Clyde	Dardanelles 1915		
River Lenn	Normandy 1944		
River Spey	Normandy 1944		
Riviera	Belgian Coast 1915		
Riviere du Loup	Atlantic 1944-45		
Robert	Sole Bay 1672		
Roberts	Dardanelles 1915-16 Salerno 1943 Walcheren 1944	North Africa 1942 Mediterranean 1943	Sicily 1943 Normandy 1944
Robin	Armada 1588*		
Robust	Chesapeake 1781	Donegal 1798	'*Chevrette*' 1801
Rochester	Passero 1718 Atlantic 1939-44	Quiberon Bay 1759 North Africa 1942	Martinique 1762 Normandy 1944
Rockcliffe	Atlantic 1945		

Rocket	Baltic 1855 Burma 1944-45	English Channel 1943 East Indies 1945	Sabang 1944
Rockhampton	New Guinea 1944		
Rockingham	Atlantic 1941-43	Biscay 1943	
Rockrose	Atlantic 1941-42		
Rockwood	Sicily 1943 English Channel 1944	Aegean 1943	Atlantic 1944
Rodney	Quebec 1759 Norway 1940 Malta Convoys 1941-42 Salerno 1943 Normandy 1944	Syria 1840 Atlantic 1940-41 North Africa 1942-43 Mediterranean 1943 Arctic 1944	Crimea 1854-55 *Bismarck* 1941 Sicily 1943 English Channel 1944
Roe	Texel 1673		
Roebuck	Armada 1588* Gabbard 1653 Martinique 1794 Sabang 1944	Cadiz 1596* Barfleur 1692 Egypt 1801 Burma 1944-45	Portland 1653 Velez Malaga 1704 China 1860 East Indies 1944-45
Roger and Katherine	Cadiz 1596*		
Rohilkhand	Burma 1945		
Romeo	Sicily 1943		
Romney	*Sibylle* 1794 Sicily 1943	Egypt 1801 Normandy 1944	Diego Suarez 1942
Romsey	English Channel 1942		
Romulus	Genoa 1795	Egypt 1801	
Ronaldsay	North Africa 1942		
Rorqual	Mediterranean 1940-43 Sicily 1943	Crete 1941 Aegean 1943	Malta Convoys 1941-42 Atlantic 1944
Rosa	Egypt 1801		
Rosalind	North Sea 1941		
Rosamund	Guadeloupe 1810	Baltic 1854	
Rosario	South France 1944		
Rosaura	Atlantic 1940	Libya 1941	
Rose	Armada 1588* Martinique 1794 Atlantic 1941-44	Texel 1673 Camperdown 1797	Martinique 1762 Navarino 1827

Rose Lion	Armada 1588*		
Rosebay	Atlantic 1943		
Rosemary	Atlantic 1940		
Rosevean	English Channel 1944-45		
Ross	Dunkirk 1940	North Sea 1942	Normandy 1944
Rosthern	Atlantic 1941-45		
Rother	Atlantic 1942-44	North Africa 1942-43	
Rotherham	Sabang 1944	Burma 1945	East Indies 1945
Rothesay	English Channel 1942 Salerno 1943	North Africa 1942-43 Anzio 1944	Sicily 1943 South France 1944
Rotoiti	Korea 1950-53		
Rousay	English Channel 1942	North Sea 1942	North Africa 1942
Rover	Mediterranean 1941		
Rowan	English Channel 1942-45		
Rowe	Cadiz 1596		
Rowena	North Sea 1944		
Rowley	Normandy 1944	English Channel 1944-45	Atlantic 1945
Roxano	Normandy 1944		
Roxborough	Atlantic 1941-43		
Royal Albert	Crimea 1854-55		
Royal Charles	Lowestoft 1665 Schooneveld 1673	Four Days' Battle 1666 Texel 1673	Orfordness 1666
Royal Daffodil	Dunkirk 1940*		
Royal Defence	Armada 1588*		
Royal Eagle	Dunkirk 1940	English Channel 1942	
Royal Exchange	Lowestoft 1665		
Royal George	Quiberon Bay 1759 Groix Island 1795	St. Vincent 1780 Baltic 1854-55	First of June 1794
Royal James	Lowestoft 1665 Sole Bay 1672	Four Days' Battle 1666	Orfordness 1666

Royal Katherine	Lowestoft 1665	Four Days' Battle 1666	Orfordness 1666
	Sole Bay 1672	Schooneveld 1673	Texel 1673
	Barfleur 1692	Gibraltar 1704	Velez Malaga 1704
Royal Marine	Atlantic 1944-45		
Royal Mount	Atlantic 1944-45		
Royal Oak	Lowestoft 1665	Orfordness 1666	Velez Malaga 1704
	Passero 1718	Chesapeake 1781	The Saints 1782
	Jutland 1916		
Royal Prince	Lowestoft 1665	Four Days' Battle 1666	
Royal Scotsman	North Africa 1942-43	Sicily 1943	Salerno 1943
	Atlantic 1944		
Royal Sovereign	Orfordness 1666	Vigo 1702	First of June 1794
	Cornwallis' Retreat 1795	Trafalgar 1805	Dunkirk 1940*
	Calabria 1940	Atlantic 1940-41	
Royal Ulsterman	Diego Suarez 1942	North Africa 1942-43	Sicily 1943
	Salerno 1943	Mediterranean 1943	Anzio 1944
	Normandy 1944		
Royal William	Barfleur 1692	Louisburg 1758	Quebec 1759
	Baltic 1854		
Royalist	'*Weser*' 1813	Jutland 1916	South France 1944
	Aegean 1944	Burma 1945	East Indies 1945
Ruben	Cadiz 1596*		
Ruby	Cadiz 1596	Dover 1652	Kentish Knock 1652
	Portland 1653	Gabbard 1653	Santa Cruz 1657
	Orfordness 1666	Sole Bay 1672	Schooneveld 1673
	Texel 1673	Barfleur 1692	Cape of Good Hope 1795
	Baltic 1855	English Channel 1942-43	Normandy 1944
Ruler	Atlantic 1944	Okinawa 1945	
Runnymede	Atlantic 1944-45		
Rupert	Orfordness 1666	Sole Bay 1672	Schooneveld 1673
	Texel 1673	Barfleur 1692	Passero 1718
	Normandy 1944	English Channel 1944	Arctic 1944
	Atlantic 1945	North Sea 1945	
Rushen Castle	Atlantic 1944-45		
Ruskholm	North Sea 1942	English Channel 1942	North Africa 1942-43
Russell	St. Kitts 1782	The Saints 1782	First of June 1794
	Groix Island 1795	Camperdown 1797	Copenhagen 1801
	Baltic 1855	Belgian Coast 1914	Dardanelles 1915-16
Ruth	Portland 1653		

Rutherford	Atlantic 1944	English Channel 1944	North Sea 1944-45
Rutlandshire	Norway 1940		
Ryde	Normandy 1944		
Rye	Malta Convoys 1942 Normandy 1944	Atlantic 1942	Sicily 1943
Rysa	Mediterranean 1940	North Africa 1942	
Sabina	Atlantic 1942		
Sable	Atlantic 1940		
Sabre	Dunkirk 1940	Atlantic 1940-43	
Sackville	Atlantic 1942-44		
Safari (P.211)	Malta Convoys 1942	Sicily 1943	Mediterranean 1943
Sagitta	Atlantic 1940		
Saguenay	Atlantic 1939-42		
Sahib (P.212)	Arctic 1942	Mediterranean 1943	
St. Albans	Barfleur 1692 St. Kitts 1782 English Channel 1942	Lagos 1759 The Saints 1782 Arctic 1942	St. Lucia 1778 Atlantic 1941-43 North Sea 1943
St. Andrew	Lowestoft 1665 Schooneveld 1673 Dunkirk 1940*	Orfordness 1666 Texel 1673	Sole Bay 1672 Barfleur 1692
St. Apollo	Atlantic 1940-41		
St. Barbe	Normandy 1944		
St. Boniface	Atlantic 1944-45		
St. Brides Bay	Korea 1950-53		
St. Cathan	Atlantic 1941		
St. Catherines	Atlantic 1943-44		
St. Clair	Atlantic 1940-43		
St. Croix	Atlantic 1940-43		
St. Day	North Africa 1942-43		
Saint Edmund	Falkland Islands 1982*		
St. Elstan	Atlantic 1940-44	North Sea 1942	Arctic 1942-43

St. Fiorenzo	*'Résistance'* 1797	*'Psyché'* 1805	*'Piédmontaise'* 1808
St. Francis	Atlantic 1941-43		
St. George	Lowestoft 1665 Sole Bay 1672 Velez Malaga 1704 Baltic 1854	Four Days' Battle 1666 Schooneveld 1672 Genoa 1795 Benin 1897	Orfordness 1666 Texel 1673 Copenhagen 1801
St. Goran	Norway 1940		
St. Helena	English Channel 1945		
St. Helier	Dunkirk 1940*	Normandy 1944	
St. Jacob	Cadiz 1596*	Orfordness 1666	
St. Jean d'Acre	Baltic 1854	Crimea 1855	
St. John	Atlantic 1944 Arctic 1944	English Channel 1944 North Sea 1945	Normandy 1944
St. Julien	Dunkirk 1940*		
St. Kenan	Atlantic 1940-44	Arctic 1942-43	
St. Kilda	North Sea 1942 Anzio 1944	English Channel 1942-43	Salerno 1943
St. Lambert	Atlantic 1944-45		
St. Laurent	Atlantic 1939-45	Normandy 1944	
St. Leger	Armada 1588*		
St. Loman	Atlantic 1940		
St. Magnus	Norway 1940		
St. Mary's	Atlantic 1942	North Sea 1943	
St. Mellons	North Africa 1942-43		
St. Michael	Sole Bay 1672 Barfleur 1692	Schooneveld 1672	Texel 1673
St. Minver	Normandy 1944		
St. Nectan	North Africa 1942	Atlantic 1942-44	
St. Paul	Four Days' Battle 1666		
St. Peter	Cadiz 1596*		
St. Pierre	Martinique 1809	Atlantic 1945	Arctic 1945
St. Seiriol	Dunkirk 1940*		

St. Stephen	Atlantic 1944-45		
St. Sunniva	Norway 1940		
St. Thomas	Atlantic 1944-45		
St. Vincent	Baltic 1854	Jutland 1916	
St. Wistan	Atlantic 1944		
St. Zeno	Atlantic 1940-41		
Sainte Therese	Atlantic 1945	North Sea 1945	
Saladin	Dunkirk 1940 English Channel 1944	Atlantic 1940-44	Arctic 1942-43
Salamander	Armada 1588* Dunkirk 1940	Lagos 1759 Arctic 1941-42	Burma 1852 Normandy 1944
Salamine	Egypt 1801		
Salisbury	Sadras 1758 Atlantic 1941-43	Negapatam 1758	Porto Novo 1759
Salmon	North Sea 1939-40		
Salopian	Atlantic 1939-40		
Saltarelo	North Sea 1941-43	Mediterranean 1944	
Saltash	Dunkirk 1940	Normandy 1944	
Salvageman	Falkland Islands 1982*		
Salvia	Atlantic 1940 Crete 1941	Spartivento 1940 Libya 1941	Greece 1941 Malta Convoys 1941
Salvini	Normandy 1944		
Samarang	Amboina 1810	Java 1811	China 1841
Samaritan	Armada 1588*	Gabbard 1653	
Samphire	Atlantic 1941-42	North Africa 1942-43	
Sampson	Armada 1588* China 1856-60	Portland 1653	Crimea 1854
Samuel	Armada 1588*	Orfordness 1666	
Samuel and Anne	Schooneveld 1673		
Samuel Talbot	Gabbard 1653		
San Carlos	Trincomalee 1782		
Sancroft	Normandy 1944		

Sancta Maria	Orfordness 1666		
Sanda	Atlantic 1942		
Sandfly	Heligoland 1914	Dogger Bank 1915	
Sandown	Dunkirk 1940	Normandy 1944	
Sandray	Burma 1945		
Sandwich	Barfleur 1692 Atlantic 1939-44	Belle Isle 1761 North Africa 1942	St. Vincent 1780
Sans Pareil	Groix Island 1795	Crimea 1854	China 1856-60
Santa Dorothea	Egypt 1801		
Santa Margarita	Martinique 1794	'*Tamise*' 1796	Bay of Biscay 1805
Santa Teresa	Egypt 1801		
Saon	Dunkirk 1940	Atlantic 1943	
Sapper	Atlantic 1943-45	Normandy 1944	
Sapphire	Dover 1652 Lowestoft 1665 Belgian Coast 1914	Portland 1653 Quiberon Bay 1759 Dardanelles 1915	Gabbard 165 China 1842 North Sea 1941-42
Sappho	'*Admiral Jawl*' 1808		
Saracen (P.247)	Cattaro 1814 Arctic 1942	Belgian Coast 1915 Mediterranean 1942	North Sea 1942 Sicily 1943
Sarah	Gabbard 1653		
Sarawak	Atlantic 1944		
Sardonyx	Atlantic 1940-42	Arctic 1942	
Sargasso	Dunkirk 1940		
Sargetta	Belgian Coast 1915		
Sarnia	Atlantic 1942-43		
Sasebo	English Channel 1942		
Saskatchewan	Atlantic 1943-44	Biscay 1944	Normandy 1944
Saskatoon	Atlantic 1942-45		
Satellite	Abyssinia 1868		
Satisfaction	Portland 1653	Lowestoft 1665	
Satsa	South France 1944		

Saturn	Copenhagen 1801		
Satyr	Belgian Coast 1917	Norway 1940	
Saulte Sainte Marie	Atlantic 1944-45		
Saumarez	Arctic 1943-44 East Indies 1945	North Cape 1943 Malaya 1945	Normandy 1944 Burma 1945
Savage	Guadeloupe 1810 Normandy 1944	Arctic 1943-45	North Cape 1943
Sawfly	Mesopotamia 1916-17		
Saxifrage	Arctic 1942 Mediterranean 1943	Atlantic 1942-43 Aegean 1944	Biscay 1943
Saxonia	Falkland Islands 1982*		
Scalpay	North Sea 1942	English Channel 1943	Normandy 1944
Scampavia	Egypt 1801		
Scarab	Mesopotamia 1917 Adriatic 1944	Sicily 1943 South France 1944	Mediterranean 1943-44
Scaravay	Burma 1945		
Scarba	Atlantic 1942		
Scarborough	Louisburg 1758 North Africa 1942 English Channel 1944	Quebec 1759 North Sea 1943	Atlantic 1939-44 Normandy 1944
Scarron	English Channel 1942		
Scawfell	Normandy 1944		
Sceptre	Trincomalee 1782 Norway 1944	Cape of Good Hope 1795 Atlantic 1944	Guadeloupe 1810 Biscay 1944
Scimitar	Dunkirk 1940 English Channel 1943-44	Atlantic 1940-44	Arctic 1942
Scipion	Java 1811		
Scomber	Normandy 1944		
Scorpion	Quebec 1759 Guadeloupe 1810 North Cape 1943	'*Athalante*' 1804 Dardanelles 1915-6 Normandy 1944	'**Oreste**' 1810 Arctic 1943-45
Scotia	Dunkirk 1940*		
Scott	Zeebrugge 1918	Norway 1941	Normandy 1944
Scottish	North Africa 1942	Atlantic 1943	

Scottish Eagle	Falkland Islands 1982*		
Scourge	Dardanelles 1915	Arctic 1943-45	Normandy 1944
Scout	Armada 1588	China 1860	
Scylla	'*Weser*' 1813 Atlantic 1943 Normandy 1944	Arctic 1942-43 Biscay 1943	North Africa 1942 Salerno 1943
Scythian	Atlantic 1944	Malaya 1945	
Sea Cliff	Atlantic 1944-45		
Sea Rover	Malaya 1944	Atlantic 1945	
Seadog	Arctic 1942-43	Atlantic 1944	
Seaflower	Martinique 1794		
Seaford	Atlantic 1944		
Seagull	Ashantee 1873	Arctic 1941-44	Normandy 1944
Seaham	Atlantic 1942	Sicily 1943	Normandy 1944
Seahorse	Quebec 1759 Negapatam 1782	Sadras 1782 Trincomalee 1782	Providien 1782 '*Badere Zaffer*' 1808
Seal	Atlantic 1939		
Sealion	Norway 1940-41	North Sea 1940	Arctic 1941-42
Sealyham	Atlantic 1942-45		
Seanymph	Arctic 1942-43	Biscay 1943	Atlantic 1945
Searcher	Atlantic 1943-44 Norway 1944-45	Aegean 1944	South France 1944
Seascout	Atlantic 1944	Malaya 1945	
Seawolf	Norway 1940-41	Arctic 1941-42	
Sedgefly	Mesopotamia 1917		
Seine	'*Vengeance*' 1800		
Seksern	Libya 1942	Aegean 1944	
Selene	Malaya 1945		
Selkirk	Atlantic 1939	North Sea 1942	Normandy 1944
Sennen	Atlantic 1941-43	North Africa 1942-43	
Sensible	Egypt 1801		

Seraph (P.219)	North Africa 1942-43 Aegean 1943	Mediterranean 1943	Sicily 1943
Serapis	'*Bonhome Richard*' 1779	Normandy 1944	Arctic 1944-45
Serpent	Burma 1852		
Setter	Atlantic 1942-43		
Settsu	Normandy 1944		
Seven Brothers	Dover 1652	Scheveningen 1653	
Sevenoaks	Four Days' Battle 1666		
Severn	Algiers 1816 Norway 1940 Aegean 1943	Belgian Coast 1914 Atlantic 1940-41	'*Königsberg*' 1915 Sicily 1943
Seychelles	Atlantic 1945		
Seymour	Normandy 1944	North Sea 1944-45	
SGB 3	See **Grey Seal**		
SGB 4	See **Grey Fox**		
SGB 5	See **Grey Owl**		
SGB 6	See **Grey Shark**		
SGB 8	See **Grey Wolf**		
SGB 9	See **Grey Goose**		
Shah	East Indies 1944	Burma 1945	
Shaitan	Mesopotamia 1914-15		
Shakespeare (P.221)	Arctic 1942 Salerno 1943 English Channel 1943	North Africa 1942 Aegean 1943 Atlantic 1944	Sicily1943 Mediterranean 1943 East Indies 1944
Shalimar	Atlantic 1944		
Shamrock	Glückstadt 1814		
Shannon	Lousiburg 1758 Lucknow 1857-58	Lagos 1759 Jutland 1916	'*Chesapeake*' 1813
Shark	Crimea 1854	Jutland 1916	North Sea 1940
Sharpshooter	Belgian Coast 1917 Atlantic 1942-44	Dunkirk 1940 Sicily 1943	Arctic 1941-43
Shawinigan	Atlantic 1942-44		
Shearwater	North Sea 1940-45		

Shediac	Atlantic 1941-44		
Sheerness	Lagos 1759	Egypt 1801	
Sheffield	Norway 1940 '*Bismarck*' 1941 Arctic 1941-43 Biscay 1943 Falkland Islands 1982	Spartivento 1940 Mediterranean 1941 North Africa 1942 Salerno 1943	Atlantic 1941-43 Malta Convoys 1941 Barents Sea 1942 North Cape 1943
Sheldon	North Sea 1942		
Sheldrake	North Sea 1941-45	Atlantic 1942	
Shell Eburna	Falkland Islands 1982*		
Shepparton	New Guinea 1943-44		
Sheppey	North Sea 1942	Salerno 1943	Anzio 1944
Sherbrooke	Atlantic 1941-45		
Sherwood	Atlantic 1941-43	North Sea 1943	
Shiant	Atlantic 1942	North Africa 1942-43	Sicily 1943
Shiel	Atlantic 1944	Burma 1945	
Shielburn	Normandy 1944		
Shikari	Dunkirk 1940	Atlantic 1940-43	
Shipmates	Dunkirk 1940		
Shippigan	North Sea 1942 English Channel 1944	Atlantic 1943	Normandy 1944
Shoalhaven	Korea 1950		
Shoreham	East Indies 1940 Burma 1944-45	Sicily 1943	Mediterranean 1943
Shrewsbury	Velez Malaga 1704 St. Kitts 1782	Passero 1718	Quebec 1759
Shropshire	Atlantic 1941 New Guinea 1943-44 Pacific 1945	Arctic 1941 Leyte Gulf 1944	East Indies 1941 Lingayen Gulf 1945
Shusa	Arctic 1942		
Shushan	Mesopotamia 1915		
Sibyl (P.217)	St. Kitts 1782 Aegean 1943-44	North Africa 1942-43	Sicily 1943
Sickle	Mediterranean 1943	Aegean 1943-44	

Sidmouth	Dieppe 1942	Normandy 1944	
Sidon	Crimea 1854-55	Atlantic 1945	
Sigma	Normandy 1944		
Sikh	Norway 1940 Cape Bon 1941 Sirte 1942	Atlantic 1940-41 Libya 1941 Mediterranean 1942	*'Bismarck'* 1941 Malta Convoys 1941-42
Silja	Arctic 1942		
Silver Dawn	Dunkirk 1940		
Silvio	Burma 1945		
Simoom	Crimea 1854-55 Sicily 1943	China 1860 Aegean 1943	Ashantee 1873-74 Mediterranean 1943
Sinbad	Baltic 1855		
Sindonis	Libya 1941		
Siona	Libya 1941		
Sioux	Normandy 1944 Korea 1950-52	Arctic 1944-45	Atlantic 1945
Sir Agravaine	Normandy 1944		
Sir Bedivere	Falkland Islands 1982**	Kuwait 1991**	
Sir Charles Forbes	China 1856-60		
Sir Francis Drake	Java 1811		
Sir Galahad	North Sea 1942 Kuwait 1991**	Normandy 1944	Falkland Islands 1982**
Sir Gareth	Normandy 1944		
Sir Geraint	North Sea 1942	Normandy 1944	Falkland Islands 1982**
Sir John Moore	Belgian Coast 1915-18		
Sir Kaye	Normandy 1944		
Sir Lamorak	Normandy 1944		
Sir Lancelot	Normandy 1944	Falkland Islands 1982**	
Sir Percivale	Falkland Islands 1982**	Kuwait 1991**	
Sir Sydney Smith	Egypt 1801		
Sir Thomas Picton	Dardanelles 1915-16		
Sir Tristram	Normandy 1944	Falkland Islands 1982**	Kuwait 1991**

Sirius	Trafalgar 1805	Belgian Coast 1914	Zeebrugge 1918
	Arctic 1942	Malta Convoys 1942	Mediterranean 1942
	North Africa 1942-43	Sicily 1943	Salerno 1943
	Aegean 1943-44	Normandy 1944	South France 1944
Skagi	Atlantic 1943		
Skate	Atlantic 1940-44	Arctic 1943	English Channel 1944
Skeena	Atlantic 1939-44	Biscay 1944	Normandy 1944
Skilful	Belgian Coast 1917		
Skipjack	Dunkirk 1940		
Skokolm	South France 1944		
Skomer	Normandy 1944	Atlantic 1945	
Skudd III	Libya 1941		
Skudd IV	Libya 1941		
Skudd V	Libya 1941		
Skye	Normandy 1944		
Skylark	Baltic 1855		
Slaney	Burma 1824-26	China 1856-60	
Sleuth	Malaya 1945		
Slinger	Okinawa 1945		
Slothany	Orfordness 1666		
Smilax	Atlantic 1944		
Smiter	Atlantic 1944		
Smiths Falls	Atlantic 1945		
Snaefell	Dunkirk 1940		
Snake	St. Lucia 1778	Crimea 1855	China 1860
Snakefly	Mesopotamia 1916-17	Atlantic 1940	
Snap	Martinique 1809	Guadeloupe 1810	Baltic 1854-55
	China 1860		
Snapdragon	Libya 1942		
Snapper	Baltic 1855	Norway 1940	Atlantic 1940
Snowberry	Atlantic 1941-44	Biscay 1943	English Channel 1945

Snowdrop	Atlantic 1941-44		
Snowflake	Atlantic 1941-44	North Sea 1941	Arctic 1942
Society	Gabbard 1653	Lowestoft 1665	Texel 1673
Soika	Libya 1941-42		
Soira	Libya 1941		
Solebay	St. Kitts 1782		
Solent	Malaya 1945		
Solomon	Armada 1588*		
Somali	Norway 1940-41 Malta Convoys 1942	'*Bismarck*' 1941	Arctic 1941-42
Somaliland	Atlantic 1944	Arctic 1944	
Somerset	Vigo 1702 Quebec 1759	Velez Malaga 1704	Louisburg 1758
Sonnet	Normandy 1944		
Sophia	Gabbard 1653	Scheveningen 1653	Burma 1824-26
Sorel	Atlantic 1941-45	North Sea 1942	
Sotra	Libya 1941-42		
Southampton	'*Émeraude*' 1757 St. Vincent 1797 Jutland 1916 Malta Convoys 1941	Belle Isle 1761 Heligoland 1914 Norway 1940	First of June 1794 Dogger Bank 1915 Spartivento 1940
Southdown	North Sea 1941-45	Normandy 1944	
Southern Floe	Libya 1941		
Southern Flower	Atlantic 1942-44		
Southern Gem	Atlantic 1940-44	North Sea 1943	
Southern Isle	Libya 1941-42 Mediterranean 1944	Sicily 1943	Atlantic 1943
Southern Maid	Libya 1941-42	Mediterranean 1942-44	Aegean 1944
Southern Pride	Atlantic 1941-44		
Southern Prince	Atlantic 1940-41	Normandy 1944	
Southern Sea	Libya 1941-42 Mediterranean 1944	Sicily 1943	Atlantic 1944
Southern Shore	Atlantic 1940-44		

Southward Ho	Normandy 1944		
Southwold	Libya 1942	Malta Convoys 1942	Sirte 1942
Sovereign	Kentish Knock 1652 Texel 1673	Solebay 1672 Barfleur 1692	Schooneveld 1673
Spanker	South France 1944		
Spark	Armada 1588*	Atlantic 1944	
Sparrow	San Sebastian 1813	Korea 1953	
Sparrowhawk	China 1860	Jutland 1916	
Spartan	Bay of Naples 1810 Atlantic 1943 Falkland Islands 1982	Burma 1852-53 Mediterranean 1944	China 1856-57 Anzio 1944
Spartiate	Trafalgar 1805		
Speaker	Dover 1652 Gabbard 1653 Okinawa 1945	Kentish Knock 1652 Santa Cruz 1657	Portland 1653 Atlantic 1944
Speaker's Prize	Portland 1653		
Spearfish	Norway 1940	North Sea 1940	
Spearhead	Atlantic 1945		
Speculator	Camperdown 1797		
Speedwell	Armada 1588* Atlantic 1941-43 Normandy 1944	Barfleur 1692 Arctic 1942-44	Dunkirk 1940 North Africa 1942-43
Speedy	'Gamo' 1801 Arctic 1942	North Sea 1942	Malta Convoys 1942
Spencer	Gut of Gibraltar 1801	San Domingo 1806	
Spey	Atlantic 1942-44	North Africa 1942-43	Burma 1944-45
Sphene	Atlantic 1940-43		
Sphinx	Cape of Good Hope 1795 Crimea 1854-55	Burma 1852-53 China 1860	Baltic 1854
Spider	Egypt 1801		
Spikenard	Atlantic 1941-42		
Spirea	Atlantic 1942-45 North Sea 1943	Malta Convoys 1942	North Africa 1942
Spiteful	Martinique 1794	Crimea 1854-55	

Spitfire	Crimea 1854-55	Jutland 1916	
Splendid (P.228)	Mediterranean 1942	North Africa 1942	Falkland Islands 1982
Sportsman	Sicily 1943 Atlantic 1945	Aegean 1943-44	Mediterranean 1944
Sposa	Atlantic 1942-44		
Spragge	Normandy 1944	English Channel 1944	
Spread Eagle	Four Days' Battle 1666		
Springbok	Belgian Coast 1917		
Spry	North Sea 1943		
Spurs	Dunkirk 1940	North Sea 1942-45	
Spy	Armada 1588	Barfleur 1692	
Squirrel	Louisburg 1758	Quebec 1759	
Staffa	English Channel 1942	North Sea 1942	Atlantic 1943
Stafnes	Atlantic 1942-44		
Stag	Martinique 1762		
Stalker	Atlantic 1943-4 Aegean 1944	Salerno 1943 East Indies 1945	South France 1944 Burma 1945
Stanley	Atlantic 1941		
Star	Dover 1652	Martinique 1809	Guadeloupe 1810
Star of India	English Channel 1942		
Starfish	Belgian Coast 1917		
Starling	China 1841-42 Atlantic 1943-45 Normandy 1944	Baltic 1855 Biscay 1943-44	China 1856-60 Arctic 1944
Starwort	Atlantic 1941-45 Mediterranean 1942 Normandy 1944	North Sea 1942-44 Arctic 1942-44 English Channel 1944	North Africa 1942 Sicily 1943
Stata	English Channel 1942		
Stately	Cape of Good Hope 1795	Egypt 1801	
Statesman	Malaya 1945		
Statice	Normandy 1944	English Channel 1944-45	Atlantic 1944-45
Statira	Guadeloupe 1810		

Staunch	China 1856-60	Dardanelles 1915-16	Normandy 1944
Stavoreen	Schooneveld 1673	Texel 1673	
Stawell	New Guinea 1943-44	Pacific 1945	
Stayner	Normandy 1944	English Channel 1944	North Sea 1944
Steadfast	Normandy 1944	Atlantic 1944	
Steepholm	Normandy 1944		
Stella	North Sea 1944		
Stella Canopus	North Sea 1944		
Stella Capella	Atlantic 1940-41	Arctic 1942	
Stella Carina	Atlantic 1941-43	Sicily 1943	Salerno 1943
Stella Dorado	Dunkirk 1940		
Stella Leonis	Normandy 1944		
Stella Pegasi	Atlantic 1944		
Stella Polaris	North Sea 1942		
Stella Rigel	North Sea 1943	Normandy 1944	
Stellarton	Atlantic 1945		
Stena Seaspread	Falkland Islands 1982*		
Stevenstone	English Channel 1943-44	North Sea 1944	Normandy 1944
Stirling Castle	Barfleur 1692 Havana 1762	Quebec 1759	Martinique 1762
Stockham	English Channel 1944	Normandy 1944	
Stoic	Malaya 1944	Atlantic 1945	
Stoke	Libya 1941		
Stoke City	Atlantic 1940	North Sea 1943-45	
Stonecrop	Atlantic 1941-45	English Channel 1945	
Stonefly	Mesopotamia 1916-17		
Stonehenge	Malaya 1944		
Stonetown	Atlantic 1944-45		
Stora	Atlantic 1942-44		

Stork	Gabbard 1653 Zeebrugge 1918 Atlantic 1940-44	Martinique 1809 Norway 1940 North Africa 1942	Baltic 1855 North Sea 1940 Normandy 1944
Storm	East Indies 1944	Malaya 1944	Atlantic 1945
Stormcloud	South France 1944		
Stormont	Normandy 1944 Atlantic 1944-45	English Channel 1944	Arctic 1944
Stornoway	Dieppe 1942 North Africa 1942-43 South France 1944	English Channel 1942 Sicily 1943	North Sea 1942 Salerno 1943
Strafford	Puerto Bello 1739		
Strahan	New Guinea 1944		
Stratagem	English Channel 1944	Malaya 1944	
Stratford	Atlantic 1942-44		
Strathadam	Atlantic 1945		
Strathalladale	Normandy 1944		
Strathella	Atlantic 1943-44		
Strathfina	Normandy 1944		
Strathmartin	Normandy 1944		
Strathroy	Atlantic 1945		
Striker	Atlantic 1943-44 Okinawa 1945	Arctic 1944	Norway 1944
Stroma	Atlantic 1942	North Africa 1942-43	Sicily 1943
Stromboli	Syria 1840	Baltic 1854	Crimea 1854-55
Strombolo	Barfleur 1692	Quebec 1759	
Stromness	Falkland Islands 1982**		
Strongbow	Scandanavian Convoys 1917	Atlantic 1944	Malaya 1944
Stronsay	English Channel 1942	North Africa 1942-43	
Strule	Normandy 1944	Arctic 1944	Atlantic 1944
Stuart	Calabria 1940 Matapan 1941 New Guinea 1942-44	Libya 1940-41 Greece 1941	Mediterranean 1940 Crete 1941
Stuart Prince	South France 1944	Atlantic 1944	

Stubborn	Biscay 1943 Malaya 1945	Norway 1944	Atlantic 1945
Sturdy	Atlantic 1940	Malaya 1945	
Sturgeon	North Sea 1940	Arctic 1942	North Africa 1942-43
Sturton	North Sea 1942	Normandy 1944	
Stygian	Atlantic 1944	Malaya 1945	
Styx	Burma 1853		
Subtle	Martinique 1809	Guadeloupe 1810	Malaya 1944-45
Success	Portland 1653 Lowestoft 1665	Gabbard 1653 Sole Bay 1672	Porto Farina 1655 Texel 1673
Sudbury	Atlantic 1941-44		
Suffolk	Barfleur 1692 Norway 1940 East Indies 1944-45	Gibraltar 1704 'Bismarck' 1941 Burma 1945	Velez Malaga 1704 Arctic 1941-42
Sulina	Crimea 1855		
Sulist	English Channel 1942		
Sulla	Arctic 1942		
Sulphur	Copenhagen 1801	China 1841	
Sultan	Providien 1782 Alexandria 1882	Negapatam 1782	Trincomalee 1782
Sultana	Egypt 1801		
Sumana	Mesopotamia 1915-16		
Sumba	Arctic 1942		
Summerside	Atlantic 1941-44	English Channel 1944-45	Normandy 1944
Sun	Armada 1588		
Sunderland	Porto Novo 1759		
Sunfish	North Sea 1940	Norway 1940-41	
Sunflower	Atlantic 1941-45 Normandy 1944	North Sea 1944	English Channel 1944-45
Superb	Passero 1718 Negapatam 1782 San Domingo 1806 Jutland 1916	Sadras 1782 Trincomalee 1782 Algiers 1816	Providien 1782 Gut of Gibraltar 1801 Alexandria 1882
Superieure	Martinique 1809	Guadeloupe 1810	

Supply	Texel 1673		
Supreme	Atlantic 1944		
Surf	Aegean 1943	Atlantic 1944	
Surface	North Sea 1942		
Surinam	Martinique 1809	Guadeloupe 1810	
Surly	Baltic 1855		
Surprise	Dogger Bank 1781 Belgian Coast 1917	*'Hermione'* 1799 Atlantic 1941	China 1856-60
Surveillante	San Sebastian 1813		
Susan	Armada 1588*		
Susan Parnell	Armada 1588*		
Sussex	Portland 1653 Burma 1945	Gabbard 1653	Norway 1940
Sussexvale	Atlantic 1945	English Channel 1945	
Sutherland	Louisburg 1758 Havana 1762	Quebec 1759	Martinique 1762
Sutlej	Sicily 1943	Burma 1945	
Sutton	Armada 1588* Normandy 1944	Dunkirk 1940	English Channel 1942-43
Svana	Libya 1941		
Swale	Atlantic 1942-44	North Africa 1942	
Swallow	Armada 1588 Orfordness 1666 Marbella 1705	Lowestoft 1665 Texel 1673 Crimea 1854-55	Four Days' Battle 1666 Velez Malaga 1704
Swan	Cadiz 1596*	Gabbard 1653	New Guinea 1942-44
Swansea	Atlantic 1943-44	Normandy 1944	English Channel 1944
Swansea Castle	English Channel 1942		
Sweepstakes	Sole Bay 1672	Schooneveld 1673	Texel 1673
Sweetbriar	Atlantic 1941-45	Arctic 1942	Normandy 1944
Swift	Dover 1917 Normandy 1944	Belgian Coast 1917-18 Arctic 1944	Zeebrugge 1918
Swift Current	Atlantic 1943-44		

Swiftsure	Armada 1588	Cadiz 1596	Santa Cruz 1657
	Lowestoft 1665	Four Days' Battle 1666	Schooneveld 1673
	Texel 1673	Barfleur 1692	Vigo 1702
	Gibraltar 1704	Velez Malaga 1704	Lagos 1759
	Quiberon Bay 1759	Belle Isle 1761	Nile 1798
	Egypt 1801	Trafalgar 1805	Suez Canal 1915
	Dardanelles 1915-16	Okinawa 1945	
Swinger	Martinique 1809	Baltic 1855	
Switha	North Sea 1942-43	Normandy 1944	
Sword Dance	North Sea 1941-42		
Swordfish	English Channel 1940		
Sybil	Atlantic 1945		
Sybille	'*Forte*' 1799	China 1856-60	
Sydney	'*Emden*' 1914	Calabria 1940	Spada 1940
	Mediterranean 1940	'*Kormoran*' 1941	Korea 1951-52
Sylvana	Normandy 1944		
Sylvia	'*Echo*' 1810		
Symbol	Atlantic 1943		
Syren	'*Williamstadt*' 1793	Belgian Coast 1914-17	
Syvern	Crete 1941		
Taciturn	Atlantic 1945	Malaya 1945	
Tactician	Sicily 1943	Mediterranean 1943	
Tadoussac	North Sea 1943	Atlantic 1943-45	Normandy 1944
Taff	East Indies 1944	Burma 1945	
Taipo	Normandy 1944		
Taku	Norway 1940-44	Mediterranean 1941	
Talbot	Armada 1588*	Navarino 1827	Syria 1840
	Dardanelles 1915-16		
Talisman	Mediterranean 1941	Malta Convoys 1941	
Tally-Ho	Biscay 1943	Malaya 1943-44	
Talybont	English Channel 1943-44	North Sea 1943-44	Normandy 1944
Tamar	Burma 1824-26	Ashantee 1873-74	
Tamarisk	Atlantic 1942-43		

Tanatside	Atlantic 1943 Normandy 1944	English Channel 1943-45	Biscay 1944
Tango	North Sea 1941-42 Sicily 1943	Arctic 1942 Salerno 1943	Atlantic 1942-43
Tantalus	Sabang 1944	Malaya 1944	
Tantivy	Malaya 1944	Atlantic 1945	
Tapir	Norway 1945		
Tarantella	Atlantic 1940	North Sea 1941-43	
Tarantula	Mesopotamia 1916-17		
Tarleton	Genoa 1795		
Tarpon	Norway 1940		
Tartan	North Sea 1942		
Tartar	Velez Malaga 1704 South Africa 1899-1900 '*Bismarck*' 1941 North Africa 1942-43 Mediterranean 1943 Biscay 1944	Ushant 1781 Belgian Coast 1914-16 Arctic 1942 Sicily 1943 Normandy 1944 Burma 1945	Baltic 1855 Norway 1940-41 Malta Convoys 1942 Salerno 1943 English Channel 1944 Malaya 1945
Tartar's Prize	Lagos 1759		
Tartarus	Egypt 1801		
Tasajera	North Africa 1942-43	Normandy 1944	
Tattoo	Atlantic 1944		
Taupo	Korea 1951-52		
Taurus	Belgian Coast 1917 Mediterranean 1943	Arctic 1942-43 Malaya 1943-44	Sicily 1943 Atlantic 1944-45
Tavy	Atlantic 1943-44 Arctic 1944	Normandy 1944	English Channel 1944
Tay	Atlantic 1942-45		
Teazer	Zeebrugge 1918 South France 1944	Mediterranean 1943 Aegean 1944	Adriatic 1944
Tedworth	Atlantic 1939		
Tees	Burma 1824-26	Atlantic 1943-45	
Telegraph	'*Hirondelle*' 1799		
Telemachus	Malaya 1944	Korea 1953	

Teme	Normandy 1944		
Temeraire	Belle Isle 1761 Trafalgar 1805	Martinique 1762 Alexandria 1882	Havana 1762 Jutland 1916
Tempest	Zeebrugge 1918		
Templar	Sicily 1943	Sabang 1944	Malaya 1944
Temple	Quiberon Bay 1759	Martinique 1762	Havana 1762
Tenacious	Adriatic 1944 Okinawa 1945	Mediterranean 1944 Japan 1945	South France 1944
Tenby	Dieppe 1942	Normandy 1944	
Tenth Whelp	Portland 1653	Gabbard 1653	
Termagant	Egypt 1801 Zeebrugge 1918 Mediterranean 1943-44 Aegean 1944	Baltic 1854 Belgian Coast 1918 Adriatic 1944 Okinawa 1945	Jutland 1916 Arctic 1943 South France 1944 Japan 1945
Terpsichore	'Mahonesa' 1796 Aegean 1944	Adriatic 1944 Japan 1945	South France 1944
Terrapin	Norway 1944	Malaya 1944-45	
Terrible	Vigo 1702 St. Vincent 1780 South Africa 1899-1900	Louisburg 1758 Genoa 1795 China 1900	Quebec 1759 Crimea 1854-55
Terror	Velez Malaga 1704 Zeebrugge 1918	Copenhagen 1801 Libya 1940-41	Belgian Coast 1916-18 Mediterranean 1941
Test	Atlantic 1943	Sicily 1943	Burma 1945
Tetcott	Libya 1942 Salerno 1943 Adriatic 1944	Mediterranean 1942 Aegean 1943-44	Sicily 1943 Anzio 1944
Tetrarch	Zeebrugge 1918	Norway 1940	Mediterranean 1940-41
Teviot	Sicily 1943	Burma 1944-45	
Texada	Atlantic 1943	Normandy 1944	
Thalassa	Atlantic 1943-44		
Thalia	Groix Island 1795		
Thames	Gut of Gibraltar 1801		
Thames Queen	North Sea 1942	Normandy 1944	
Thane	Atlantic 1944		

The Boys	Dunkirk 1940		
The Pas	Atlantic 1942-44		
The Way	Normandy 1944		
Theseus	Nile 1798 Benin 1897	Acre 1799 Dardanelles 1915-16	Basque Roads 1809 Korea 1950-51
Thetford Mines	Atlantic 1945	North Sea 1945	
Thetis	Lagos 1759 Egypt 1801	*'Bouffonne'* 1761 Guadeloupe 1810	*'Prévoyante'* 1795 Zeebrugge 1918
Thirlmere	Norway 1940	Atlantic 1941-44	North Sea 1942
Thisbe	Egypt 1801		
Thistle	*'Havick'* 1810	Baltic 1855	Norway 1940
Thomas Bartlett	Dunkirk 1940		
Thomas Bonaventure	Armada 1588*		
Thomas Drake	Armada 1588*		
Thomas and Edward	Sole Bay 1672		
Thomas and Elizabeth	Barfleur 1692		
Thomas and Lucy	Portland 1653	Gabbard 1653	
Thomas and William	Portland 1653	Gabbard 1653	
Thorbryn	Libya 1941		
Thorgrim	Libya 1941		
Thorlock	Atlantic 1945		
Thorn	Mediterranean 1941-42		
Thornborough	Normandy 1944 North Sea 1945	English Channel 1944	Atlantic 1945
Thorough	Malaya 1944-45		
Thrasher	Mediterranean 1941-42	Atlantic 1944	
Three Rivers	Atlantic 1942-44		
Thruster	Belgian Coast 1917 Anzio 1944	Sicily 1943 South France 1944	Salerno 1943 Aegean 1944

Thule	Atlantic 1944	Malaya 1944-45	
Thunder	Martinique 1762 Atlantic 1941-44	Havana 1762 Normandy 1944	Basque Roads 1809
Thunderbolt	Biscay 1940	Malta Convoys 1941-42	Mediterranean 1942
Thunderer	'*Achille*' 1761 St. Lucia 1796 Jutland 1916	Lake Champlain 1776 Trafalgar 1805	First of June 1794 Syria 1840
Thuringia	Dunkirk 1940		
Thyme	North Sea 1941	Atlantic 1941-42	Diego Suarez 1942
Tidepool	Falkland Islands 1982**		
Tidespring	Falkland Islands 1982**		
Tiger	Armada 1588 Scheveningen 1653 Sole Bay 1672 Negapatam 1758 Jutland 1916	Portland 1653 Lowestoft 1665 Marbella 1705 Porto Novo 1759	Gabbard 1653 Orfordness 1666 Sadras 1758 Dogger Bank 1915
Tiger Prize	Barfleur 1692		
Tigre	Acre 1799	Egypt 1801	
Tigress	Dogger Bank 1915		
Tigris	Norway 1941	Arctic 1941-42	Mediterranean 1942
Tilbury	Velez Malaga 1704	Ushant 1747	
Tillsonburg	Atlantic 1944-45		
Timmins	Atlantic 1942-45		
Tintagel Castle	Atlantic 1944-45		
Tipperary	Jutland 1916		
Tiptoe	Malaya 1945		
Tiree	North Sea 1942	Atlantic 1943-44	
Tisiphone	Ushant 1781		
Tobago	Atlantic 1944		
Tobruk	Korea 1951-53		
Toby	Armada 1588*		
Tocsin	Normandy 1944		
Toneline	Libya 1941-42		

Tonnant	Trafalgar 1805		
Tor Caledonia	Falkland Islands 1982*		
Torbay	Vigo 1702	Velez Malaga 1704	Quiberon Bay 1759
	Belle Isle 1761	St. Kitts 1782	The Saints 1782
	Mediterranean 1941-43	Arctic 1942-43	Sicily 1943
	Aegean 1943	Atlantic 1944	English Channel 1944
	Malaya 1945		
Torbay II	Dunkirk 1940		
Tormentor	Martinique 1794		
Torrington	Normandy 1944	Atlantic 1944	English Channel 1944
	North Sea 1944-45		
Tortola	Arctic 1944	Atlantic 1944-45	
Totland	Atlantic 1941-44		
Tourmaline	Atlantic 1943		
Tourterelle	Egypt 1801		
Townsville	New Guinea 1944		
Towy	Atlantic 1943-45	English Channel 1945	
Tracker	Atlantic 1943-44	Arctic 1944	Normandy 1944
Tradewind	Malaya 1944-45		
Trafalgar	Crimea 1854		
Trail	Atlantic 1941-45		
Tramontana	Armada 1588	Cadiz 1596	
Transcona	Atlantic 1943-45		
Transfer	Egypt 1801		
Treern	Libya 1940	Aegean 1944	
Tremendous	First of June 1794	Cape of Good Hope 1795	
Trenchant	Malaya 1944-45		
Trent	Louisburg 1758	Quebec 1759	Havana 1762
	Sicily 1943	Atlantic 1943	Burma 1945
Trentonian	Normandy 1944	Atlantic 1944	English Channel 1944-45
Trespasser	Sicily 1943	Aegean 1943	Malaya 1944
Triad	Dardanelles 1915	Norway 1940	Mediterranean 1940

Tribune	Baltic 1854 Arctic 1942	Crimea 1854-55 North Africa 1942	China 1856-60 Sicily 1943
Trident	Quebec 1759 Ostend 1918 North Sea 1942 Atlantic 1944	Cape of Good Hope 1795 Norway 1940-41 Sicily 1943	Zeebrugge 1918 Arctic 1941-42 Mediterranean 1943
Trillium	Atlantic 1940-45		
Trinidad	Arctic 1942		
Tritellia	Atlantic 1943		
Triton	Velez Malaga 1704 Crimea 1854-55	St. Vincent 1780 Norway 1940	The Saints 1782 Mediterranean 1940
Triumph	Armada 1588 Gabbard 1653 Four Days' Battle 1666 Schooneveld 1673 Camperdown 1797 Mediterranean 1941	Dover 1652 Scheveningen 1653 Orfordness 1666 Texel 1673 Dardanelles 1915 Korea 1950	Portland 1653 Lowestoft 1665 Sole Bay 1672 Cornwallis' Retreat 1795 Malta Convoys 1941
Trollope	Normandy 1944	English Channel 1944	
Trondra	Atlantic 1943-44		
Trooper	Sicily 1943	Aegean 1943	Mediterranean 1943
Troubridge	Sicily 1943 Aegean 1944 Okinawa 1945	Salerno 1943 South France 1944	Mediterranean 1943 Adriatic 1944
Trouncer	Atlantic 1944		
Truant	Norway 1940	Mediterranean 1940-41	Atlantic 1944
Truculent	Belgian Coast 1917 Atlantic 1944	Zeebrugge 1918 Malaya 1944	Arctic 1943
Truelove	Cadiz 1596	Schooneveld 1673	Texel 1673
Trump	Malaya 1945		
Trumpeter	Atlantic 1943-44	Arctic 1944	Norway 1944-45
Truro	Atlantic 1942-45		
Trusty	Egypt 1801	Malta Convoys 1941	
Tudor	Malaya 1944-45		
Tui	Atlantic 1942	Guadalcanal 1942-43	
Tulip	Portland 1653	Gabbard 1653	Scheveningen 1653
Tumby	North Sea 1942		

Tumult	Atlantic 1943 Aegean 1943-44 South France 1944	Sicily 1943 Mediterranean 1943-44	Salerno 1943 Adriatic 1944
Tuna	Biscay 1940-43	Norway 1941	Arctic 1943
Tunsberg Castle	Atlantic 1944	Arctic 1944	
Turbulent	Jutland 1916	Mediterranean 1942	
Turcoman	Atlantic 1942		
Turkey Merchant	Orfordness 1666		
Turquoise	North Sea 1942-43		
Tuscan	Adriatic 1944	South France 1944	Aegean 1944
Tutira	Korea 1950-51		
Tweed	Biscay 1943	Atlantic 1943-44	
Twostep	Anzio 1944		
Tyler	Normandy 1944	English Channel 1944-45	Atlantic 1945
Tyne	Baltic 1854	Korea 1953	
Tynedale	St. Nazaire 1942	English Channel 1942-43	Sicily 1943
Tynwald	Dunkirk 1940*	North Africa 1942	
Typhoon	North Sea 1942		
Typhoon	Falkland Islands 1982**(RMAS)		
Tyrian	Atlantic 1943 Mediterranean 1943 Aegean 1944	Sicily 1943 Adriatic 1944	Salerno 1943 South France 1944
Uganda	Atlantic 1943 Mediterranean 1943	Sicily 1943 Okinawa 1945	Salerno 1943 Falkland Islands 1982*
Ugiebank	Normandy 1944		
Ulleswater	Zeebrugge 1918		
Ullswater	Atlantic 1940	English Channel 1942	
Ulster	English Channel 1943 Normandy 1944	Adriatic 1944 Okinawa 1945	Mediterranean 1944
Ulster Monarch	North Africa 1942 Normandy 1944	Sicily 1943 English Channel 1944	Salerno 1943
Ulster Prince	Greece 1941		

Ulster Queen	Arctic 1942 Anzio 1944 Atlantic 1944	Sicily 1943 Aegean 1944	Salerno 1943 South France 1944
Ultimatum (P.34)	Malta Convoys 1942 Atlantic 1944	Mediterranean 1942-44	Aegean 1944
Ultor	Sicily 1943 Aegean 1944	Mediterranean 1943-44 Atlantic 1944	Anzio 1944
Ulva	Normandy 1944		
Ulysses	Martinique 1794 Arctic 1944	Egypt 1801 Normandy 1944	Martinique 1809 Japan 1945
Umbra (P.35)	Mediterranean 1942		
Una	Burma 1945		
Unbeaten	Mediterranean 1941-42	Malta Convoys 1941-42	Biscay 1942
Unbending (P.37)	Mediterranean 1942		
Unbroken (P.42)	Malta Convoys 1942	Mediterranean 1942	Sicily 1943
Undaunted	Dogger Bank 1915 Okinawa 1945	Belgian Coast 1916	Normandy 1944
Undine	Mediterranean 1944 Okinawa 1945	Normandy 1944 Japan 1945	Adriatic 1944
Ungava	Atlantic 1942-44		
Unicorn	Armada 1588* Santa Cruz 1657 Sole Bay 1672 'Vestale' 1761 Salerno 1943	Cadiz 1596* Lowestoft 1665 Schooneveld 1673 'Tribune' 1796 Okinawa 1945	Porto Farina 1655 Orfordness 1666 Texel 1673 Basque Roads 1809 Korea 1950-53
Union	Quiberon Bay 1759	Ushant 1781	
Unique	Mediterranean 1941 Arctic 1942	Malta Convoys 1941	Biscay 1942
Unison (P.43)	Malta Convoys 1942	Sicily 1943	
Unité	Pelagosa 1811		
United (P.44)	Malta Convoys 1942	Sicily 1943	Mediterranean 1943
United Boys	English Channel 1942		
Unity	Armada 1588*	Orfordness 1666	Jutland 1916
Universal	Sicily 1943	Atlantic 1944	Mediterranean 1944
Unrivalled (P.45)	Arctic 1942 Aegean 1943	North Africa 1942 Mediterranean 1943	Sicily 1943

Unruffled (P.46)	Malta Convoys 1942 Sicily 1943	Mediterranean 1942	North Africa 1942
Unruly	Arctic 1942-43 Atlantic 1944	Sicily 1943	Aegean 1943-44
Unseen (P.51)	North Africa 1942-43 English Channel 1944	Sicily 1943	Mediterranean 1943
Unshaken (P.54)	Arctic 1942 Mediterranean 1943	North Africa 1942	Sicily 1943
Unsparing	Sicily 1943	Aegean 1943-44	Atlantic 1944
Unst	Atlantic 1943		
Unswerving	Aegean 1944	Atlantic 1945	
Untiring	Mediterranean 1943-44	Atlantic 1944	
Upholder	Malta Convoys 1941-42	Mediterranean 1941-42	
Upright	Malta Convoys 1941	Mediterranean 1941	
Uproar (P.31)	Mediterranean 1941-44	Malta Convoys 1942	Sicily 1943
Upstart	Mediterranean 1944	Atlantic 1944	
Urania	Normandy 1944	Okinawa 1945	Japan 1945
Uranie	'Chevrette' 1801		
Urchin	Egypt 1801 Normandy 1944	Anzio 1944 Adriatic 1944	Mediterranean 1944 Okinawa 1945
Ure	Belgian Coast 1915-16		
Urge	Malta Convoys 1941	Mediterranean 1941-42	
Urgent	China 1860		
Ursa	Biscay 1944	Normandy 1944	Okinawa 1945
Ursula	North Sea 1939 Mediterranean 1941	Norway 1940 Arctic 1942	Malta Convoys 1941 North Africa 1942
Usk	Dardanelles 1915-16	Atlantic 1943-44	
Usurper	Sicily 1943		
Ut Prosim	Dunkirk 1940		
Utmost	Mediterranean 1941	Malta Convoys 1941-42	
Valentine	Atlantic 1939		

Valiant	Belle Isle 1761	Havana 1762	Ushant 1781
	The Saints 1782	First of June 1794	Groix Island 1795
	Basque Roads 1809	Jutland 1916	Norway 1940
	Mediterranean 1940-43	Matapan 1941	Crete 1941
	Malta Convoys 1941	Sicily 1943	Salerno 1943
	Sabang 1944	Falkland Islands 1982	
Valleyfield	Atlantic 1944		
Valorous	Baltic 1854	Crimea 1854-55	North Sea 1940-45
Valse	North Sea 1941-45		
Vampire	Calabria 1940	Libya 1940-41	Greece 1941
	Crete 1941	Aegean 1944	
Vancouver	Aleutians 1942-3 (RCN)	Atlantic 1944-45	
Vandyk	Norway 1940		
Vanessa	Atlantic 1939-43		
Vanguard	Armada 1588	Cadiz 1596	Portland 1653
	Gabbard 1653	Scheveningen 1653	Lowestoft 1665
	Four Days' Battle 1666	Orfordness 1666	Barfleur 1692
	Louisburg 1758	Quebec 1759	Martinique 1762
	Nile 1798	Syria 1840	Jutland 1916
Vanity	North Sea 1939-45	English Channel 1943	
Vanoc	Atlantic 1939-44	Norway 1940	North Africa 1942-43
	English Channel 1943-44		
Vanquisher	Atlantic 1939-45	Dunkirk 1940	English Channel 1943-44
	Normandy 1944		
Vansittart	Atlantic 1939-43	Norway 1940	Malta Convoys 1942
	North Africa 1942		
Varanga	Atlantic 1942-44		
Varna	Crimea 1854		
Vascama	Atlantic 1941-45	North Sea 1941-42	
Vatersay	English Channel 1945		
Vega	North Sea 1940-45		
Vegreville	Atlantic 1944	Normandy 1944	
Veleta	North Sea 1941-42	Atlantic 1943-44	Normandy 1944
Velox	Zeebrugge 1918	Ostend 1918	Belgian Coast 1918
	Atlantic 1940-43	North Africa 1942-43	

Vendetta	Libya 1940-41 Crete 1941 Vietnam 1969-70	Matapan 1941 Mediterranean 1941	Greece 1941 New Guinea 1943-44
Venerable	Camperdown 1797 Dardanelles 1915	Gut of Gibraltar 1801	Belgian Coast 1914-15
Venetia	Atlantic 1939-40		
Vengeance	Quiberon Bay 1759 Crimea 1854	Martinique 1794 Dardanelles 1915	St. Lucia 1796
Vengeful	Atlantic 1945		
Venom	Martinique 1794		
Venomous	Dunkirk 1940 Malta Convoys 1942	Atlantic 1940-43 North Africa 1942-43	Arctic 1942 Sicily 1943
Venturer	Norway 1944-45		
Venus	Quiberon Bay 1759 Arctic 1942-44 Burma 1945	St. Lucia 1778 Normandy 1944 East Indies 1945	First of June 1794 Malaya 1945
Verbena	Atlantic 1941		
Verdun	North Sea 1940-45	Arctic 1942	
Verity	Atlantic 1939-45 North Africa 1942-43	Dunkirk 1940	North Sea 1940
Veronica	Atlantic 1941		
Versatile	Atlantic 1939-45 Normandy 1944	North Sea 1941-45	English Channel 1944-45
Verulam	Arctic 1944 Malaya 1945	Normandy 1944 Burma 1945	Norway 1944 East Indies 1945
Vervain	Atlantic 1941-45	Normandy 1944	
Vesper	Atlantic 1939-45 Normandy 1944	English Channel 1940-45	North Sea 1941-42
Vestal	'Bellone' 1759 Normandy 1944	Egypt 1801 Burma 1945	Belgian Coast 1914
Vesuvius	Barfleur 1692 Martinique 1794	Quebec 1759 Syria 1840	Belle Isle 1761 Crimea 1854-55
Vetch	Atlantic 1941-43 Mediterranean 1943	North Africa 1942-43	Sicily 1943
Veteran	Martinique 1794 Atlantic 1939-42	Camperdown 1797 Norway 1940	Copenhagen 1801 North Sea 1940
Viceroy	North Sea 1942-45	Sicily 1943	

Victor	Egypt 1801		
Victor Emmanuel	Ashantee 1874		
Victoria I	Libya 1942		
Victoriaville	Atlantic 1945		
Victorieuse	St. Lucia 1796	Egypt 1801	
Victorious	*'Rivoli'* 1812 Arctic 1941-42 Biscay 1942 Palembang 1945	*'Bismarck'* 1941 Malta Convoys 1942 Sabang 1944 Okinawa 1945	Norway 1941-44 North Africa 1942 East Indies 1944-45 Japan 1945
Victory	Armada 1588 Gabbard 1653 Orfordness 1666 Texel 1673 St. Vincent 1797	Dover 1652 Scheveningen 1653 Sole Bay 1672 Barfleur 1692 Trafalgar 1805	Portland 1653 Four Days' Battle 1666 Schooneveld 1673 Ushant 1781
Victrix	Atlantic 1940-44	English Channel 1942-43	Normandy 1944
Vidette	Spartivento 1940 English Channel 1944	Atlantic 1940-44 Normandy 1944	Malta Convoys 1942
Vienna	North Africa 1942-43		
Vigilant	Arctic 1943-44 Burma 1945	Normandy 1944 East Indies 1945	Malaya 1945
Vigorous	Aegean 1944		
Viking	Belgian Coast 1914-15		
Viking Deeps	Normandy 1944		
Ville de Paris	*'Chevrette'* 1801		
Ville de Quebec	Atlantic 1942-44	Mediterranean 1943	English Channel 1944-45
Vimiera	Guadeloupe 1810	North Sea 1941-42	
Vimy	Atlantic 1939-45 Normandy 1944	Dunkirk 1940 English Channel 1944-45	Biscay 1943 North Sea 1944-45
Vincejo	*'Guillaume Tell'* 1800	Egypt 1801	
Vindex	Atlantic 1944	Arctic 1944-45	
Vindictive	Zeebrugge 1918	Ostend 1918	Norway 1940
Vineyard	Armada 1588*	Cadiz 1596*	
Violet	Armada 1588* Atlantic 1941-44	Cadiz 1596* North Africa 1942-43	Gabbard 1653 North Sea 1943-44
Viper	Havana 1762	*'Cerbère'* 1800	Crimea 1854-55

Virago	Arctic 1943-44 Malaya 1945	North Cape 1943 Burma 1945	Normandy 1944 East Indies 1945
Virgin	Orfordness 1666	Martinique 1762	
Virgin God **save her**	Armada 1588*		
Virginia	Burma 1945		
Virginie	'*Gelderland*' 1808		
Virtue	Aegean 1944		
Viscol	North Africa 1942**		
Viscount	Atlantic 1939-44	Biscay 1943	
Visenda	Atlantic 1941-45 Salerno 1943	North Sea 1942	Sicily 1943
Visigoth	Atlantic 1944		
Viva II	Atlantic 1940		
Vivacious	Atlantic 1939-40 Arctic 1943	Dunkirk 1940 English Channel 1943-44	North Sea 1942-45 Normandy 1944
Viviana	Arctic 1942	Atlantic 1942-43	
Vivid	Aegean 1944		
Vivien	North Sea 1940-45		
Vixen	China 1842		
Vizalma	Atlantic 1940-45	North Sea 1942	Arctic 1942-43
Volage	Lissa 1811 Arctic 1944	Aden 1839 East Indies 1945	Baltic 1855
Volcano	Copenhagen 1801	Baltic 1854-55	China 1856-60
Voltaire	Atlantic 1940-41		
Volunteer	Atlantic 1939-45 Biscay 1943	English Channel 1940-45 Normandy 1944	Arctic 1942 North Sea 1945
Voracious	Atlantic 1944		
Vortigern	Atlantic 1939-40	North Sea 1941-42	
Vox	Aegean 1944		
Voyager	Calabria 1940 Crete 1941	Libya 1940-41 Mediterranean 1941	Greece 1941 Pacific 1942

Vulcan	Barfleur 1692 Crimea 1854-55 Libya 1942	Velez Malaga 1704 China 1860	Finisterre 1747 Atlantic 1940
Vulture	Barfleur 1692 Baltic 1854-55	Vigo 1702	Velez Malaga 1704
Wager	East Indies 1944	Okinawa 1945	
Wagga	New Guinea 1943-44		
Wakeful	Atlantic 1939-40 East Indies 1944	Dunkirk 1940	North Sea 1944
Waldegrave	Normandy 1944	English Channel 1944	
Walker	Atlantic 1939-43 Normandy 1944	Norway 1940 Arctic 1944-45	English Channel 1944
Wallace	North Sea 1941-45	Sicily 1943	
Wallaceburg	Atlantic 1944-45		
Wallflower	Atlantic 1941-45 Normandy 1944	North Sea 1942	Arctic 1943-44
Walney	Atlantic 1941-42	North Africa 1942	
Walnut	English Channel 1942-44		
Walpole	Atlantic 1939-43 Normandy 1944	English Channel 1942-44	North Sea 1942-44
Wanderer	Guadeloupe 1810 Norway 1940 English Channel 1944	China 1842 Sicily 1943 Arctic 1944	Atlantic 1939-44 Normandy 1944
War Star	Normandy 1944		
Warramunga	New Guinea 1942-44 Pacific 1945	Leyte Gulf 1944 Korea 1950-52	Lingayen Gulf 1945
Warrego	Lingayen Gulf 1942	New Guinea 1942	Pacific 1945
Warrior	The Saints 1782	Copenhagen 1801	Jutland 1916
Warrnambool	Pacific 1945		
Warspite	Cadiz 1596 Schooneveld 1673 Velez Malaga 1704 Quiberon Bay 1759 Narvik 1940 Mediterranean 1940-43 Malta Convoys 1941 Normandy 1944 Biscay 1944	Orfordness 1666 Texel 1673 Marbella 1705 Jutland 1916 Norway 1940 Matapan 1941 Sicily 1943 Walcheren 1944	Sole Bay 1672 Barfleur 1692 Lagos 1759 Atlantic 1939 Calabria 1940 Crete 1941 Salerno 1943 English Channel 1944

Warwick	Zeebrugge 1918 Biscay 1943	Ostend 1918	Atlantic 1939-44
Warwickshire	Norway 1940		
Wasaga	Atlantic 1944	Normandy 1944	
Waskesiu	Atlantic 1943-45	Arctic 1944	Normandy 1944
Wasp	Syria 1840	Crimea 1854-55	
Wastwater	Arctic 1942		
Watchful	China 1856-60		
Watchman	China 1860 Normandy 1944	Atlantic 1940-44 English Channel 1944-45	Arctic 1944
Waterfly	Mesopotamia 1916-17	English Channel 1942	
Waterhen	Libya 1940-41	Greece 1941	Crete 1941
Waterhound	Portland 1653	Gabbard 1653	
Waterwitch	Anzio 1944		
Wave Baron	Korea 1952**		
Wave Chief	Korea 1951-53**		
Wave Knight	Korea 1951-53**		
Wave Laird	Korea 1950-51**		
Wave Premier	Korea 1950-52**		
Wave Prince	Korea 1950-53**		
Wave Sovereign	Korea 1952-53**		
Waveney	Atlantic 1942-43 Burma 1945	Biscay 1943	Normandy 1944
Waverley	Dunkirk 1940		
Wear	Dardanelles 1915-16	Atlantic 1943-4	Biscay 1943
Weasel	Baltic 1855	China 1860	
Weazel	Ushant 1747 Boscaline Bay 1813	St. Lucia 1778	*'Mercure'* 1812
Webb	Armada 1588*		
Wedgeport	North Sea 1942 Normandy 1944	Atlantic 1943	English Channel 1942-44

Welcome	Portland 1653 Schooneveld 1673	Gabbard 1653	Orfordness 1666
Welfare	South France 1944		
Welland	Dardanelles 1915-16		
Wellard	North Sea 1941	Atlantic 1941-42	
Wellesley	China 1841		
Wellington	Atlantic 1939-45		
Wells	Atlantic 1941-42	Arctic 1942	North Sea 1943-44
Welshman	Malta Convoys 1942		
Wensleydale	Atlantic 1943-44 Normandy 1944	English Channel 1943-44	North Sea 1943-44
Wentworth	Atlantic 1944-45		
Weser	Crimea 1855		
Wessex	Atlantic 1939-40	East Indies 1944	Okinawa 1945
West York	Atlantic 1945		
Westcott	Norway 1940 North Africa 1942-43 Normandy 1944	Atlantic 1940-43 English Channel 1943	Malta Convoys 1942 Arctic 1943-45
Westella	Dunkirk 1940		
Westminster	North Sea 1940-45	English Channel 1943	
Westmount	Atlantic 1944		
Weston	North Sea 1940	Atlantic 1940-44	English Channel 1945
Westray	North Sea 1942	North Africa 1942-43	
Westward Ho	Belgian Coast 1915	Dunkirk 1940	
Wetaskiwin	Atlantic 1941-45		
Weyburn	Atlantic 1942	North Africa 1942-43	
Weymouth	Sadras 1758	Negapatam 1758	Porto Novo 1759
Whaddon	North Sea 1941-43 Mediterranean 1943 Adriatic 1944	Sicily 1943 South France 1944	Salerno 1943 Aegean 1944
Whalsey	English Channel 1942		
Wheatland	Arctic 1942 Sicily 1943	North Africa 1942-43 Salerno 1943	Mediterranean 1943 Adriatic 1944

Whelp	East Indies 1944	Okinawa 1945	
Whimbrel	Sicily 1943 Normandy 1944	Atlantic 1943-44 Arctic 1944	English Channel 1944 Okinawa 1945
Whippet (ex **KOS 21**)		Crete 1941	Libya 1941
Whippingham	Normandy 1944		
Whirlwind	Zeebrugge 1918 Norway 1940	Ostend 1918 Okinawa 1945	Atlantic 1939-40
Whitaker	Atlantic 1944	Normandy 1944	English Channel 1944
Whitby	Atlantic 1944-45		
White Bear	Burma 1944-45		
(White) Bear	Armada 1588		
White Hind	Armada 1588*		
White Lion	Armada 1588		
Whitehall	Atlantic 1939-43 English Channel 1944	Dunkirk 1940 Normandy 1944	Arctic 1943-45
Whitehaven	Atlantic 1942	Sicily 1943	Normandy 1944
Whitehorn	Atlantic 1942-43		
Whitesand Bay	Korea 1950-53		
Whitethroat	Atlantic 1945		
Whiting	Basque Roads 1809 Sicily 1943	China 1900	North Sea 1942
Whitshed	Dunkirk 1940 English Channel 1942-44	Atlantic 1940 Normandy 1944	North Sea 1941-45
Whyalla	New Guinea 1942-44	Okinawa 1945	
Widgeon	Benin 1897	North Sea 1941-45	
Widnes	Crete 1941		
Wild Goose	Atlantic 1943-44 Arctic 1944	Biscay 1943 English Channel 1945	Normandy 1944
Wild Swan	Dunkirk 1940	Atlantic 1940-42	
Wildflower	Atlantic 1940		
Wilhelmina	Egypt 1801		
William	Armada 1588*	Gabbard 1653	Scheveningen 1653

William and John Portland 1653 Gabbard 1653

William and Mary Velez Malaga 1704

William Scoresby Atlantic 1940

William Stroud Normandy 1944

Willowherb Atlantic 1943-45

Wilton	Arctic 1942	Malta Convoys 1942	North Africa 1942-43
	Sicily 1943	Aegean 1943	Mediterranean 1944
	Adriatic 1944	North Sea 1945	

Wimpey Seahorse Falkland Islands 1982*

Winchelsea	Martinique 1794	Egypt 1801	Atlantic 1939-44
	Dunkirk 1940	North Sea 1942	

Winchester	Burma 1852-53	China 1856-60	North Sea 1940-44
	English Channel 1943	Atlantic 1944	

Winchester Castle Diego Suarez 1942*

Windemere Atlantic 1941-45

Windflower Atlantic 1941

Windrush Atlantic 1943-44

Windsor	Finisterre 1747	Ushant 1747	Atlantic 1939-40
	Dunkirk 1940	Arctic 1942	English Channel 1942-43
	North Sea 1942-45	Normandy 1944	

Windsor Castle Barfleur 1692 Genoa 1795

Winnipeg Atlantic 1943-45

Winsby Santa Cruz 1657

Wishart	Atlantic 1939-44	Spartivento 1940	Malta Convoys 1942
	Mediterranean 1942	North Africa 1942-43	Sicily 1943

Wistaria Norway 1940 Atlantic 1942-44

Witch Atlantic 1939-43 Norway 1940 North Sea 1944

Witham Normandy 1944

Witherington Atlantic 1939-44 Norway 1940 English Channel 1940

Witness Cadiz 1596

Wivern Atlantic 1939-43 North Africa 1942-43 North Sea 1944-45

Wolborough Libya 1941-42 Sicily 1943 Atlantic 1944

Wolf Barfleur 1692

Wolfe	Atlantic 1941-43		
Wolfhound	Dunkirk 1940	North Sea 1943-45	
Wollongong	Sicily 1943	Mediterranean 1943	East Indies 1943
Wolsey	Dunkirk 1940 English Channel 1943	Atlantic 1940-42	North Sea 1941-45
Wolverine	Martinique 1809 Norway 1940	Dardanelles 1915-16 Malta Convoys 1942	Atlantic 1939-45
Wolves	Dunkirk 1940	North Sea 1942-45	
Woodcock	China 1856-60 Okinawa 1945	Atlantic 1943-45	English Channel 1944
Woodpecker	Atlantic 1943-44	Biscay 1943	
Woodruff	Atlantic 1941-45		
Woodstock	Atlantic 1942-44 English Channel 1944	North Africa 1942-43	Normandy 1944
Woolston	Atlantic 1941 Sicily 1943	North Sea 1941-45	Arctic 1942
Woolwich	Barfleur 1692 St. Lucia 1796	Martinique 1762 Egypt 1801	Martinique 1794
Worcester	Dover 1652 Scheveningen 1653 Porto Bello 1739 Negapatam 1782 Atlantic 1940 Arctic 1942-43	Portland 1653 Porto Farina 1655 Sadras 1782 Trincomalee 1782 North Sea 1940-43	Gabbard 1653 Santa Cruz 1657 Providien 1782 Dunkirk 1940 English Channel 1942-43
Worcestershire	Atlantic 1940-41	North Sea 1943	
Worthing	Dunkirk 1940* Normandy 1944	North Sea 1942	Atlantic 1943
Wrangler	Baltic 1854	Crimea 1855	
Wren	Atlantic 1939-45 Normandy 1944	Norway 1940	Biscay 1943-44 Arctic 1944
Wrestler	Atlantic 1940-43 North Africa 1942 Normandy 1944	Mediterranean 1940-42 Sicily 1943 English Channel 1944	Malta Convoys 1942 Arctic 1943-44
Wryneck	Greece 1941	Libya 1941	Mediterranean 1941
Wye	North Sea 1944		
X. 6	'*Tirpitz*' 1943		
X. 7	'*Tirpitz*' 1943		

X. 20	Normandy 1944		
X. 23	Normandy 1944		
X. 24	Norway 1944		
XE.1	'*Takao*' 1945		
XE.3	'*Takao*' 1945		
XE.4	Malaya 1945		
XE.5	Malaya 1945		
Yager	Cadiz 1596*		
Yana	Libya 1941		
Yarmouth	Lowestoft 1665	Orfordness 1666	Sole Bay 1672
	Schooneveld 1673	Texel 1673	Gibraltar 1704
	Velez Malaga 1704	Finisterre 1747	Ushant 1747
	Sadras 1758	Negapatam 1758	Porto Novo 1759
	The Saints 1782	Jutland 1916	Falkland Islands 1982
Yarra	Libya 1941		
Yes Tor	North Sea 1942	Atlantic 1942-44	
Yonge	Armada 1588		
York	Lowestoft 1665	Orfordness 1666	Sole Bay 1672
	Schooneveld 1673	Texel 1673	Louisburg 1758
	Martinique 1809	Atlantic 1939	Norway 1940
	Mediterranean 1940-41	Malta Convoys 1941	
York City	Atlantic 1940		
Yorkshire Lass	Dunkirk 1940		
Yorkshireman	Atlantic 1944	Falkland Islands 1982*	
Young Hebe	China 1842		
Young Lion	Lowestoft 1665		
Young Mun	Dunkirk 1940		
Young Prince	Four Days' Battle 1666		
Zambesi	Norway 1944	Arctic 1945	
Zanzibar	Atlantic 1944	English Channel 1945	
Zealand	Orfordness 1666		
Zealous	Nile 1798	Norway 1945	Arctic 1945

Zebra	The Saints 1782 Syria 1840	Martinique 1794 Arctic 1945	Copenhagen 1801
Zephyr	Quebec 1759 Baltic 1854	Martinique 1762 Arctic 1945	Copenhagen 1801
Zest	Arctic 1945	Norway 1945	
Zetland	Atlantic 1942-45 Mediterranean 1943-44 South France 1944	Malta Convoys 1942 Aegean 1944	North Africa 1942-43 Adriatic 1944
Zinnia	Atlantic 1941		
Zodiac	Arctic 1945		
Zubian	Zeebrugge 1918		
Zulu	Belgian Coast 1915-16 Atlantic 1941 Mediterranean 1942	Norway 1940 Malta Convoys 1941-42 Libya 1942	'*Bismarck*' 1941 Sirte 1942

PART 4
FAA SQUADRONS AND THEIR BATTLE HONOURS

The following Battle Honours are awarded to FAA Squadrons:

700
River Plate 1939	Norway 1940	Spartivento 1940
Atlantic 1940-41	Matapan 1941	East Indies 1941
Mediterranean 1942	North Africa 1942-43	Normandy 1944

701 Norway 1940

723 Vietnam 1967-71

737 Falkland Islands 1982

767 Mediterranean 1940

800
Norway 1940-44	Mediterranean 1940-41	Spartivento 1940
Malta Convoys 1941-42	'Bismarck' 1941	Diego Suarez 1942
North Africa 1942	South France 1944	Aegean 1944
Normandy 1944	Burma 1945	Malaya 1945
East Indies 1945	Korea 1950	Falkland Islands 1982

801
Norway 1940-44	Dunkirk 1940	Atlantic 1940
Malta Convoys 1942	Japan 1945	Korea 1952-53
Falkland Islands 1982		

802
Norway 1940	Atlantic 1941	Arctic 1942
North Africa 1942	Korea 1952	

803
North Sea 1939	Norway 1940	Libya 1940-41
Matapan 1941	Mediterranean 1941	

804
Norway 1940-44	Atlantic 1941	North Africa 1942
Normandy 1944	Burma 1945	East Indies 1945
Korea 1951-52		

805
Crete 1941	Libya 1941-42	Korea 1951-52

806
Norway 1940	Dunkirk 1940	Mediterranean 1940-41
Libya 1940-41	Matapan 1941	Diego Suarez 1942
Malta Convoys 1942		

807
Atlantic 1940	Malta Convoys 1941-42	North Africa 1942-43
Sicily 1943	Salerno 1943	South France 1944
Aegean 1944	Burma 1945	Malaya 1945
Korea 1950-53		

808
Spartivento 1940	'Bismarck' 1941	Malta Convoys 1941
Atlantic 1943	Salerno 1943	Normandy 1944
Burma 1945	East Indies 1945	Korea 1951-52

809
Arctic 1941	Malta Convoys 1942	North Africa 1942
Salerno 1943	South France 1944	Aegean 1944
Burma 1945	East Indies 1945	Falkland Islands 1982

810	Norway 1940	Mediterranean 1940-41	Spartivento 1940
	Atlantic 1941	*'Bismarck'* 1941	Diego Suarez 1942
	Salerno 1943	East Indies 1944	Korea 1950-3
811	English Channel 1942	North Sea 1942	Atlantic 1943-4
	Arctic 1944		
812	North Sea 1940	English Channel 1940-42	Mediterranean 1941
	Malta Convoys 1941	Korea 1951-52	
813	Calabria 1940	Mediterranean 1940-41	Taranto 1940
	Libya 1940-41	East Indies 1941	Malta Convoys 1942
	Atlantic 1942-44	Arctic 1944-45	
814	Atlantic 1940		
815	Mediterranean 1940-41	Taranto 1940	Libya 1940-41
	Matapan 1941	Burma 1944	East Indies 1944
	Falkland Islands 1982	Kuwait 1991	
816	Norway 1940	Malta Convoys 1941	Mediterranean 1941
	Atlantic 1943	Arctic 1944	Normandy 1944
817	Norway 1941	North Africa 1942	Biscay 1942
	Sicily 1943	East Indies 1944	Korea 1951-52
818	Norway 1940	Spartivento 1940	Mediterranean 1940-41
	'Bismarck' 1941	Atlantic 1941	
819	Taranto 1940	Libya 1940	Mediterranean 1940-41
	English Channel 1942	Normandy 1944	Arctic 1944
820	Norway 1940-44	Spartivento 1940	Mediterranean 1940
	'Bismarck' 1941	Atlantic 1941	Malta Convoys 1941
	North Africa 1942-43	Sicily 1943	Salerno 1943
	East Indies 1945	Palembang 1945	Okinawa 1945
	Japan 1945	Falkland Islands 1982	
821	Norway 1940	Libya 1942	Mediterranean 1942-43
	Korea 1952-53		
822	North Africa 1942-3	Arctic 1943	East Indies 1944
823	Norway 1940		
824	Calabria 1940	Mediterranean 1940	Taranto 1940
	Libya 1940-41	East Indies 1941	Malta Convoys 1942
	Atlantic 1942	Arctic 1944	Falkland Islands 1982
825	Dunkirk 1940	English Channel 1940-42	Norway 1940
	'Bismarck' 1941	Malta Convoys 1941	Arctic 1942-45
	Atlantic 1944	Korea 1952	Falkland Islands 1982
826	Dunkirk 1940	North Sea 1940-44	Atlantic 1940
	Matapan 1941	East Indies 1941	Mediterranean 1941-43
	Libya 1941-42	Falkland Islands 1982	Kuwait 1991

1700	Burma 1945		
1770	Norway 1944 Okinawa 1945	East Indies 1945	Palembang 1945
1771	Norway 1944	Japan 1945	
1772	Japan 1945		
1830	East Indies 1944 Okinawa 1945	Sabang 1944	Palembang 1945
1832	Norway 1944	Atlantic 1944	Arctic 1944
1833	Sabang 1944 Okinawa 1945	East Indies 1944	Palembang 1945
1834	Norway 1944 Palembang 1945	Sabang 1944 Okinawa 1945	East Indies 1944-45 Japan 1945
1836	Norway 1944 Palembang 1945	Sabang 1944 Okinawa 1945	East Indies 1944-45 Japan 1945
1837	Sabang 1944	East Indies 1944	
1838	Sabang 1944		
1839	East Indies 1944-45	Palembang 1945	Okinawa 1945
1840	Norway 1944	Okinawa 1945	
1841	Norway 1944	Okinawa 1945	Japan 1945
1842	Norway 1944	Okinawa 1945	Japan 1945
1844	East Indies 1944-45	Palembang 1945	Okinawa 1945
1845	Okinawa 1945		

PART 5
ROYAL MARINES BATTLE HONOUR

Gibraltar

LIST OF SOURCES/BIBLIOGRAPHY

Admiralty Fleet Order 2565 of 1954

Naval Staff Histories (BR1736 series)

10	The Tobruk Run June 1940-January 1943
20-	Naval Aircraft attack on the Tirpitz (Operation Tungsten) 3 April 1944
21-	Battle of the Java Sea 27 February 1942
26-	Raid on Dieppe (Naval Operations) 19 August 1942
27-	The Invasion of Sicily (Operation Husky) 10 July – 17 August 1943
30-	The Invasion of Italy – Landing at Salerno (Avalanche) (Naval Operations) 9 September 1943
31-	Invasion of North Africa (Operation Torch) November 1942 – February 1943
32-	The Evacuation from Dunkirk (Operation Dynamo) 26 May – 4 June 1940
33-	Burma 1941-45 Naval Operations
40-	Aegean Operations 1943
42-	Operation Neptune – Landings in Normandy June 1944 (2 Volumes)
44-	Arctic Convoys 1941-1945
48-	Home Waters and Atlantic (2 Volumes)
49-	Mediterranean (2 Volumes)
50-	War with Japan (6 Volumes)
52-	Submarines (3 volumes)
53-	The Development of British Naval Aviation 1919-1945 (2 Volumes)
54-	Korea – British Commonwealth Naval Operations 1950-1953

Various Pink Lists
Navy List September 1852
Admiralty War Diary
Various Commander-in-Chiefs' and Area Flag Officers' War Diaries
Hansard 25 October 1983
The Royal Navy, A History, Sir W. Laird Clowes (7 volumes) Sampson Low, Marston & Company 1903
The War at Sea 1939-1945 by Captain S.W. Roskill, D.S.C., Royal Navy, (HMSO)
Various unpublished documents